THE MONGOLS OF MANCHURIA

OWEN LATTIMORE

THE MONGOLS
OF MANCHURIA

THEIR TRIBAL DIVISIONS

GEOGRAPHICAL DISTRIBUTION

HISTORICAL RELATIONS WITH MANCHUS

AND CHINESE AND

PRESENT POLITICAL PROBLEMS

With Maps

NEW YORK

Howard Fertig

1969

First published in 1934
Copyright 1934 by O. Lattimore;
renewal copyright © 1962 by Owen Lattimore

H OWARD F ERTIG, I NC. E DITION 1969
Reprinted by special arrangement with The John Day Company, Inc.

Library of Congress Catalog Card Number: 68-9626

PRINTED IN THE UNITED STATES OF AMERICA
BY NOBLE OFFSET PRINTERS, INC.

To

R. LeM. Barrett

In earnest of caravan days to come

Contents

CONTENTS

Introduction

THE following brief study was compiled chiefly from notes made in the course of research work on a broader study of the whole frontier region from the Pacific to Chinese Central Asia and Tibet. I wish therefore to acknowledge my indebtedness to the Social Science Research Council, the Harvard-Yenching Institute, the John Simon Guggenheim Memorial Foundation and the American Geographical Society, under whose auspices I worked from 1929 to 1933, in Manchuria, Peiping and Inner Mongolia.

The material here presented is derived partly from standard sources, partly from my own travel and observation and partly from information given to me by Mongols and Chinese. Standard information of the kind to be found in the *Meng-ku Yu-mu Chi* and *Ta Ch'ing Hui Tien* has too long awaited recognition in an easily accessible English source. A beginning was made by the late Lieutenant G. C. Binsteed, but his promising career was cut short by his death in action in 1914.

There is much information available in Japanese and Russian sources, but these I have been unable to consult, except for the admirable maps, printed in Chinese, which are based on the work of the South Manchuria Railway's research department. This is the first time, I believe, that the painstaking work of the Japanese cartographers in regard to Mongol Banner frontiers has been made available in English.

My sources for information derived from written material are fully indicated in the notes and bibliography. The material derived from what I have seen and what I have been told is offered with due reservation, and without claiming that it is either infallible or complete. Information regarding Mongol insurrections, for instance, is extremely hard to clarify, even though I have talked with a number of men who led or took part in different rebellions and political movements. In a period of general unrest, separate risings in different regions are often remembered as if they had been a coordinated movement; on the other hand, a general rising affecting a wide region is often remembered locally as a local event, and associated only with the names of local leaders.

The really essential information about colonization in Mongol territories in Manchuria, during the latter years of the Manchu Empire and in the period between the founding of the Chinese Republic in 1911-12 and the founding of Manchukuo in 1931-32, is even harder to assess. Large-scale colonization has always tended to be an "inside business," controlled by the political, military and family groups who were on the inside, with the result that it is practically impossible to estimate some of its most important processes by reference to published data. Colonization is here treated, in the main, from the Mongol point of view—a point of view which has been insufficiently emphasized (to say the least of it) in the past.

Mongol affairs being in a state of change, I have especially aimed at presenting a study that will be true to the general character of the Mongol question, as well as accurate in particular facts, so that, whatever the changes that may occur in the next few years, the reader who consults this book may find a reliable guide to the general aspect and the essential conditions which affect particular changes. The Mongols are a people whose problems and interests are too little understood or cared for by the world at large. I sincerely hope that the information I have here collated may eventually work to the benefit of the Mongols themselves.

I should perhaps mention that the name "Manchuria" is used in this book as a geographical and historical term, while "Manchukuo" is used as the name of the new State comprising the provinces of Fengt'ien, Kirin, Heilungchiang, Jehol and Hsingan.

Extracts from the book have appeared in *Asia,* to whose editor I wish to make special acknowledgment, and in *Pacific Affairs.*

THE MONGOLS OF MANCHURIA

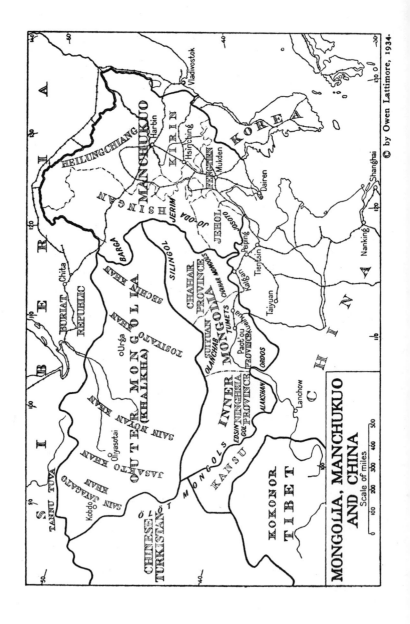

MONGOLIA, MANCHUKUO
AND CHINA

Scale of miles

0   100   200   300   400   500

© by Owen Lattimore, 1934.

MANCHUKUO
showing
HSINGAN PROVINCE
and Mongol Territories colonized by Chinese

Scale of miles

0   50   100   150   200

"Lost" Territory of the Mongols   Railroads

Nonni Valley tribes   ———— In operation

Jerim League Mongols   ----- Under construction

Jehol Mongols   -·-·- Projected

© By Owen Lattimore, 1934.

G. Schweizer

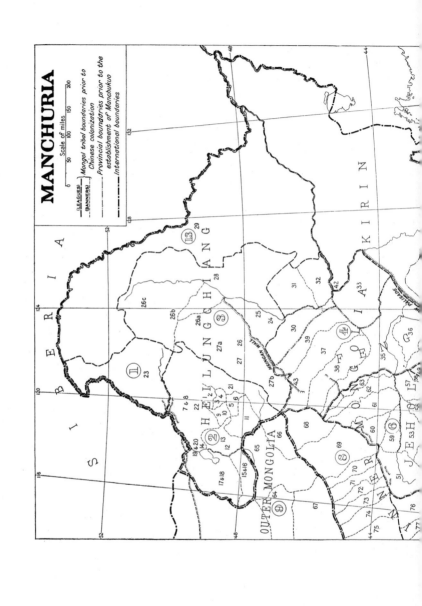

MANCHURIA

Scale of miles

0   50   100   150   200

(LEAGUES)
(BANNERS) Mongol tribal boundaries prior to
           Chinese colonization
           Provincial boundaries prior to the
           establishment of Manchukuo
           International boundaries

© By Owen Lattimore, 1934.

LEAGUES, BANNERS AND OTHER TRIBAL TERRITORIES AS NUMBERED ON THE MAP

(1) NORTHERN BARGA

23. "Unorganized" Tungusic groups.

(2) THE BARGA TRIBES

1. 2. Solon "Old Barga" East Wing Bordered Yellow and All White Banners.
3. 4. Olöt "Old Barga" East Wing Bordered Yellow Banner; now 2 Banners.
5. 6. Solon "Old Barga" East Wing Bordered Red and Bordered Blue Banners.
7. 8. Chipchin "Old Barga" West Wing All Blue and Bordered White Banners.
9. 10. Solon "Old Barga" West Wing All Yellow and All Red Banners.
11. Buriat "New Barga" East Wing All Blue Banner.
12. 13. Buriat "New Barga" East Wing Bordered Yellow and All White Banners.
14. Buriat "New Barga" East Wing Bordered White Banner.
15. 16. Buriat "New Barga" West Wing Bordered Blue and Bordered Red Banners.
17. 18. Buriat "New Barga" West Wing All Yellow and All Red Banners.
19. 20. "Refugee Buriat," Old and New, 2 Banners.
21. Oronchon, 1 Banner.
22. Hailar Daghors, 1 *Hsieh-ling.*

(3) THE NONNI VALLEY TRIBES

24. 25. Yeghe Minggan Mongols; Tsitsihar Solons and Daghors.
26. 26a. 26b. 26c. Butcha East Wing; Moroi Daba, Bayan, Non groups.
27. 27a. 27b. Butcha West Wing; Aron and Khiiagar groups.
28. Mergen Banners; Daghors and affiliated tribes.

(4) JERIM LEAGUE, AND ADDITIONAL GROUPS

30. Jalaid Banner.
31. Durbet Banner.
32. North Gorlos Banner.
33. South Gorlos Banner.
34. Khorchin East Wing South Banner (Bintu Wang).
35. Khorchin East Wing Center Banner (Darkhan Wang).
36. Khorchin East Wing North Banner (Bo Wang).
37. Khorchin West Wing South Banner (Jasakto Khan).
38. Khorchin West Wing Center Banner (Tosiyeto Wang).
39. Khorchin West Wing North Banner (Tusiye Gung).

40. 41. East and West Suruk Mongols.
42. Sibe (Sibege) Mongols.
43. "Manchu-Mongols" (attached to 37 above).

(5) JOSOTO LEAGUE

44. Kharchin West Wing Banner.
45. Kharchin Center Banner.
46. Kharchin East Wing Banner.
47. Tumet West Wing Banner.
48. Tumet East Wing Banner or Monggoljin.
49. Shiretu Khurie Lama Banner.
50. Tanggot Khalkha Banner.

(6) JO-ODA LEAGUE

51. Keshikten Banner.
52. Ongniod West Wing Banner.
53. Ongniod East Wing Banner.
54. Aokhan West Wing Banner.
55. Aokhan South Banner.
56. Aokhan East Wing Banner.
57. Naiman Banner.
58. Chokhor Khalkha Banner.
59. Bairin West Wing Banner, or Great Bairin.
60. Bairin East Wing Banner, or Little Bairin.
61. Aro-Khorchin Banner.
62. Jarod West Wing Banner.
63. Jarod East Wing Banner.

(7) THE CHAHAR MONGOLS

76. All Blue Banner.
77. Bordered White Banner.
78. All White Banner.
79. Adochin (Horse-herd) Banner

(8) SILINGOL LEAGUE

68. East Ujumuchin Banner.
69. West Ujumuchin Banner.
70. East Hochit Banner.
71. West Hochit Banner.
72. East Abahanar Banner.
73. East Abaga Banner.
74. West Abahanar Banner.
75. West Abaga Banner.

(9) KHALKHAS OF OUTER MONGOLIA; SECHIN KHAN AIMAK

64. East Wing Rear Banner (Uichen Beise).
65. East Wing Center West Banner (Ildon Wang).
66. East Wing Front Banner (Erkhimsen Beile).
67. West Wing Rear Banner (Khorcha Wang).

(10) THE OLD CHINESE PALE IN MANCHURIA

(11) THE IMPERIAL HUNTING PARK IN JEHOL PROVINCE

(12) THE OLD CHINESE PALE IN JEHOL

(13) TRANS-HSINGAN DAGHORS AND AFFILIATED TRIBES

29. Banners of Aigun, Taheiho, etc.

Chapter I

MONGOLIA ENTERS WORLD AFFAIRS

I F the creation of Manchukuo means anything, it means an attempt to set up a continental power in Asia, based on the territories north of the Great Wall, as an alternative to the maritime power exercised over China by the Western nations, as represented in the last hundred years of history by the "unequal treaties" and the treaty-port positions of advantage held by foreign nations. This means, in turn, that Vladivostok and the Siberian frontier of Manchukuo are of minor significance compared with its Mongolian frontier. It means that even if war should break out over some question of the Siberian frontier, it would be decided by operations along the Mongolian frontier. For the "Manchurian question" in the new form symbolized by the State of Manchukuo is a completely senseless product of violence unless it means the opening up of the far more comprehensive question of Mongolia.

There has been no period in all history when the Chinese have conquered, or even controlled, the whole of Mongolia. The modern relations between China and Mongolia derive from a double line of history, that of the Manchu conquest of China and that of the Manchu overlordship in Mongolia. An alliance between the Manchus and the Eastern Mongols was one of the essential preliminaries to the Manchu conquest of China. Starting from this alliance with some of the Mongols, the Manchu Emperors created for themselves a position as overlords of all the Mongols. This came about as the result of a curious and involved series of wars and alliances, in which the Manchus appeared consistently as participants in Mongol affairs, rather than as conquerors of the Mongols. There has always been a cleavage between Inner and Outer Mongolia, which goes back to fundamental factors of geography and tribal history; but the modern distinction dates also from Manchu history. The first series of Manchu-Mongol alliances built up a frontier power in Inner Mongolia which protected the Manchu conquests in China; and it was only later, by using their position in Inner Mongolia as a fulcrum, that the Manchus extended their power into Outer Mongolia.

With the fall of the Manchu Empire, the essential link between China and Mongolia was broken. The Mongols in Outer Mongolia promptly undertook to create a nation of their own. They have been virtually independent of China ever since 1911, except for a brief period in 1919 and 1920, although the outside pressure of international relations has prevented all nations except Soviet Russia from dealing with Outer Mongolia as an independent state.

Independence led inevitably to an internal social revolution in Outer Mongolia, largely because the hereditary ruling princes failed to produce a leader who would put the nation first and the class interests of the aristocracy second. Owing to the hostility between Outer Mongolia and China, Russian influence has become paramount; but it is not exactly fair to say that Outer Mongolia is being "absorbed" by the Soviet Union, since neither Mongol ideology nor that of Soviet Russia works exactly in the familiar channels of Western political terminology. Economically, the Mongols are thrown within the Russian sphere by their hostility to China; and "reform" and "progress" are necessarily based largely on Russian models, because there is no other source from which they can be borrowed.

Outer Mongolia is a Republic, governed under a form of state socialism.[1] The old privileged classes have been dispossessed, but a surprisingly large number of the new leaders derive from the old aristocracy. "Communism" cannot be said to exist; rather, it would appear that political, social and economic questions are being handled in such a manner as to create a society which in the future can be adapted to some form of communism, which in turn has been adapted to a nation composed almost entirely of herdsmen, with little agriculture and no manufacturing industry.

In 1911, when the Manchu Empire broke up, the old tribal cleavage between Inner and Outer Mongolia at once became evident. Revolutionary movements actually began earlier in Inner Mongolia than in Outer Mongolia, but

[1] For a note on the new political divisions of Outer Mongolia (with map) see Krijanovsky, in *Geog. Rev.*

17

never made so much headway; with the result that many early leaders of anti-Chinese risings in Inner Mongolia withdrew eventually to Outer Mongolia.

At the time of the Chinese Revolution several attempts were made to assert Inner Mongolian independence and to unite with Outer Mongolia; but they came to nothing, partly because the Inner Mongolian princes believed that independence would lead to their being overshadowed by the princes of Outer Mongolia, and partly because of greater economic dependence on China. Many Inner Mongolian princes were heavily interested in Chinese trading firms which handled the trade of the Mongols, and did not want to risk the loss of the large revenues thus obtained. Undoubtedly, however, the most important single reason was the feeling, among the Southern Mongols, that China, under the Republic, would be a weak state with which they could manage their relations as they liked. There can be no doubt that they also feared the spread of Russian influence in Outer Mongolia, and believed that they would have more real freedom in nominal association with China than under a nominal independence, controlled in reality from Russia. Thus, during the first independence movements in Inner Mongolia the Chinese troops were everywhere defeated and driven out with startling ease, but independence was never really clinched, and in the end certain of the Inner Mongolian princes "sold out," by accepting high office under the Republic of China.

The hope that the Chinese Republic would prove weak in its relations with Inner Mongolia was disappointed, because of two factors which the Mongols had not been in a position to anticipate—modern arms and railways. Both of these represented, essentially, not the independent power of China, but an illusory Chinese power which was a phase, primarily, of the control which Western nations indirectly exercised over China; but they worked in favor of the Chinese. Modern arms gave the Chinese an immediate military advantage over the Mongols, but railways gave them a permanent advantage. By making possible the export of agricultural produce over distances which had been prohibitive in the age of carts and caravans, they enabled the Chinese to settle permanently in Mongol territory.

Before this time there had been a gradual immigration of Chinese into Inner Mongolia, especially into Manchurian Inner Mongolia. This was the territory, occupying in the seventeenth century about a half of what is now Manchuria and most of Jehol, held by the Mongols who first joined the Manchus as allies. Chinese immigration first affected what is now Jehol, and the region south and southwest of Ch'angch'un (now Hsinching or Hsinking, the capital of Manchukuo). The Manchus opposed it, because they wished to keep the Mongols "tribal" and thus better available as military reserves, but the Mongols themselves favored it, because they then had land to spare, and wanted the grain-supplies and land-rentals of the Chinese, and because the Mongol princes wanted to live at ease as overlords of the Chinese, like their Manchu allies.

With the building of railways, Chinese penetration became quite different in character. It started to overwhelm the Mongols, and the Mongols, though alarmed, were help-less. The Peking-Suiyüan railway started colonization among the Chahar Mongols, north of Kalgan, and in the Olanchab League, north of Kueihua; but the chief railway construction was in Manchuria, and the chief sufferers were the Manchurian Mongols. The problems of Jehol, in this respect, are identical with those of Manchuria, since the only railways that open up Jehol approach it from the Manchurian side. The Mongols were pushed back from a frontier that had reached as far east as Harbin and Ch'ang-ch'un (Hsinching), and to within 80 miles of Mukden, until they had lost about two-thirds of their territory in Jehol and about a third of their territory in Manchuria.

The sudden dominance of the Chinese made the Mongols irresolute. A number of desperate uprisings did something to slow down the rate of the Chinese advance, but Mongol princes capitulated too often to the Chinese, with the idea of saving what they could for themselves, at the expense of the Mongols as a whole. The Chinese adopted a policy of supporting the princes in such territory as had not yet been reached by colonization, and of giving them a share in the profits of colonization. This divided the interests of princes and commoners, and ensured that the princes, as a class, would work against "revolutionary" Mongol movements. It should however be said, to the credit of the princes, that almost every Mongol rising in defense of Mongol soil was led either by ruling princes or by men of princely family.

THE MONGOLS OF MANCHURIA

The hopelessness of Mongol efforts to hold back the Chinese provided Japan with a ready-made Mongol policy in Manchukuo, and apparently it has been executed with a good deal of success. All of the uncolonized Mongol territory in Manchukuo has been set aside as an autonomous Mongol province, under the name of Hsingan province, from the Hsingan range which runs through it. Land in which Chinese decidedly outnumber the Mongols has not been included within Hsingan, but Mongol interests are protected by local "offices of Mongol affairs." The autonomous province itself has a greater degree of freedom in its internal affairs than any other part of Manchukuo. The Mongols are ruled partly by their hereditary princes and partly by elective and appointive officials. They are even allowed to maintain their own troops.

The province thus organized is the largest province in Manchukuo, and its domestic importance to Manchukuo is obvious. It lies almost entirely west of the railway network in Manchukuo, and thus forms a marginal territory beyond the zones in which troops can be moved easily by rail. It sets up a framework for controlling Manchukuo by dividing the interests of the Chinese, naturally more hostile to Japan, from those of the Mongols, naturally more friendly to Japan because of being saved from the all-extinguishing effects of Chinese colonization. In its frontier aspects it is comparable, at least to a certain extent, with the Northwest Frontier of India—a border region of separate economic and social character, with a population of warlike tradition from which may be recruited troops to hold down the more numerous but less warlike Chinese population of the southeast.

Economically, this great Mongol province within Manchukuo has possibilities which the world at large has not yet appreciated. The Chinese exploitation of Manchuria was weak in manufacturing, mining, forestry—everything but agriculture. It was not only overbalanced by agriculture, but the agriculture was predominantly of a low-grade type—the hand-cultivation of the great estates of absentee landlords by refugee colonists with no capital and no economic independence. For the raising of livestock the Chinese had no tradition and no aptitude. It is indeed a regular characteristic of the Chinese colonization of Mongol land that first-rate pasture land is ploughed under for crops and exhausted within a few years, by the blowing away of the top soil, after which it is unproductive either for farming or for pasture.

This meant that Manchuria, under Chinese control, was lacking in economic diversification. Japanese control will certainly tend to remedy this, because Japan needs not only the grain and beans of Manchukuo, but its minerals, timber, meat, wool and hides. Japan at present buys wool from Australia. Nothing can be more certain than that a serious effort will be made to develop a supply of wool in Manchukuo. The segregation of Mongol territory, with laws protecting the Mongols against Chinese colonization, opens the way for experiments in the improvement of livestock that will benefit both Japan and the Mongols. The agricultural experiment stations of the South Manchuria Railway

THE MONGOLS OF MANCHURIA

succeeded years ago in "stabilizing" a cross-bred Mongol-merino sheep, and other kinds of livestock, which never made headway because of the decline of the Mongols and Chinese lack of interest. With the experimental stage already completed, breeding on a large scale can begin at once.

All of these considerations might be thought interesting primarily to Manchukuo and Japan, were it not for the peculiar frontier position of Manchukuo and the crucial importance of the Mongol part of that frontier. In its larger aspect, the establishment of Manchukuo means a new chapter in the history of Asia; a new chapter, however, in continuation of an old chronicle. It is a cast back to the two thousand years in which the tides of Chinese history were set and controlled by the frontier of the Great Wall, before the brief interlude of the Western "sea-barbarians."

The problem would be comparatively simple if Japan, alone, were the dominating continental power, balancing the sea-power of the Western world represented by America and the members of the League of Nations. There is, however, an inevitable opposition between Japan and Russia. It is probably absurd to say that either Japan or Russia *wants* a war. The real question is whether war can be avoided. If it cannot be avoided, then either nation may "want" war, in the sense of preferring to fight at a time convenient for itself and awkward for its opponent.

In the event of a war between Russia and Japan, the strategic capacities of the Siberian-Manchukuo frontier are reasonably well known to both nations. The railway mileages are known; the number of troops that each nation could bring into action, and the time it would take to get them into action, can be calculated without gross inaccuracy. It is obvious that Japan must have taken into account the possibilities of a Russian air offensive based on Vladivostok and directed against Osaka and Tokyo, and that something must have been done, in the way of preparation, to discount the effectiveness of such an attack. It is ridiculous, on the other hand, to assume that Japan could dispose of Russia by occupying Vladivostok and the Maritime Province of Siberia. In fact a frontal defeat for either nation would only mean a straight-line withdrawal; it would not radically change their basic relationship. That, after all, is why the Russo-Japanese war of 1904-5 was indecisive. It was only the first round.

The only flank which either nation could turn by a sweeping and decisive movement is the Outer Mongolian flank of Siberia, or the Inner Mongolian flank of Manchukuo. The problems of Vladivostok and the Ussuri-Amur frontier are local and tactical: the problem of Mongolia is one which allows room for strategy. The terrain is open: the Trans-Siberian Railway flanks it, the railways of Manchukuo point straight at it, the scope of movement covers many hundreds of miles. Mongolia, therefore, of which the world knows less than it knows of China, Siberia or Manchukuo, is the key to the destiny of the whole Far East.

There are certainly not more than five million Mongols all told. Of these about a million are in Outer Mongolia, occupying a territory as large as the United States east of the Mississippi. About a million are in the part of Inner Mongolia lying north of Suiyüan and Kalgan. About two million are in the Hsingan province of Manchukuo, in a territory of roughly 100,000 square miles—about half the size of France. Perhaps a million more are scattered through Chinese Turkistan, the Kokonor province of Tibet, the Buriat Republic of Siberia (contiguous with Outer Mongolia) and far away in the Astrakhan region, on the lower Volga, in Russia. Thus there are actually about twice as many Mongols in Manchukuo as there are in Outer Mongolia.

The weakness of the Mongols, as a scattered people of limited economic development in an enormous territory— nearly as large as the United States, in all—is obvious. Their strategic position, however, is remarkably strong; so strong that in the event of a war between Russia and Japan they might, by vigorous action on behalf of one nation or the other, be able to influence the result, perhaps decisively.

Manchukuo holds about half of Inner Mongolia, consisting of Barga (the western part of Heilungchiang province); part of the Nonni valley (also in Heilungchiang); Jerim League (covering practically all of Fengt'ien province west of the Shanhaikuan-Mukden Railway, and parts of Heilungchiang and Kirin as well) and Josoto and Jo-oda Leagues (in Jehol province). About two-thirds of Jerim League, all of Josoto League and half of Jo-oda League have been thickly settled by Chinese, and have not been included in the estimated 100,000 square miles of Hsingan province.

Chinese Inner Mongolia, as it may now be called, is about as large as Manchurian Mongolia. It is divided between the provinces of Chahar and Suiyüan; the inclusion within the Chinese provincial system being designed to hasten colonization and the obliteration of the Mongols. These Mongol territories consisted originally of the three Leagues of Silingol, Olanchab and Ordos or Yeghe Jo, together with the Chahars and the Suiyüan Tumets. Alashan (properly Alakshan) and Edsin Gol (properly Ejen-ni Gol) which are contiguous to Inner Mongolia on the west, and politically are now affected by the same conditions, belong historically to Western or Central Asian Mongolia.

Of these territories, the Chahar Mongol country, in the south of Chahar province, and extending westward into Suiyüan province, has been 70 per cent colonized. The Tumet country, adjacent to the city of Kueihua in Suiyüan province, has been almost wholly colonized. All the best land in the Ordos, in the west of Suiyüan province, has been colonized. About 40 per cent of the land in Olanchab League, in the north of Suiyüan province, has been colonized. The Silingol territory, a long strip in the north of Chahar province, bordered on the north by Outer Mongolia and on the east by Hsingan province, is the only region in Chinese Inner Mongolia that has entirely escaped colonization. The Mongols of the ten Banners of Silingol are therefore the backbone of the present movement of resistance against Chinese aggression.

It can thus be seen how the creation of Hsingan province in Manchukuo has tightened up all the latent tensions in Mongolia. Until the Japanese intervention of 1931, two main forces were at work among the Mongols. In Outer Mongolia, a Mongol nation was being built, under strong Russian influence but none the less nationalistic in character. Throughout Inner Mongolia, the Chinese were encroaching and the Mongols were being wiped out. The princes were supported by the Chinese authorities, and were encouraged to assume absolute powers (powers a good deal greater than those they had exercised under the old, pure Mongol tradition) in the domains that were left to them; but at the same time they were forced to yield fresh grants of land to the Chinese every year.

This deprived the Mongols of their natural leaders, and faced them with the bitter choice of extinction if they remained under Chinese domination, as against combined rebellion and social revolution if they should attempt to break away. The princes, as a class, were necessarily opposed to union with Outer Mongolia, because it would have meant that many of them would have been killed and the rest deprived of all their powers and revenue.

By the creation of Hsingan province, however, a fresh alternative was made possible. Since the Mongols of Manchukuo have been given regional autonomy, with a status which approximates to alliance with the Japanese, the princes have been able to assume once more the position of natural leaders of their people, in a movement which may yet restore unity and nationality to the Mongols. The princes therefore are no longer defeatists by the necessity of their position, and Inner Mongolia has emerged into open and dangerous rivalry with Outer Mongolia. The choice before the Mongols, as a whole, is between revolutionary nationalism, in association with Russia, and conservative nationalism, in association with Japan, but led by their own princes, descendants of the holy House of Chingghis, and fortified by their own religion, which as part of the old "feudal" system has suffered heavily in Outer Mongolia.

The regions of Inner Mongolia still under Chinese overlordship have responded promptly to the new hope. Their most active leader has been the Prince of West Sunid, in Silingol League, who has been referred to in news despatches under his Chinese name and title of Te Wang. He stands for the new feeling that the Mongols of Inner Mongolia, if they are determined enough, may now win independence and safety.

He stands also for the feeling, not yet obvious to the outer world, that a general restoration is at hand which may sweep from Inner Mongolia into Outer Mongolia. The symbol of this feeling was the coronation of P'u Yi as the monarchical ruler of Manchukuo. The status of P'u Yi as "Chief Executive" was undoubtedly felt by all the people of Manchukuo, but especially by the Mongols, to be ambiguous. A Chief Executive in a quasi Civil Service position could be much too easily removed if it were decided to annex Manchukuo to Japan. The coronation of a sovereign commits Japan much more definitely to maintenance of the independence of Manchukuo. (There is no analogy here between Manchukuo and Korea, because the Korean sovereign who was deposed by Japan had not been created by Japan.)

For the Mongols especially the recognition of the legitimist heir of the Manchu Emperors as the sovereign of Manchukuo is significant. The Mongols had never looked on the Manchu Emperors as alien conquerors. The Manchurian Mongols in particular, because they had been allies of the Manchus even before the Manchu conquest of China, felt that they were equals of the Manchus as founders of the Manchu Empire. Moreover a Manchu Emperor, or Ejen Khagan to use the Mongol term,[2] is a better focus of unity among the Mongols than any Mongol candidate could be. The Mongol ruling princes are all descendants of different sons or brothers of Chingghis Khan; or, in the case of the Kharchin princes in Jehol, of his daughter. There is no convincing reason why one of them should be made supreme over the others. The original recognition of the Manchu Emperors as overlords of the Mongols was largely the result of negotiations to end the fighting among different descendants of the heirs of Chingghis, and consequently the heir of the Manchu line is still regarded by

[2] The Mongol term is of importance, because it was the term used when the Manchu Emperor ruled all China, Manchuria, Mongolia, Chinese Turkistan and Tibet. It is thus a "restoration" term, and will inevitably be used by all Mongols, even though the official *Chinese* characters for the title of the sovereign of Manchukuo will not restore the exact title used for the former Manchu Emperors.

conservative Mongols as the natural Emperor of the Mongols.

The autonomy movement in Chinese Inner Mongolia represents, as might be expected, an effort to find out, in the first place, whether better terms can be obtained from China than from Manchukuo. The Nanking Government appears to be willing to guarantee immunity from further colonization, and even from provincial supervision. The Chinese border provinces, however, object strongly to a "generous" policy toward the Mongols. Formerly, Mongol affairs were supervized by a central bureau in the National Government at Nanking, but at the same time were dealt with by the local authorities of the provinces among which Mongol territories had been divided. The result was that Chinese pressure on the Mongols remained constant, while Mongol demands for negotiation were shuttled back and forth between the provincial governments and the central Government, without ever being fairly answered. The Mongols now demand the right to go over the heads of the provincial authorities, and to deal directly and finally with Nanking.

Obviously, however, such late and unwilling concessions by the Chinese, even if they are granted in full, are no permanent solution for the Mongol question. They merely enable the Mongol leaders to take a little more time in which to work out a policy toward Manchukuo and Outer Mongolia.

It is also plain enough that from the point of view of Manchukuo it would be better not to instigate a rising in

Chinese Inner Mongolia, but to come to the support of a rising which the Mongols themselves had begun. If the Mongols were to rebel outright against China, they would have to appeal to Manchukuo for support. From the point of view of the Mongols, however, it would be better to make Manchukuo (and therefore Japan) commit itself first by supplying arms and offering open support. This would be a guarantee that the Mongols were not being used simply to bring bargaining pressure on China, and would commit Japan and Manchukuo to a permanent policy of support for the conservative Mongols, under terms favorable to the Mongols themselves.

These, however, are details, and are unimportant in comparison with the fact that no Japanese continental policy can be complete without an active Mongol policy. Japan, having created the state of Manchukuo, and given it a Mongol policy by setting aside the province of Hsingan, can no longer avoid extending its interest into the western part of Inner Mongolia.

If a Japanese forward policy in Inner Mongolia is inevitable, a clash between Inner and Outer Mongolia is no less inevitable. It is inherent in both the geographical and political conditions. Inner Mongolia encloses Outer Mongolia on the east and south. It offers, through the railways and ports of Manchukuo, a route for the export of Outer Mongolian products, which in recent years have been monopolized by Siberia. The unification of Inner Mongolia, again, in association with Manchukuo, will create a new Mongolian frontier so vulnerable for both Siberia and Manchukuo that it cannot stand long without a test of strength.

Above all, the Mongols themselves are bound to look for war. All Mongols must think inevitably in terms of Mongol unification; and the ancient cleavage between Inner and Outer Mongolia does not alter this innate urge toward unity. The Mongol Empire brought about a unification of the Mongols based on Outer Mongolia; the Manchu Empire also unified the Mongols, but it began with Inner Mongolia. In the modern phase, the tribes of Inner Mongolia hung back because they had something to lose as well as to gain. Socially and politically, unification meant submission to the revolutionary Government of Outer Mongolia. Now it is possible to think of unification in terms of a counter-revolution in Outer Mongolia, leading to the restoration of the hereditary princes, the Lama Church and the old tradition.

While the Government of Outer Mongolia is a strong one, and has proved its ability to rule without the support of Russian troops, it is undeniably a minority government, and its ability to prevent counter-revolution rests undeniably on the supply of Russian arms. Its leaders are probably the pick of the nation, but they will not represent a national majority until the generation which remembers the old days and the old ways dies out, and is replaced by one which has grown up entirely under the new order.

The anti-revolutionary Mongol leaders are aware of this. They know that if a counter-revolution is to be successful, it must be begun while the men of the older generation are still vigorous. Many of them believe that it would not require a large army to win over Outer Mongolia to the new movement of "conservative nationalism"; that it would be necessary only to supply arms and leadership. Thus, for the first time since Outer Mongolian independence became effective, Outer Mongolia has more to gain by temporizing and evasion, and Inner Mongolia more to gain by decisive action.

It is impossible for a friend of the Mongols to consider the almost certain prospect of Mongol civil war without pity and regret. Undoubtedly, the pick of the Mongol nation to-day are the young intellectuals who believe that a successful revival of the Mongols cannot be achieved by patching up the old order; that it demands the "liquidation" of the hereditary princes and at least a thorough reform of the Lama Church. These leaders of the younger men are to be found throughout Inner Mongolia as well as in Outer Mongolia.

On the other hand the conservative leaders, the princes and the high lamas, are most of them honest and patriotic men, and some of them are very able. Their trouble is that they are born out of time, for the old tradition is now decayed, and it will be hard, though it may be possible, to make it clean and strong again in time to lead the nation as tribal feeling believes that it should. Its greatest disadvantage is the bad repute that it has among the younger men, because of the known fact that the princely class, in recent years, has on the whole set its class interests above the national interest—although it failed through despair, and because of the feeling that even good leadership was hopeless, much more than through dishonesty. Another disadvantage is the inevitable opposition of the conservatives to education and reform, because of the fear that "progressiveness" will mean revolutionary ideas.

As the matter now stands, the initiative lies with Japan rather than with Russia. The whole Russian policy is necessarily defensive, in order to gain time while the young, the thoroughly Sovietized generation matures, and the economic sinews of the nation are strengthened. It is easy enough to suggest alternatives of disaster. Japan, for instance, may not be in a good position to make a frontal attack on Russia; but it might be good policy to start a tribal war in Mongolia, and to follow it up if there seemed a good chance of bringing Outer Mongolia under Japanese control. If that were accomplished, in fact, there would be no need for Japan to force war on Russia, for the whole of Siberia and the Trans-Siberian Railway would be outflanked.

But could Russia let Mongolian events go so far without intervening? For the most imminent danger is that Japan and Russia, even if they both wish to avoid war, may be drawn into war through Mongolia. Japan cannot afford not to organize and support the Mongols who are within Manchukuo, and this necessarily involves Japan in the affairs of all the Mongols. Nor can Russia afford not to support Outer Mongolia. While, however, both Russia and Japan may wish to stop short of war, the general trend of events among the Mongols themselves makes for war.

THE MONGOLS OF MANCHURIA

There is no telling when or how, or on what frontier, a tribal war may start in Mongolia. Still less can it be foreseen how far that war might spread. The powers of the world may plan for peace, but Manchukuo was fashioned under the star of war, and the star shines now toward Mongolia. Empires, in the end, are masters of the men who build them: you cannot claim a great destiny and then refuse to follow it up.

Chapter II

IMPORTANCE AND HISTORICAL BACK-
GROUND OF THE MANCHURIAN MONGOLS

IT is evident from the maps published in Manchukuo
that the boundaries of the autonomous Mongol province of Hsingan have not been decided only by the present
distribution of Mongol population within Manchukuo.
"Railway politics" and strategy must also have been taken
into consideration. The frontier between Chinese and
Mongols has been drawn so as to leave to the Chinese
population of Manchukuo, as far as possible, all land
opened up by the new railways, the Mongols being confined to the unexploited western territory. In fact, if Manchukuo be considered a buffer state, then Hsingan is the
buffer province of the buffer state. The frontiers of Hsingan
province are therefore of the greatest interest, ethnically,
politically, economically and historically. The maps here
used are based on an original map published by the authorities of Hsingan province, dated 13 October 1932. This
map in turn is physically based on the South Manchuria
Railway map of Manchuria, current before the founda-

tion of Manchukuo, which is issued in various forms.

The Mongols of Manchuria are important for three chief reasons: their numbers, the extent of their territory, and the strategic position they hold in relation to Outer Mongolia and to the part of Inner Mongolia still nominally under the control of China. In all three respects their importance in recent years has been obscured by Chinese policy; with the result that their present emergence into the affairs of Manchukuo and China appears comparatively sudden and perplexing.

In the early years of the Manchu Empire (1644-1911), the importance of the Mongols was always emphasized, together with the fact that Mongol territories were different in character from the Chinese part of the Empire. This was because the Manchu Empire was founded on a coalition of frontier powers, which made possible the conquest of China. After the Manchus had transferred their capital to Peking, and as the Manchus of the Court became Chinese in culture, they developed gradually an "antihistorical" conception of the Empire, treating China as the center and base and the frontier dominions, which had originally been the base, as auxiliaries. This tendency was made positive by the assertion of Western maritime power in the nineteenth century, transferring the main focus of Chinese international affairs from the Great Wall, where historically it had always rested, to the sea coast.

The tendency was hardened again by the course of events under the Republic of China. Manchus, Mongols, Moslems (who have always functioned in Chinese history rather as a nation than as a faith) and Tibetans were treated at first as participants in the Republic, on a sort of federative basis. Because, however, the new Republic was treated internationally as essentially a *Chinese* Republic, and because the introduction of armaments and railways, under Western pressure, developed an outward thrust against the frontiers which was a totally new phenomenon in Chinese history, there arose inevitably a tendency to subordinate all "tribal" interests to the predominant interests of the Chinese.

From 1927, when the Kuomintang or Nationalist Party came into power, this tendency was frankly asserted as a policy. The Manchus already had virtually disappeared, by absorption among the Chinese, although the regionalism of Manchuria remained a serious problem. This regionalism, together with the quasi-national interests of Mongols, Moslems and Tibetans was to be suppressed and denied. All racial, cultural and linguistic minorities were to be smothered and absorbed by the Chinese, and the semi-independent outer dominions were to be converted into provinces homogeneous with China proper. Thus the name of Peking (Pei-ching, Northern Capital) was altered to Peiping (Pei-p'ing, Northern Peace) in reminiscence of the name it had borne for a short while after the downfall of the Mongol Empire in China, and as a symbol of the "pacification" of the reactionary North by the nationalist South. The name of Fengt'ien province in Manchuria (Feng-t'ien, Ordained by Heaven) with its imperial connotation, was altered to Liao-ning (Tranquillity of Liao, from the Liao River), indicating its complete assimilation to China. (The name, under Manchukuo, has been changed to Fengt'ien once more.)

The Mongol territories in Manchuria had already been divided among the different provinces, and the rest of Inner Mongolia was similarly apportioned in 1929 among the "normal" Chinese provinces of Jehol, Chahar, Suiyüan and Ninghsia, after having been, for some years, administered under the preliminary form of "Special Administrative Areas." Thus the *Tung Pei Nien Chien,* the official yearbook of Manchuria published under the auspices of the Kuomintang, just before the Japanese intervention of 1931, contains lists of Mongol "Banners" and "Leagues," but no definition of Mongol territory or separate figures of Mongol population, much less any acknowledgment of the "Mongol question" affecting a great part of Manchuria. The standard Japanese maps of Manchuria, published by the South Manchuria Railway, carried much more detail about the distribution and tribal boundaries of the Mongols than did Chinese maps, even before the creation of Manchukuo.

The Mongols are important numerically as the largest racial minority in Manchuria, though it is impossible to detect this from any standard work of reference, or even in the Lytton Report. No exact figures are available, but the fairest estimate is probably two million. The importance of the Mongol population has usually been minimized in order to enhance the importance of the Chinese character of Manchuria. The Mongols are referred to as forming from three to five per cent of the population, or in terms of population per square mile, which makes them appear inconsiderable and creates the impression that all that surplus land ought to be taken away and given to somebody who could use it. This is unfortunate, since the Mongol question cannot be properly understood unless land, people, history, and position are all considered, and unless possibilities of economic development other than colonization are fairly appraised.

Mongol territory, in spite of the way it has been eaten into by colonization, is still the largest territorial unit in Manchukuo, as can be seen from the map of Hsingan province. This was true even before the inclusion of Jehol within Manchukuo. Indeed, it is of great importance to have it clearly understood that "Eastern Inner Mongolia" does not consist of Jehol province and Barga, and nothing else, as is so often assumed; the Mongol territories in Jehol are only about a quarter of the total Mongol territories in Manchukuo.

Strategically, the Mongol territory of Manchuria is of cardinal importance. Its main axis is the Hsingan range, which runs from the Amur basin southward all the way into Jehol province. The Mongol land lying east of this range is the Eastern Inner Mongolia made familiar by Japanese usage, while the Barga region, lying west of the Hsingan range and now included in Hsingan province, is historically a separate Mongol territory, never fully identified with either Inner or Outer Mongolia. Bordering both on Western Inner Mongolia and on Outer Mongolia, the Mongol territory of Manchuria affords the easiest line of communication between these major divisions of the old Mongol domain. The Gobi desert, lying east and west, has always been recognized both tribally and internationally as the natural line of cleavage between Inner and Outer Mongolia. The desert itself, though not an absolute barrier, is a kind of barrier zone, and has been of great importance ever since Outer Mongolia declared itself independent of China in 1912, and especially since 1921, when the policies of Soviet Russia and Outer Mongolia were coördinated.

The Gobi divides the revolutionary Mongols of the north from the conservative Mongols of the south and east. The Gobi, however, is bounded on the east by the southern reaches of the Hsingan range, and along the flanks of this range there is good pasture and passage from north to south, and easy communication between Outer and Inner Mongolia. Whoever controls the Mongols of the Hsingan range can therefore exercise an influence on both Inner and Outer Mongolia, in terms of tribal politics which have a plain meaning for the people of the country, in a way that cannot be done from any other region.

Historically, the Mongols of Manchuria are an overflow from Outer Mongolia. The Hsingan mountains appear to have formed, in the most ancient times, a barrier between Tungus tribes on the east and Mongols, or tribes from which the modern Mongols eventually developed, on the west. The Tungus are related to the Mongols in race, language and culture, but at the same time are distinct from them in all these respects. In the great forests and along the great rivers of Manchuria the Tungus groups differentiated themselves from the Mongol groups at a very early period. In the north they developed both a reindeer-economy and a dog-economy (in the use of dog-sleds for travel and transport) which set them apart from the pastoral Mongols. In the south, they adapted themselves to agriculture more readily than did the Mongols; but in the south, also, because the geographical cleavage between Mongols and Tungus was much less abrupt, and the two groups were therefore closer to each other, they merged with each other more readily in race and culture.

Of the great dynasties that have originated in Manchuria, the Liao or Khitan of the tenth and eleventh centuries were probably of an intermediate Mongol-Tungusic stock, whose political power was based on the upper Liao valley, in what is now the northern half of Jehol province. They conquered China as far as the Yellow River, but in the twelfth century were displaced by the dynasty of the Chin or Nüchen, the founders of which were probably of purer Tungusic stock, originating in the forests to the east and northeast of the Liao valley, in what is now Kirin province. They took over and enlarged the conquests of the Liao dynasty, pushing on into China as far as the Yangtze valley.

It was the Chin, in all probability, who built the Hsingan Wall, although this wall is in the south sometimes popularly attributed to Yüeh Fei, a Chinese hero who fought against the "barbarians," and in the north to Chingghis

Khan—simply because the Chin is a half-obliterated dynasty in the folk-memory of both Chinese and Mongols. The Hsingan Wall can only have been built to defend an empire based on Manchuria against invasion from Mongolia. It runs from a point in Jehol province along the eastern slope of the Hsingan range to a point in the Nonni valley. Crossing the Hsingan range diagonally from this point, traces of another wall can be picked up, running roughly east and west across the northern part of the Barga territory; this is quite possibly a part of the same frontier fortification system. It can be traced even farther west, near the frontier of Outer Mongolia and Siberia. In the south, some of the Japanese maps mark the Hsingan Wall as ending near the town of Solun. I have myself, however, seen it continuing past Solun, where I followed it for about twenty miles, and have added this extra length to the map. One of my companions, a Jehol Mongol, said that it continued "a long way" into Jehol. Some of the Japanese maps continue the Wall, after a gap, near the frontier between Jehol and Chahar. Near this southernmost part of the Hsingan Wall, the remnants of another wall can be found, running from west to east across Jehol, on the southerly side of the Shira Muren or upper Liao valley. This wall, however, (not marked on the map) was probably a frontier between the Liao or Khitan dynasty and the Northern Sung dynasty of China, before the Liao began their southward expansion.

The line of the Hsingan range and Hsingan Wall, representing as it does the reinforcement of a natural boundary by a military frontier, may be regarded as the "classic" or normal ancient frontier between tribes of Mongol type and tribes of Tungus type. This ancient frontier was overwhelmed by the Mongols in the thirteenth century, in the course of the conquests begun by Chingghis Khan, which destroyed the Chin Empire and eventually brought the whole of China under Mongol rule.

It was during this period that the Mongols reached their maximum territorial expansion in Manchuria. It is probable that they did not move directly east from Outer Mongolia through Barga, but spread first over Southern Hsingan, occupied the whole great central plain of Manchuria, and then expanded east and north until they were held up, not by military action, but by heavy forests, which were unsuitable both for the movement of Mongol cavalry and for permanent Mongol occupation. Although they established political control beyond these limits, their tribal migration did not go so far as their imperial power.

On the southeast, the establishment of a Mongol population was checked along the line of the Willow Palisade (itself a very old frontier) by agricultural regions occupied by Chinese, where the Mongols could conquer but could not settle. Within the great forest regions the "wild" Tungusic tribes, outliers of the Chin people, continued their ancient life as nomadic hunters, of whom some at least were also reindeer herdsmen, and some were riparian tribes, using canoes in summer and dog-sleds in winter. The "tame" Tungusic tribesmen, whose economy and customs had been modified by their Chinese conquests, were absorbed partly among the Chinese, in the enclave between the Willow Palisade and Inner Willow Palisade, and partly among the Mongols themselves, in the region about Ch'angch'un.

A remnant of the Chin people, however, in the Kirin region, preserved their ethnic identity, and an economy which was a compromise between the "tribal" and the Chinese. It was from this remnant that the Manchus arose, after several centuries, building a nation on the nucleus of the old "tame" or semi-civilized tribes, which were thereafter distinguished within the Manchu organization as "Old Manchus," with accretions from such tribes as the "Fishskin Tatars" (Hêjê), Daghors and Solons, who were differentiated as "New Manchus."

The fact that the thirteenth century Mongol conquests in Manchuria were backed up so largely by tribal migration well to the east of the "classical" frontier may have been due in part to the disappearance of the forests which had once covered the Southern Hsingan. Under the Liao and the Chin many cities had been founded in the central plain of Manchuria (although it is probable that they were more important as trading centers than as the centers of large agricultural populations) and it is likely that there was a considerable destruction of forests in this period. South of the headwaters of the T'ao or T'ao-erh River (Tor or Tora in the original Mongol; said to be from the name of a kind of shrub, but possibly from a word meaning a fort, and used for old ruins) the forests have now almost totally disappeared. Still farther to the south, however, in Jehol province, one stand of timber remained in the (Manchu)

Imperial Hunting Park, to show the old extent of the forest. It has been cut off by the Chinese only in recent years, and a little of it still remains.

The Mongol or Yüan dynasty was followed, in China proper, by that of the Ming (1368-1644) which filled the interval between the Mongol Empire and the Manchu conquest. Great as was the resurgence of Chinese power under the Ming, it did not succeed in materially altering the Mongol situation north of the Great Wall. It is true that Ming generals campaigned far to the north, in Outer Mongolia, and that great victories were recorded. These victories, however, never amounted to conquest, for the Mongols remained in fact independent. Indeed, from the nature and results of the Chinese campaigns, it may be inferred that the armies concerned were not genuine invading Chinese armies, but that the Chinese operated by backing one Mongol tribal group against another, and claimed their victories as Chinese conquests. The Mongols were driven from China in the first place largely because of disputes (especially between Northern and Southern Mongols) over the succession to the throne, and these disputes were continued, after the loss of the empire in China, in wars for tribal hegemony. They continued, in fact, for three centuries, and were only terminated by recognition of the Manchu line as Emperors of the Mongols, or rather paramount overlords of the Mongol princes.

The Ming dynasty fell so far short of breaking the power of the Mongols that in 1449, only eighty years after the

47

establishment of the dynasty, the Mongols actually invaded China, captured the Chinese Emperor and held him for eight years.[1] In 1554 Peking was again besieged, though not taken, by Anda, famous as the Altan Khan or Golden Khan of the Tumets,[2] who were not barbarians, from distant Outer Mongolia, but a comparatively small tribe, semi-civilized and semi-agricultural, established on the very borders of China, in the Kueihua-Suiyüan region. The name Kueihua, which may be interpreted as "the Return to Civilization," was in fact bestowed on the capital of Altan Khan by the Ming, after the conclusion of peace; one of the terms being the grant of a title of honor to Altan Khan.[3] The name Suiyüan, originally given to the walled Manchu garrison town standing alongside the trading town of Kueihua, but now the name of the province as well, means "Rehabilitation of the Distant (Regions)" and is thus the mark of a later stage in the growth of the Manchu Empire, when the distinctions between conquered China and the dominant Frontier were being reduced to terms of balance of power.

In Manchuria itself the Chinese power must have been confined, in direct administration, to the most ancient "Chinese pale," bounded on the west by the Willow Palisade and on the north and northeast by the Inner Willow Palisade. Here, in the lower valley of the Liao and the

[1] Howorth, Vol. I.

[2] The date of this siege is taken from Baddeley, Vol. I.

[3] *Mongol Pastures,* I, 2, 21b. This source does not record any siege of Peking, merely saying that Altan Khan attacked the Ming borders, whereupon the Ming were frightened and sent an emissary to grant the title of Loyal Prince, and a golden seal, and to urge peace.

Liaotung ("East of Liao") peninsula, the Chinese had been permanently established for centuries, though at intervals they had been ruled by barbarian conquerors. Their presence in this extreme southeastern part of Manchuria was based on sea-communication with Shantung and the use of the lower Liao River for the transport of grain and goods, which gave an economic range permitting the standard Chinese social economy of groups of cities in close touch with a well-developed agricultural countryside.

The distribution and character of the Mongol tribes in Western Manchuria were certainly affected very little at this time. Among the Tungusic tribes of the northern forests, it would appear that the Ming Chinese operated by the device (standardized from of old) of granting titles and subsidies to certain of the chiefs, and supporting them against possible tribal rivals. The subsidized chiefs were then listed as "tribute bearers." By this means the Chinese cultural influence penetrated far beyond the limits of true political authority; but unfortunately, it has become the custom to take any kind of evidence of Chinese penetration as proof of government control.

Thus in a pamphlet by Dr. Li Chi [4] it is claimed that two stone tablets found near the mouth of the Amur are decisive evidence of Chinese conquest and administration, as the result of an expedition led by a Chinese eunuch in 1411. Yet from the form of administration it appears that these regions were still, properly speaking, tribal. "The administration of these garrisons was left to native chiefs

[4] *Manchuria in History.*

with hereditary rights," and "if they should become dis-
obedient, the appointment might be transferred to another
family at any moment." In other words, control was by
manipulation rather than by decree, and could not be asserted independently of tribal rivalries. Moreover, it is
claimed, in the same study, that the original Great Wall lay
north of the present work, the eastern part of which was
in the main constructed under the Ming. This, it might be
thought, would be evidence, of the most important kind,
of the limits of real power under the Ming; for if their campaigns in the north had been at all satisfactory, they need
not have constructed an enormous defensive system far
to the south of the region claimed, and south even of the
ancient Great Wall alignment. As for the "original Great
Wall," it may well have run through what is now Jehol
province. The fortification in the Shira Muren valley has
already been mentioned; there are also traces of other
walled frontiers in Inner Mongolia, north of the present
Great Wall. I have discussed elsewhere [5] one interpretation
of these outer wall-systems; but whether any of them was
the line of the earliest *main* wall can hardly be decided
without extensive archæological work.

The rise of the Manchus in the seventeenth century revealed the true power of the Mongols, and also made it
plain that the Mongols had maintained, through the period
of Chinese ascendancy, approximately the same territories,
tribal groupings and potential power. Only two important
changes had taken place. In the Nonni valley (and also,

[5] *Manchuria, Cradle of Conflict.*

it would appear, on the Argun and upper Amur [6]) outlying Mongols had begun to coalesce with Tungus tribes, thus founding the people later to be known as Daghors (called sometimes, after the Russian usage, Daurs). Where the Kirin forests touched the central plain a similar fusion had formed, apparently, the tribe usually called (following the Chinese transliteration) Yehonala. This name is possibly derived from a Mongol form, Yeghe Nere, Great Name; which would be a clan name rather than a tribal name.

The formation of the Manchu power began as a process of welding together a large number of small tribes, kin to each other in race and speech, but widely scattered and possessing almost no sense of political or tribal unity, and ranging in culture and economy from settled people in walled towns, which were the centers of agricultural districts enclosed by the forest—the Old Manchus—to semi-agricultural, semi-hunting people in forest clearings not yet quite permanently settled, and to reindeer nomads and remote hunting groups altogether "wild"—the New Manchus. It was the half-Mongol Yehonala who held out most stubbornly, in the first phase, against Manchu unification, and it was the subjugation of this tribe, resulting in its complete detachment from the Mongols and absorption into the growing Manchu nation, which gave the Manchus an initial ascendancy over the Mongols as the rising non-Chinese power in Manchuria. It may be mentioned here that it was from the extermination of the ruling house of Yehonala that there sprang the prophecy (said to have

[6] Lindgren.

been spoken by the last of the Yehonala chiefs before he
died in his burning stronghold) that the Yehonala would
yet be the destroyers of the Manchu house. As only the
immediate family of the chiefs had been killed, it was
made a house law of the Manchu Imperial line that no
Empresses might be taken from the stock of the Yehonala,
who were listed thenceforth as Manchus. At last, however,
a woman of the Yehonala came to be Empress; this was
the great Empress Dowager, Tzŭ Hsi, who is held to have
fulfilled the prophecy, though she was taken in the first
place as a "secondary consort," not as Empress.

After the Yehonala had been overcome, the Manchu
power spread rapidly along the fringe of the Mongol
regions in Manchuria, and the Nonni tribes, believing evidently that the future belonged to the Manchus rather
than the Mongols, began to join them voluntarily, and thus
became known as Daghors (the commonest Chinese transliteration is Ta-hu-li), from a Mongol word which is
roughly equivalent to our term "feudatory."

The early relations between Mongols and Manchus in
Manchuria are of the greatest interest. It is because they
have not been properly understood that the whole course
of Manchu, Manchurian and Mongol history (and therefore of Chinese history also), from the seventeenth century
onward has never been adequately interpreted. These early
relations are, or should be, indispensable material for the
study of the process of formation of tribal power, the type
of strategic power inherent in a nomad society, the type of
opposition between settled and nomadic peoples, the proc-

esses by which Empires founded north of the Great Wall have expanded into China, the process of political decay among nomads when, after victory in the field, they are associated with the exercise of power over an agricultural nation; and, finally, the degrees by which typical Chinese power, in periods when the frontiers of China have been cleared, breaks down as it expands beyond the Great Wall. The character of early Manchu-Mongol history has been obscured chiefly by later "official" interpretations, written in *Chinese* (a point of great importance, especially psychologically) at a period when the Manchus had come to regard their position in China as more important than their origins in Manchuria; but it has also suffered from mere neglect, because Western students of Chinese history have naturally and unconsciously interpreted Chinese affairs in the light of the *maritime* values which have been predominant in the foreign relations of China ever since the late eighteenth century.

The history of the Manchu conquests has been oversimplified, and the chief point which has been passed over without notice is that the Manchus were only one group among several possible claimants to power over China. At the close of the Ming dynasty, China had degenerated to a pitiful condition, both politically and economically, and the whole "outer barbarian" territory, from Tibet to the Liaotung Peninsula, was in turmoil. This was a state of affairs which had been known before in Chinese history. The general trend of the evidence is, that at such a period "barbarian" conquests in China do not depend on "pressure" among the northern tribes. The importance of famine and climatic change in disturbing the nomadic tribes have especially been overemphasized. Drought, for instance, affecting the pasturage, may be a stimulus toward migration and conquest; but it is not in itself a *creative* power. The barbarian conquest, at such a period, is not "necessary" in type; the barbarians are not forced to attempt invasion.

Politically, in the typical period of which the end of the Ming is an example, the peoples outside the Great Wall are not in the least afraid of China. Economically, they are affected to a certain extent in that their chiefs do not draw their subsidies regularly, and their people do not enjoy cheap trade in Chinese goods and in the purchase of grain for winter supplies—which, though not an essential to nomadic life, is a luxury which for centuries has been demanded. In such periods, the preliminary warfare that leads to conquest is never the warfare between Chinese and barbarians (though this may also be present, and confuse the issue). The preliminary wars do not originate in self-defense, nor is it intended to test the relative strength of nomads and settled people. Everything depends on the accident of the emergence of a leader of the right caliber; and the essential qualification of the leader is not the ability to raid and plunder China, for that has always been a commonplace of such periods. The single necessary qualification is the ability to hold the conquests made, and to guard the plunder.

In order to establish this qualification and win a dependable following, the ambitious barbarian leader must prove his worth, not to the Chinese but to his peers—the other possible barbarian invaders. It therefore follows as an axiom of Chinese history that successful invasions of China must be preceded by severe tribal fighting to the north of China; and that such fighting is much more serious, in a military sense, than the subsequent operations attending the actual invasion. It is not necessary to the present thesis to draw parallels from modern or contemporary Chinese history, though it would be interesting to draw them; but it may be pointed out that in the problems of Manchukuo the Chinese frontier offers no difficulties. The dangerous frontiers are those of Siberia and Mongolia. If they can be held, or expanded, then the problems of the Chinese frontier can be dealt with as matters of routine.

This also explains the readiness of a people like the Mongols to engage in the bitterest kind of fighting among themselves. Tribal war among the Mongols has always tended to result in the emergence of a great leader, while civil war in China has tended to result in giving some one man the largest profit in making terms with the conqueror from beyond the Great Wall. Deeply engrained in the Mongol consciousness is the feeling that any Mongol horde which can master other Mongols, can master anyone else in the world, so that in spite of totally changed conditions, their political instinct continues to function in its old channels. Even at a time like the present, when the issue to be decided is not the power of the Mongols, but their very existence, the average Mongol cannot think of Mongol unification except as the result of a war between Inner and Outer Mongolia, to determine the right of leadership. The world has changed, and with it the bases of military power, without the Mongols realizing it.

Historically, the success of barbarian invasions of China from the north has been so much a foregone conclusion that the invasions have tended to follow almost a fixed routine. The decisive events of such an invasion are those of the preliminary struggle. If a number of tribes of fairly equal strength emerge, then the succeeding conquests in China will be only partial. From such partial conquests arose the states and dynasties known as the Wei (386-535; Middle Inner Mongolia, Shansi and Honan); the Liao (907-1115; South Manchuria and North China to the Yellow River); the Chin (1115-1234; most of Manchuria and most of China north of the Yangtze); the Hsia (1036-1227; the Kokonor region of Tibet, Kansu and Western Shensi) and so forth.

If the preliminary fighting produces a leader of real genius, then the succeeding conquests are tidal in character —such as the conquests initiated by Chingghis Khan. It is noteworthy, in judging the importance of this kind of preliminary fighting, that the non-Chinese kingdom of Hsia, mentioned above, was considered worth the personal attention of Chingghis himself (who died in his final campaign against it); while the subjugation of that part of the Chin Empire which lay within China proper, and of the remnants of the Sung Empire to the south of it, was left to the lesser genius of his grandson and successor

THE MONGOLS OF MANCHURIA

Khublai Khan, known to the Mongols as Khobilai Sechin, or the Immortal and Wise.

At the end of the Ming dynasty, while the Manchus were rising in the east, the Mongols and Tibetans were disputing power in the west, and different groups of Mongols in the center. The Mongols produced a number of remarkable leaders, but so unconquerable, by Mongols or anyone else, were the different major divisions of the Mongol people, that none of them succeeded in winning complete mastery. It was this deadlock among the Mongols which allowed the Manchus, originally much inferior to them in power, to conquer China; but the Manchus were never strong enough to conquer the Mongols outright. Every major extension of Manchu power in Mongolia had therefore to be prepared by compromise, and the effect of this series of compromises was traceable thereafter throughout the history of the Manchu Empire—not only in China, but even more in Mongolia, Central Asia and Tibet.

In the mid-seventeenth century the Mongols occupied about one half of Manchuria and nearly the whole of what is now the province of Jehol. The Eastern Mongols formed a definite and at that time already well-recognized major division of the Mongol people, their territory and tribal organization, as has already been pointed out, being in the main a result of the thirteenth century Mongol expansion. They held a very strong position with regard to China, for they controlled access to the Kupeik'ou (Old North Pass) entry into the Peking plain, and to several other passes. They also held the hills flanking and overlooking the narrow coastal corridor which is the approach from Manchuria to the Great Wall at Shanhaikuan (the Sea and Mountain Barrier).

To the east of them were the Manchus, and the old Chinese Pale of Liaotung. To the west were the Chahar Mongols, whose approach to China was through Kalgan (the Barrier, from the Mongol word *khalaga*). The Chahars were under Likdan or Lingdan Khan (the Chinese transliteration of his name is Lin-tan), who was born in 1592 and ruled from 1603 (or 1604) to 1634, when he was defeated by the Manchus.[7] The Eastern Mongols feared the Chahars more than they feared either Chinese or Manchus—a fact which decided the fate of China, but which is not properly brought out in any standard history. Because of their preoccupation with Likdan, whose ambition was to form a new Mongol Empire and who started out in the traditional manner by campaigning against other Mongols, they were unable to use their full strength against the Manchus.

The wars between the Manchus and Eastern Mongols therefore took the following course. Nurhachih and his Manchus won a few victories over the Mongols, none of them really decisive, while the Mongols were taken up with affairs on the Chahar frontier. It is evident, however, even from the official Manchu records of the manner in which the Mongols offered allegiance, that unwillingness to come under Likdan Khan was a more important factor than the victories of the Manchus. Following up this ad-

[7] Baddeley, Vol. II.

vantage, the Manchus offered alliance to the Eastern Mongols, and were able, as a result of the alliance, to defeat Likdan Khan.

The natural development thereafter would have been a war of elimination between Manchus and Mongols; but in the meantime the Manchus had secured control of the old Chinese Pale in Liaotung, within the Willow Palisades. This Manchu success, also achieved by a mixed process of conquest and alliance, in which alliance and the enlistment of Chinese troops, resulting in the formation of the "Chinese Bannermen," was at least as important as conquest, immeasurably fortified the basis of Manchu power. The Manchu army, almost as mobile as Mongols and welded together by many campaigns, was now backed by the wealth and resources of the Chinese Pale. The combination of Manchu mobility and Chinese solidity was too much for the Eastern Mongols, who therefore remained content with the advantages they derived from the Manchu alliance, rather than risk the attempt to overthrow the Manchus. Moreover (and this was a factor of cardinal importance) the Eastern Mongols never produced a great leader peculiarly their own, like Altan Khan of the Tumets (b. 1507, d. 1583) Likdan Khan of the Chahars, or Galdan Khan of the Ölöts (d. 1745).

The Eastern Mongols therefore supported the foundation of the Manchu Empire in China; and the Manchus, working from the advantage of this initial Mongol alliance, were able thereafter to extend their Empire gradually until it included the Mongols of Outer Mongolia and Central

Asia. This is not the place to discuss in detail the relations of the Manchus with the Mongols as a whole; but it should be pointed out, and indeed cannot be too strongly emphasized, that Manchu sovereignty was not achieved by outright conquest, but was always based on alliance with some one group of Mongols against another group, and that the status of the Mongols within the Empire was different from, and higher than, that of the Chinese. The Manchus in almost every case made important concessions to each Mongol group that came within the Empire, using the favorable terms first accorded to the Eastern Mongols as a precedent.

The result was that the Mongols never regarded themselves as conquered subjects, but as free allies. "Among some ancient Mongolian archives," according to Giles, "there has recently been discovered a document, dated 1636, under which the Mongol chiefs recognized the suzerainty of the Manchu Emperor. It was, however, stipulated that, in the event of the fall of the dynasty, all the laws existing previously to this date should again come into force." [8] As this is only two years later than the defeat of Likdan Khan, the agreement must have applied specifically to the princes of the Manchurian Mongols. The high standing of all Mongols was, however, later confirmed in practical administration, decisions in Mongol cases being referred to the ancient Mongol code—essentially the same as the codification of tribal law drawn up in the time of Chingghis, and recognized also by the Russians as "Steppe

[8] Giles, 1912.

60

Law." [9] Under this practice the Mongols were granted a form of extraterritoriality, and the right of entry of Chinese into Mongolia was limited and regulated. Intermarriage between Mongols and Chinese was also prohibited, but this law was of course nullified by the habit of the Chinese traders in Mongolia of taking temporary Mongol wives.

It is on definite considerations of the specific relations between Mongols and Manchus that Outer Mongolia bases its claim to independence—the case being, in its most brief form, that China and Mongolia each owed allegiance to the Manchu Emperor, but on different grounds; that Mongolia did not "belong" to China, and that therefore the fall of the Manchu House broke the only link between China and Mongolia, the Mongols automatically becoming an independent nation. The same case could be stated for Inner Mongolia, but the Mongols of Inner Mongolia have not been strong enough to assert and carry it.

[9] *China Year Book.*

Chapter III

EARLY COLONIZATION: THE MONGOLS AS
THE PRIVILEGED PEOPLE

IT has already been pointed out that the plain between
the Hsingan Wall and the Willow Palisade is a region
which geographically favors contact and cultural exchange
between pastoral and agricultural communities; provided,
that is, that social and political conditions are also favorable. The spread of agriculture into this region, and the
foundation of cities, had intermittently been promoted in
the past by the existence of "barbarian" Empires based on
the Frontier, which exercised their power over China. The
Empires of Liao and Chin, which have already been mentioned, are good examples; but the same phenomenon had
been known in much earlier times.

Now the character of "colonization" and the "spread of
Chinese civilization" in such periods needs to be correctly
understood. It does not mean a merging of "barbarian" and
Chinese, with a consequent infusion of urbanity into the
barbarian and of virility into the Chinese, followed by an
outward surge of civilizing Chinese colonists into the raw

barbarian lands—at least, not at first. It means, on the contrary, that when a barbarian people successfully invades China, it divides into two classes. An administrating, controlling, garrisoning body moves into the conquered Chinese territory, but the main body remains behind in the original barbarian territory, because this barbarian territory has always been essential to dominion over China and therefore cannot be abandoned, for fear that another barbarian people will break in through it and challenge the newly founded power in China.

Since, however, the barbarians who move into China at once become a privileged class, enjoying all kinds of new luxuries, the barbarians who remain behind also feel entitled to luxuries. They therefore build little, provincial, half-barbarous imitations of the luxury-cities of China, and import a servile class of artisans to build the cities, traders to bring them the goods of China, and a servile, or at least dependent class of farmers to feed the cities, the artisans and the traders. The initial spread of city-building and agriculture of Chinese type into regions north of the Great Wall, controlled by barbarians, is therefore, in the *normal* historical cycle, a phenomenon of self-indulgence on the part of the barbarians and of parasitic dependence on the part of the Chinese.

There is, however, a secondary tendency, among those of the barbarians who are in touch with the luxury-cities and artificial agriculture, to be affected by the easier, more comfortable standards of life which they represent. It is almost impossible for outside observers, whether Chinese or Western, who cannot appreciate the very deep and genuine pride of the barbarian in being a barbarian, to understand that this, from the barbarian point of view, does not necessarily mean "progress" or "civilization." Our attitude is inevitably biased by the use of the term "barbarian" for the nomad and "civilized man" for the peasant, artisan and townsman.

The barbarian, however, is not, to himself, a barbarian; he is the free man, the strong man, the man who takes and who rules. From the barbarian point of view the "civilized" Chinese, throughout history, has been the dependent man, the weak man, the man who has things taken from him and who is ruled. To become *dependent* on the comforts of agriculture and towns is, according to the barbarian tradition, to degenerate. In the vocabulary of people like the Mongols, to this day, the term "hard" is used of Mongols and the term "soft" of Chinese. These terms do not stand only for physical robustness, but for the moral "hardness" of the man who lives in the saddle and makes his camp where he pleases, as against the moral "softness" of the man who is in bondage to the land he tills or the merchandise in which he deals; to his goods and his comfort, the safety of his roof and his walled town.

There can be no doubt that these characteristics are historically important. The Mongol herdsman looks down on the Mongol farmer. Even among the Manchus, whose assimilation to the Chinese is usually regarded as complete, men of the older Manchu villages in Manchuria, though they have quite lost their Manchu speech, tend to claim that they are "hardier" and "purer" than the city Manchu of Peking, and to claim a moral superiority, even though they somewhat grudgingly admit and admire the superior sophistication of the city Manchu.

Historically, the periods which we regularly treat as "periods in which the barbarians are civilized by the conquered" become quite different if we realize that they were periods in which the barbarians consciously indulged themselves in the *morally questionable* ease of civilization. The psychological characteristic of such periods is that of the athlete who breaks training, with the feeling that he can always, at some future time, work off the effects of easy living and return to form. It is only after two or three generations that the barbarians find they have lost their grip on their old form, and themselves become subservient to the civilization which they had begun by exploiting.

At this point there is a genuine turn in Frontier relations. The barbarians have become a class of Chinese; they no longer control China from the frontier but are forced, from their position within China, to prop up the frontier as best they can from within, lest they be themselves conquered by a fresh invasion from beyond the frontier. In this new phase the Chinese who has moved beyond the frontier takes on a new character. Originally a dependent, he has become genuinely rooted in the region. In one sense, he represents the "spread of civilization." In another, he has taken on the regional feeling of the Frontier. He has become primarily a frontiersman, and consequently, so long as the central power in China continues to function strongly he will continue to push outward, but when it begins to weaken and the rise of a new frontier power is at hand, he will either fall back into China, abandoning the frontier altogether, or identify himself, in a quasi-tribal manner, with the new frontier power that is beginning to press inward on China.

The most recent historical illustration of this process is the Manchu assumption of control within the old Chinese Pale in Southern Manchuria, which was followed in the first place by a wave of "defeatist" Chinese Manchurians migrating into China, and in the second place by the formation of a Chinese group within the regional frontier power which the Manchus created; these were the Chinese Bannermen who served with the Manchus in the conquest of China. The initial hesitancy of allegiance among them is best illustrated by the history of Wu San-kuei, the Chinese commander at the Great Wall, who admitted the Manchus after negotiation, so that their final march on Peking might well be called an intervention in the civil wars of China, rather than an invasion. The decision of Wu San-kuei is usually construed as a desperate effort to "save" China; for Chinese rebels from Shensi province had desecrated the tombs of the Ming Emperors and taken Peking, and the last ruler of the Ming dynasty had hanged himself as they broke into the Forbidden City. Wu San-kuei then came to terms with the Manchus (although his father was a hostage in the hands of the rebels) and with the Manchus marched on Peking to destroy the "usurpers:"

The whole incident, however, can be very differently interpreted if it be remembered that Wu San-kuei was a native of the Chinese Pale in southernmost Manchuria. He must, considering his rank and importance, have had both personal interests in Manchuria and personal connections among the Chinese Manchurians already serving with the Manchus. The decision which he made must have been a decision between playing his own hand in China, or taking the place to which his Manchurian affiliations entitled him in the regional coalition of Manchus, Mongols and Manchurian Chinese. His later career indicates that he may even have hoped to displace the Manchus, eventually, as the leading power within the coalition. The Manchus, at any rate, insured themselves against such a possibility, for while they continued Wu San-kuei in power and honor they kept him away from the Great Wall frontier; and in the end, finding himself jockeyed out of position, and unable to play the king-maker, he turned against the Manchus, and died a rebel.

These, then, were the forces at work in the Manchurian region, as between Manchus, Mongols and Chinese, at the time when the composite racial and regional power of Manchuria was about to break through the Great Wall and set up a new Empire in China. The Mongol princes of the region, owing to their early alliance with the Manchus, had been given many Manchu princesses in marriage, and this kind of personal relation between the princely families of the Manchurian Mongols and the Manchu Imperial House was to continue important in later years. The princes of the Manchurian Mongols therefore tended increasingly to take a Manchu and dynastic, rather than a Mongol and tribal point of view. They formed a powerful regional group, intermediary between the Manchus and the outlying Mongols, and they aspired, inevitably, to the same kind of career and position that appealed to rich and highly born Manchus. They began to patronize agriculture because of the fixed type of revenue it brought in and because it made possible for them, as the "upper class" of the Mongol constituency within the Manchurian regional coalition, an approximation to the "amenities of civilization" which the conquering Manchus had themselves, very early, begun to consider a social necessity.

Manchu high policy discouraged such tendencies, especially while the Manchus retained the impetus of their first ascendancy. Even in 1635, before the actual conquest of China, the Emperor rebuked his Court for the tendency to ape the Chinese, referring them, for a warning, to the example of the decline of the Chin dynasty of the Nüchen Tatars [1]—a clear case of the old *moral* distrust of "civilization."

It soon proved impossible to keep the Manchus who entered China from "luxuriating" in civilization. Moreover it was desirable, in order to win the respect of the Chinese, that Manchus of the upper classes at any rate should endeavor to reach the standard of the Chinese in scholarship —although the Chinese always looked with warrantable suspicion on the literary degrees awarded, by a system of

[1] *Tung Hua Lu*, 1st year of Ch'ung Te.

favoritism, to Manchu scholars. An effort was made, however, to keep the Manchus left in Manchuria from being
"contaminated." In the later years of the dynasty, colonies
of Peking Manchus were actually moved to Manchuria,
in a futile effort to renew their racial and regional spirit,
and to check the increase of the "hanger-on" class in
Peking.

No decrees of policy could halt the inevitable historical
process among the Manchus; but an intelligently organized
frontier policy did slow down the spread of civilization
among the Mongols very considerably. If the Mongols
could be held to their old tribal organization and culture
then the Manchus, by retaining as much as possible of
their own Frontier character, while at the same time taking
on something of the civilized character of the Chinese,
could hope to stand between Mongols and Chinese and
control both. Their stance in China, and in the Chinese
Pale of Manchuria, gave them the resources of an old and
rich civilization, while from the Mongols they could draw
troops that were at once first class fighting men and un-
sophisticated in politics.

It was necessary therefore to protect the tribal character
of the Mongols, but at the same time to interfere with tribal
processes in such a manner as to prevent the formation of
major tribal groupings among them, and especially to prevent the emergence of any tribal leadership which might
add political direction to their obvious but uncoördinated
racial and national unity. Mongol princes and nobles were
therefore barred from political and civil careers within

China, and restricted to military and administrative careers within their own regions of the frontier. They were given important honors and subsidies; but if the career of any Mongol became too "creative," and his power among the Mongols too constructive, he was promoted to some supervisory position in Peking, which kept him in contact with the Court and away from the main current of tribal affairs; his heirs grew up with the social ideas of Peking Manchus, and the growth of coördination among the Mongols was inhibited.

Even this policy, however, could not wholly prevent the "spread of civilization" along the actual border where Chinese and Mongols met, and especially in the Mongol territories of Manchuria. While the Manchus in Peking became Chinese, and the Manchus remaining in Manchuria tended to become identical in culture and regional interest with the Chinese of the Chinese Pale, the Manchurian Mongols tended to become what the Manchus themselves had originally been—a people half-tribal and half-agricultural in character.

Chinese colonization, as has been pointed out, was in the beginning a luxury which the Mongols themselves introduced; but there was also an early tendency for Mongol tribesmen to settle down. It is probable that there was a good deal of agriculture among the Kharchins of Josoto League, in Jehol, even before the Conquest of 1644; as there was also among the Suiyüan Tumets, farther to the west, and among the Tumets who had, before the Conquest, migrated from the Suiyüan region to the territory of Josoto

71

League. The beginnings of agriculture had also appeared along the Willow Palisade, on the traditional border between the Mongols and the Chinese Pale.

No one, who has been enough among both settled and nomadic Mongols to appreciate their instinctive feelings, and who has seen the actual processes of transformation when pastoral Mongols take up agriculture, can possibly doubt that Mongol agriculture, at such a period, must have begun among the dependent classes, the hangers-on of greater men. The Mongol of wealth or family might settle down to live off the rentals of land cultivated by Chinese, but the Mongol who actually began to work on the land was the man of no particular standing among his own people—the man who, after long years of garrison service, or of attendance on his prince, had lost touch with the tribal life, or become dependent on the life of houses and streets and the undeviating, unenterprising routine of "civilization."

Mongol farming, in other words, was not in the early period the occupation of ambitious men, any more than it is now. The Mongol who settled down did not do so because he felt it was a step up in civilization; he was resigned to it as a makeshift. In the same way, at the present time, the successful Mongol is the man of tents and herds. If the Mongol settles down, it is because he has been crowded by Chinese colonization until there is no room for his herds. Nothing that he gains can compensate him for the feeling of loss. It is because he has been forced to *descend* to the Chinese level of living that he so passionately resents the way in which the Chinese looks down on him as a barbarian. He wants always to claim that he is "just as good a Mongol" as the herdsman; but feels always that he is neither as good a Mongol nor as good a man.

The first period, both of Chinese colonization among the Manchurian Mongols and of Mongol agriculture, runs from before the Conquest of 1644 to the year 1748. The Manchus, in this period, had two main problems. They had to restore economic stability within China, which had been shattered by the disorders in the last years of the Ming dynasty, and they had to maintain and extend their military control along the Great Wall frontier. They needed Mongol military contingents while completing their administrative control of China; but they needed also to complete their administrative control in Mongolia. The Northern and Western Mongols had not yet come over to the "trans-frontier coalition," and the Manchus especially feared that the Western Mongols might create an independent military power capable of challenging their own.

During these years the Manchus worked hard at "colonization" within China itself, bringing back into cultivation the acreage that had been laid waste in the civil wars under the Ming. Lands along the Great Wall, just to the north and northwest of Peking, were largely allotted to the followers of the Manchu Conquest.[2] This put a screen along the Great Wall, ensuring that the Mongol sector along the edge of the frontier should actually be controlled by the Manchus rather than the Mongols. It is probable also that

[2] *Ta Ch'ing Hui Tien;* Hu Pu 8 & 9; *chüan* 135 & 136.

73

the Manchus, while following in principle a policy of keeping the Mongols tribal, did not in this period object to a little "softening" of their own Mongol allies. Agriculture spread further among the southern Mongol tribes of Jehol, and there was an important increase of Chinese tenant-farming among the Mongols of Jerim League in Fengt'ien and Kirin provinces. This immigration must not be confused with the encroachment of later periods; it was, as can be understood from what has already been said, promoted by the Mongols themselves.

A second period can be dated from 1748. By the reign of Ch'ien Lung (1736-1796) the constructive period in the formation of the Manchu Empire was rounded out. The great wars had been fought and the great problems of organization dealt with. The menace of an independent Mongol Empire had faded with the decline of the Olöts or Western Mongols. This great branch of the Mongols, with tribes extending from the Altai region of Outer Mongolia across Chinese Turkistan into the Kokonor region of Tibet, had very nearly destroyed the balance of the Great Wall frontier. It was by supporting the Khalkhas of Outer Mongolia against the Olöts that the Manchus extended their authority into Outer Mongolia; and thereafter, by supporting one Olöt faction against another, they completed their expansion by gaining control of Chinese Turkistan. In 1750, making use of both Central Asian Turkish and Mongol allies, they defeated the ruling tribal group among the Olöts, and in 1770 they persuaded a large number of the Olöts who, because of disagreement with the dominant group, had migrated into Russia as far as the Volga, to return to Northern Chinese Turkistan.

Having created a tribal balance in Western Mongolia and Central Asia favorable to their own dynasty, the chief concern of government thenceforth for the Manchus was to maintain regional and administrative balance. For the Manchus, ruling an Empire founded on the power of the Frontier, only one conception of stability was possible. The Frontier, as a region and as a political conception, must be held in reserve in order to guarantee power over the Empire as a whole, while China was to be administered as the "exploitable" part of the Empire. The Frontier, therefore, as a world apart, must be kept in a state of poise. It must not be allowed to decline, but it must not be allowed a tribal political growth of its own, nor must it be allowed to bear down increasingly on China, because that would have started a new cycle of wars of conquest. Nor must China proper be allowed to expand into the Frontier zone, because that would have destroyed the differentiation between conquerors and conquered which kept the Manchus in place as rulers of China.

From this turning point between the period of construction and the period of attempted stabilization, and specifically from the year 1748, the Manchu policy toward the Mongols hardened in theory, although it did not grow more efficient in practice. The failure in practice was not due to the Manchus, but to the Mongols themselves. The Manchu intention was to preserve the Mongol character of the Mongols, and especially of the Manchurian Mongols, but it failed because the Mongols, taking their ease as the descendants of conquerors associated with the Manchus, insisted on living on a scale comparable with that of the Manchus.

From the conflict between Manchu policy and Mongol willingness to let things slide there arose an important development in the theory of sovereignty in Mongol territories, which can be dated to the year 1748. The basis of Mongol land tenure is that all land belongs to all the tribe, even the prince having no prescriptive right. This may undoubtedly be traced to an underlying, primitive concept of sovereignty (possibly obtaining among other nomadic peoples besides the Mongols) in which land has no place at all. The important entity is the tribe itself, not the territory of the tribe; so long as the tribe holds together, it is a power. Territory does not matter, and as a tribe could, in the "classical" period of Mongol history, increase its power by moving from one territory to another, no disgrace attached to the abandonment of territory. (It is also evident that this tradition must have something to do with the enduring Mongol distrust of a settled economy; the man who is free to move has power, and the Mongol, because of the force of his history, does not like to be tied to a piece of land.)

Thus it will be found all through Mongol history that even a tribe is not so "real" a thing as the genealogy of a princely family; because princely descent, being descent from a great chief, is the obvious nucleus on which to found a tribe. This is all the more true in that all princely genealogies, since the thirteenth century, are traceable to the House of Chingghis. The tribe itself, in the older conditions of Mongol history, might lose its name and identity by changing its allegiance from one prince to another; or a prince might found a new tribe by gathering up followers from many different tribes.

In all this, land had no part. Manchu policy succeeded, however, in establishing a degree of identification as between tribe and land. In putting an end to the characteristic Mongol processes of creating tribes, breaking them up and forming them afresh—the processes out of which arose great leaders and great conquests—the Manchus relied strongly on the assignment of definite frontiers to each tribe—or rather to each tribal unit ruled by a prince, for some tribes were subdivided among several princes. This, in turn, tended to create a new form, the "principality," superseding the true Mongol concept of a "tribal following," which might be associated with a region, in a general sort of way, but had no territorial *identity*.

While this process was never fully completed, so that even to-day the Mongol "principality" is not a petty "state," in the Western sense, it did have an important effect on the tribal unit, and on the political character of the ruling prince. Not only do all tribal boundaries of the present day derive from the comparatively modern time of the Manchus, but the functions of the prince are also largely of Manchu creation. The Manchus laid great emphasis on the boundaries which they had created; and while the Mongol prince was virtually autonomous within his own frontiers, the offense of leading his tribal following across their frontiers was one of the few acts which were likely to bring direct Imperial intervention.

The Manchus, of necessity, worked largely through the princes in their relations with the Mongols, and this had an effect of a kind familiar to other suzerain powers—to the British in India, for example. It placed a false emphasis on certain elements in the native system, which under the free play of native forces would never have had the same importance. The Mongol prince, or chief, was by origin a *leader,* whose power depended primarily on his ability to lead successfully. Under the Manchus, he became a petty sovereign, at once restrained and supported by an overlord. The unnatural fixation of the powers, prerogatives and functions of Mongol princes, thus brought about, was to have devastating results later. The rapidity and thoroughness of revolution in Outer Mongolia, for instance, was primarily due to the fact that the position of the princes was artificial; they were unable to resume rapidly enough their true function as leaders of their people, and as this made them inevitably a reactionary and negative social group in the instinctive struggle of the Mongols to adapt themselves to new conditions, they had of necessity to give way before new social forms.

The most important legal development in the eighteenth century, however, was that the prince was made responsible for the control of Chinese colonization, and of Mongol agricultural allotments, within his territory.[3] This ruling, unquestionably designed in the first place to conserve the

[3] *Ta Ch'ing Hui Tien*, Li Fan Yüan 17, *chüan* 742.

Mongol character of the Mongols, to prevent the spread of the Chinese population and Chinese ideas, and to stop Chinese colonization and check the spread of agriculture among the Mongols themselves, was later to be cited (as will be seen) for the ironical purpose of assisting Chinese encroachment in Mongol territory. Its effect in the eighteenth century, however, since the Mongols were largely in favor of the type of Chinese penetration then at work, was merely to develop a regular procedure in the evasion of the law; chiefly, it would seem, by granting or arranging "exceptions" to the standard prohibitions.

During this second period, characterized by Mongol evasions of the Manchu policy, Chinese penetration was of two kinds. In Southeastern Jehol, in the territories of the Kharchins and Tumets of Josoto League, the Mongols mortgaged land to Chinese for a term of years, in return for cash advances. The Chinese were supposed to repay themselves by farming the land, and to return the land to the Mongols at the end of the mortgage period.[4] This, in itself, is evidence that a great part of the land must have passed already from the original tribal form of Mongol ownership into the private ownership of individual Mongols; which, again, indicates that agriculture had become established among the Mongols.

The references in the *Ta Ch'ing Hui Tien* indicate that the Chinese first appeared in these regions as extra farmhands, hired by land-owning Mongols in the sowing and harvesting seasons. The situation in this part of Jehol was

[4] *Loc. cit.*

therefore parallel to that in the Chinese Pale of Manchuria, and in the Manchu region of Kirin. In all of these regions there is a short growing season, and as the sowing, cultivating and harvesting are all done by primitive hand methods, a great deal of work has to be done in a limited time, which results in a seasonal demand for extra workers. The long idle season between the harvest and the next sowing gave time, even in the age before rail transport was developed, for Chinese to reach Manchuria, work for three or four months, and return to their homes for the winter. The need for this extra labor supply was always recognized, in spite of the ordinances against free Chinese immigration; and an attempt was made to meet the situation by admitting men who came without their women and families, under a passport system.

In Southern Jehol, as in Manchuria, laborer-passports were issued, and the number of passports issued each year was limited, in order to prevent abuse of the system. The probable effect of these regulations was to put up the price of labor, and to encourage the Mongols to evade the regulations by retaining their hired laborers permanently. The "mortgaging" of land to Chinese may have served in part as a blind to cover this practice, the Chinese being given a small piece of land to work for himself and thus being available to do extra work for the Mongol landlord.

The Chinese, therefore, did not (in Jehol) colonize on large grants of land vacated for them by the Mongols, but interpenetrated the Mongol agricultural communities as settlers and small-holders. This is proved by the record of an effort to clear up the situation by exchanging lands, in order to form separate Mongol and Chinese communities; an effort which quite evidently failed. The records bear out the other indications that by 1748, while a part of these Mongol lands remained under the normal form of tribal ownership, the individual ownership of farms by Mongols was already well established.

The social results were of several kinds. In the first place a number of the Mongols degenerated from being a leisured class into a landless class, through being underlived and outbought by the Chinese who had at first been their tenants under the mortgage system, so that there was a steady transfer of smaller holdings from Mongols to Chinese. In the second place many of the Chinese, having come in without women of their own, "became" Mongols. They took Mongol wives (although this nominally was prohibited) and eventually succeeded in being listed on the records as members of the Mongol tribe. This, probably, was done in order to escape the restrictions imposed on Chinese in Mongol territory, and may often have been arranged through the bribing of Mongol officials, in order to facilitate the acquisition of land. The mortgage system in itself is an indication that there were difficulties in selling land outright to Chinese. This particular phenomenon was more common among the Kharchin Mongols than in any other region; and it is said by the Kharchin Mongols themselves that in the modern period of increased pressure on the Mongols, when it had become an advantage to be Chinese rather than Mongol, these families often took the lead in "becoming" Chinese.

In the third place, a comparatively powerful class of Mongol "capitalists" was developed, among whom the aristocracy were prominent, together with the clergy—the lama monasteries, that is, regarded as landowning corporations. These owners of large estates, by the advantage of their greater initial wealth, their strong social position and the relatively great influence they had in controlling tribal lands that had not yet passed into private ownership, actually improved their position as rich landlords, with both Mongol and Chinese tenants and laborers.

The fact that the Manchu policies, at this period, were genuinely directed toward the protection of the Mongols is proved by the references in the *Ta Ch'ing Hui Tien*. A decree was issued enjoining Chinese in Jehol to relinquish their mortgages after a term of years, to be determined in each case by the value of the holding, in order to force out as many Chinese as possible and discourage further immigration. The aristocracy and lamas were at the same time directed to distribute one-third of their holdings to poor Mongols, "to be farmed"—a wording which proves again that the situation was not one in which Chinese agriculture had encroached on the pastures of the Mongols, but one in which agricultural Mongols had lost possession of their lands to their Chinese tenants, through the mortgage system. The failure of all these Manchu attempts to keep the Mongol organization healthy, moreover, proves that it was the Mongols themselves, or the privileged classes among them, that were chiefly responsible for the encouragement of Chinese immigration.

The second important area of Chinese penetration in this period was farther north; especially among the Gorlos Mongols in the extreme northeastern angle of Jerim League, in territory that is now part of the provinces of Heilungchiang and Kirin, but to a certain extent also among the Khorchin Mongols of the same League, in territory that is now part of Fengt'ien (Liaoning) province. The region of Ch'angch'ün, now the capital of Manchukuo under the name of Hsinching, may be taken as the focus of activity. The method of transferring land differed from that in Southern Jehol, as Mongol agriculture was unimportant, and consequently there was little or no transfer by mortgage from individual Mongol holders to individual Chinese tenants. Colonization was a public enterprise; tracts of tribal land were turned over on long lease, or on perpetual lease, to communities of Chinese.

Under the terms of this practice, the heads of the Chinese communities dealt with the authorities of the Mongol tribe. The income from land rentals was a tribal fund, and was divided among the ruling prince, the officials, and the tribe as a whole. Naturally, however, it was the privileged classes among the Mongols, who had the handling of the funds, who profited most, and it was their financial interest which prompted the encouragement of colonization in spite of Manchu disapproval, and developed it beyond the point of furnishing easy money, until it threatened the whole economic and social position of the Mongols.

83

Chinese colonization as a source of profit for the Mongol upper classes was paralleled by other activities, which made it easy to evade the Manchu regulations. The region first affected, near Ch'angch'ün, was a point of departure for Manchu expansion and tribal control in Northwestern Manchuria, and especially for the strategic route from Kirin up to the Nonni valley and the Amur. The Manchus themselves were forced to introduce agricultural colonies at certain points, in order to provide supplies for their garrisons, and for troops moving between Central Manchuria, the Nonni and the Amur. Other tracts were brought under cultivation to provide grain reserves for the Mongols themselves, in years of drought, and official granaries were maintained, with a stated reserve of grain for each tribal unit. This, apparently, originated as a benevolent measure for the protection of the Mongol allies of the Manchus. The granary system spread from the agricultural Mongols of Josoto League to Jo-oda League, then to Jerim League, and later to other Mongol territories.

In Jerim League the Mongols themselves appear to have begun the system of building up grain reserves, and to have imported agricultural Mongols from Josoto League for the purpose. Later the Manchu Government backed up the system—probably as one form of compensation for the military contingents which the Mongols furnished, and in order to provide supplies both for the troops and for their families whenever the Mongol contingents were called out. It was natural, however, as they grew accustomed to the position of a privileged, subsidized people, that the Mongols should consider themselves entitled to have colonies of Chinese working for them, rather than farm the land themselves. This kind of demand among the Mongols, aided by the proximity of official colonies, made it easy to evade the Manchu regulations in extending the area under cultivation.

As for the spread of Mongol agriculture in Jerim League, this too differed from the agriculture of the Kharchins and Tumets of Josoto. Although a little had existed even before the conquest of China, the later spread was due to assimilation to the standards of the Chinese immigrants. Groups of Mongols tended to become "islanded" between tracts turned over to the Chinese, and gradually settled down to farming in the Chinese manner. As, however, these Mongols were not closely interpenetrated by the Chinese, as were the Mongols in Jehol, the tracts farmed by Mongols remained distinct from those held by Chinese colonists. Mongol villages were solidly Mongol, with no resident Chinese farmers and only a few Chinese laborers in the busy season.

Among the easternmost Gorlos Mongols, who were in contact with the Manchus of Kirin, there was a tendency for these agricultural communities to lose their language and become completely Chinese in character. This was because the Mongols tended to model themselves on the Manchus, and as the Manchus became assimilated to the Chinese, so did the Mongols. Farther south, among the Khorchins, there was less Manchu influence and the Mongols were in direct contact with the Chinese of the Chinese

Pale. Here the traditional antagonism between Mongols and Chinese was more effective, and Mongol farming villages, even though surrounded by Chinese communities, retained their language and national character with really extraordinary tenacity. It is thus possible to find, within eighty or a hundred miles of Mukden, even at the present day, Mongol villages where the people have lived for generations in the Chinese manner, and yet still preserve the Mongol language—although of course most of them, the men especially, speak Chinese as well.

It is now possible to assess the general character of this period in colonization, which may be called the period of Manchu disapproval and Mongol toleration, extending from about 1748 until about the end of the nineteenth century. It is quite plain that the Manchu policy of restriction was ineffective. There are repeated references to the concern felt by the Manchu Government.[5] The settled lands would be surveyed at intervals, and orders given that no further colonization would be allowed; but after a few years it would be found that there had in fact been a further extension of settlement, because "the Mongols, not contented with the nomadic life, get Chinese to cultivate for them. This has been going on for years, and they have lived at peace with each other for a long time. Moreover, the rentals which the Mongols get are a benefit to them economically."[6] (This does not mean that the Mongols were not satisfied with *living* the nomadic life, but that they

[5] *Ta Ch'ing Hui Tien;* Li Fan Yüan, *chüan* 742, and Hu Pu 14, *chüan* 141.

[6] *Loc. cit.* This passage is dated 1800.

86

wished, while remaining Mongols, to have the resources of Chinese civilization in addition to their own resources.)

A certain number of the Mongols "fell" to the position of cultivators, and a certain number, notably in Jehol, were pauperized by the competition of the lower Chinese standard of living, while the privileged classes drew large revenues by exploiting Chinese colonization. On the whole, however, the immigration of Chinese, and the partial displacement of Mongol pastoral economy by Chinese agricultural economy, were as favorable to the Mongols as any such radical changes could be to any people. Even where Mongols were being assimilated by the Chinese, the process was easy and gradual enough to give them adequate time for adaptation. The Mongols nowhere felt that they were being swept out by Chinese immigration. The majority of them, even within the field of Chinese penetration, were able to retain their language and racial identity. Their feeling of solidarity, and the prestige reflected on them by their own independent princes, were fortified by the class-consciousness of being the superior race, lords of the land, entitled to tribal subsidies in the form of rentals from the Chinese. There was still a definite Mongol demand for Chinese immigrants, although a majority of the profit came into the hands of a limited group among the Mongols.

Chapter IV

MODERN COLONIZATION: THE CHINESE
BECOME THE PRIVILEGED PEOPLE

BY the end of the nineteenth century, however, Chinese penetration reached a third phase, of totally different character. The spread of agriculture as a form of exploitation, bringing wealth, luxuries and unearned increment to the Mongols, had been carried so far that it was destroying the economic, social and political structure of Mongol life. The number of Mongols who made a satisfactory money profit out of the admission of Chinese immigrants had been narrowed down to a small group among the privileged classes, while the number of Mongols who suffered from being underlived and dispossessed by the Chinese had expanded until it included the majority of the people in the regions affected. Yet there was little reaction on a national scale, because the Mongols of Outer Mongolia, and of Western or Central Asian Mongolia, were hardly affected. The impact of the Chinese advance was limited to the barrier regions which had, owing to their earlier and closer political affiliation with the Manchu Empire, a peculiar political status. The Mongols who suffered were the tribes from the Ordos eastward into Manchuria, and especially the Manchurian Mongols.

The change from Mongol exploitation of Chinese immigrants to Chinese pressure on the Mongols was brought about by a competitive lowering of the standard of living, and a destruction of the standard of leisure. The Mongols were being underlived by the Chinese, and the number of Chinese in the regions affected had increased to a point where the Mongols were forced to compete with them in terms of the Chinese standard of living. This is an aspect of Chinese frontier colonization which has never been properly studied.

There is no greater fallacy than the too easy generalization that Chinese agricultural settlement brings in a "higher standard" than the "primitive" economy of the Mongols. It is based entirely on the simple-minded assumption that a hunting economy is lower than that of pastoral nomads, that the pastoral economy is lower than that of agriculture, and that the agricultural economy, in turn, is lower than that of industrialization. In point of fact, however, if Western standards be left entirely out of consideration, the *combined* economic, social and political standing of the Mongols has always been higher than that of the Chinese. The pastoral Mongol has a complete economy. His herds provide him with every necessity of housing, clothing and food. Everything which can be bought or sold for money is therefore pure surplus; and in this he is necessarily superior to the Chinese peasant, who is tied to a money economy. If he can sell the surplus of his herds to get such things as cloth, silks, grain and manufactured articles by trade, his superiority is even more obvious.

The Mongol must work with intense activity in the season when colts, calves and lambs are born, or when he is moving camp, or when the herds are scattered by storm; but he has long spells of idleness during which he can hunt, or ride away on visits. The Chinese peasant is tied to his piece of land, and even in the winter must work at anything that turns up, because of his narrow and uncertain margin of living. He must take what he is offered, because he is tied to money. The Mongol, on the other hand, if he happens to want something over and above what he really needs, may work with a caravan for a journey or two; but if he does not happen to want something, no money wages will make him work. This is commonly called laziness, but it is in fact a standard of dignity and leisure.

The felt tent of the Mongol is cool in hot weather and warm in cold weather. He can move it to shelter in winter or to a cool place in summer. The mud hut of the peasant is surrounded by puddles in the rainy weather and is bitterly cold in winter because fuel represents money and heating is therefore only a by-product of cooking. The fuel of the Mongol is the dung of his cattle, which he gathers according to his needs. The food of the peasant is the poorest part of his crops, because everything that brings money must be sold. The diet of the Mongol, with its meat and milk, and grain got by trade, is therefore more varied and more healthy than that of the Chinese.

Nor must the Mongol limit his herds to the amount of land he owns, because there is no privately owned land. There is enough of the tribal domain, unless colonization has encroached on it, to take up the increase of his herds. He need not sell his yearly surplus unless he gets his own price for it. The average Mongol therefore has more cash in hand at the end of the year than the average peasant; and since he is able to spend it as he likes, on luxuries, the Chinese trader in Mongol territory works on a margin of profit that is calculated in hundreds per cent.

The agricultural Mongol stands midway between the colonist and the pastoral Mongol. He keeps more livestock than the Chinese, because he retains at least something of the Mongol tradition of leisure and ease, and would rather use poor land to pasture animals than try, by extra labor, to get a scanty harvest from it. For this reason his economy, being more varied, is more sound. The average Chinese colonist, especially the Chinese who is not frontier bred but comes from Shantung or somewhere else within the Great Wall, knows nothing of animals except stall-fed draft animals. Rather than learn how to handle animals in herds, he will turn fair pasture into poor plough, and slave endlessly trying to get some kind of return from it.

The Chinese colonist in the early periods of settlement, with plenty of room to spare, does keep more livestock than the farmer in China; but as the settled region fills up, the inevitable tendency is to reproduce, more and more closely, the conditions in China which form the background of the Chinese peasant, forcing out livestock and substituting the slave-driving competition of manual labor and small-scale, intensive cultivation. As the pressure of this process increases, the Mongol is forced either to give up his riding animals, milk cattle, meat diet and comparatively careless farming methods, thus coming down to the Chinese level— or to get out. The Mongol suffers from being underlived by the Chinese exactly as the Californian suffers from the competition of Chinese or Japanese, and would in the same way exclude Chinese immigration if he had the power.

The whole question is therefore not one of simple opposition between the "primitiveness" of a pastoral economy and the "higher" standards of agriculture. It is a complex question of many factors, among which the political factor is of high importance. When the Mongols are an ascendant people, they are able to introduce Chinese colonization as a luxury; and they were normally an ascendant people throughout the Great Wall period of Chinese history, the rhythm of which was determined by barbarian conquests. When, however, they lose their ascendancy, their relatively high, self-contained pastoral economy is hopelessly vulnerable to the advance of the relatively low type of Chinese agricultural economy.

This has been the character of the modern period, in which Chinese colonization has advanced into Mongolia with a smothering effect; but it should be realized that the modern period, by the standards of Chinese history as a whole, has been *abnormal,* in that the relations between

THE MONGOLS OF MANCHURIA

Chinese and barbarians on the Great Wall frontier have been totally altered by the impact of the maritime powers of the West. These are points that need to be borne in mind when considering the future of Mongolia and the Mongols. It has been commonly assumed that the Chinese must, in the long run, succeed in spreading over the whole of Manchuria and Mongolia. The Chinese are now confronted, however, with an Outer Mongolia which is politically strong, and able to decide for itself between the introduction of agriculture and the improvement and modernization of its pastoral economy. In Manchuria they are confronted with an autonomous Mongol province in which Chinese are forbidden to settle and in which the development and improvement of the pastoral economy is to the interest of Japan. It is not too much to say that the Mongols are once more an ascendant people, so far as the Chinese are concerned, although they are not fully independent of either Japan or Russia. It therefore follows that not only political relations between Mongols and Chinese, but social and economic relations as well, must be considered entirely afresh.

It was in fact the operation of new political and social values in the last quarter of the nineteenth century, even more than the ill-considered self-interest of controlling groups among the Mongols themselves, which altered Chinese immigration into Inner Mongolia in the last quarter of the nineteenth century from a process largely promoted and controlled by Mongols into a process which first undermined the privileged position of the Mongols and then threatened to exterminate them as a race. This alteration is plainly marked by the change in Manchu policy, which turned from the official discouragement of Chinese expansion to the official promotion of Chinese colonizing enterprises; but the historical problems here involved are unfortunately obscured by the slipshod habit of treating all Empires in China, and especially the Manchu Empire, as *Chinese* Empires.

The Manchu Empire, in structure, and all through the first part of its history, was an Empire *over* China. It was based on the use of the Frontier peoples, and of the Frontier itself as a strategic region, for the control and domination of the Chinese. In the nineteenth century, however, and especially from 1850 onward, while the structure altered but slowly, the *policy* of the Empire altered rapidly, and became increasingly Chinese. This of course was a standard phenomenon. The "turning Chinese" of a Frontier dynasty, and its political decay, had always been synonymous.

In the case of the Manchus, however, alien forces were also at work. The immemorial cycle of expansion and invasion along the Great Wall frontier had been broken by the action of the European Powers, coming from the sea. This meant that the Manchus in China, even more than other rulers of barbarian origin, no longer considered themselves as alien conquerors. They were hardly considered aliens even by the Chinese, except for the propaganda purposes of revolutionaries, and in order to make them scapegoats for the helplessness of China in the face of Western exploitation. They were simply the Chinese ruling class. Their domestic policy still worked to maintain their class interests, but their foreign policy was a Chinese policy.

The Great Wall frontier was no longer the focus of control, either within China or over the foreign relations of China. Foreign policy, which had once meant hardly anything but Mongolian and Central Asian policy, now meant primarily policy with regard to the maritime Powers. Only Russia, by its proximity to the land frontiers of the Manchu Empire, still came within the scope of the old policy; and for this reason both Manchu Imperial and Chinese Republican policies dealing with Russia have always been organically different from policies dealing with the maritime Powers. This, incidentally, makes clear the inner meaning of Manchukuo as a historical phenomenon; it represents a shift in Japanese policy from a maritime basis to a continental basis, and therefore not only revives the cardinal importance of the Great Wall frontier, but sets it up in opposition to the maritime control of the European nations and America.

The change in position of the Manchus within China meant that the Manchus remaining in Manchuria, and such people as the Manchurian Mongols, were no longer important either for the recruitment of troops to maintain power in China or for their other historical function, the preservation of a balance of power along the Frontier, and the holding in check of such marginal regions as Outer Mongolia. They were no longer peoples of special value, as they had once been. The Frontier had changed from positive to negative; it had become, so to speak, empty. The new positive problem, from the point of view of the Imperial House, the Court, the Peking Manchus and the Chinese themselves, was the problem of pushing the power of China out into Manchuria and Mongolia, in order first to hold off the Russians and later the Japanese.

Between 1880 and 1890 the Government began actually to promote colonization; and from this time forward it is proper to speak of Imperial policy as the policy of China rather than of the Manchu Empire. According to the older understanding of Frontier history and its processes, the farthest outlying Mongols might even become dangerous, through changing their allegiance from China, or the Manchu Empire in China, to Russia. The new theory of colonization therefore contemplated the substitution of Chinese for Mongols; the Chinese had become the people of special value, and the Mongols were treated more and more as subject people. In 1876 a type of provincial government similar to that within China had been introduced into Manchuria. From then on there was an increasing tendency to divide the supervision of the Mongol territories within Manchuria among the provinces, and this tendency was confirmed in 1907, when the provincial governments of Manchuria were brought still closer to the standard within China, and the last nominal restrictions on Chinese immigration were abolished. From this time onward the Chinese officials continually increased their control over the Mongols.

The effort to change the character of the Frontier was

not altogether a success. There was, for one thing, a marked tendency among the incoming Chinese, because of historical tendencies which weakened very slowly, to take over a regional frontier feeling toward China, instead of creating a new, solid Chinese front expanding actively toward the north.[1] Colonization also suffered from lack of independent funds and centralized supervision. Land-commissioners were appointed to control the transfer of land from Mongols to Chinese, and these land-commissioners, for lack of adequate funds and according to the immemorial tradition of official procedure, paid themselves chiefly out of the opportunities offered by their official positions.

They allied themselves with land speculators, and became at one and the same time officials enforcing the regulations of land transfer and private investors taking up the land transferred—a practice which allowed them to take up the best lands at the cheapest prices. Having acquired huge grants at practically no cost, they were under no pressure to risk heavy capital investment in promoting settlement to develop their holdings. They could afford to wait indefinitely for unearned profits, until the spontaneous progress of colonization approached their property, enabling them to realize enormous profits on the rise in land values, without risk or cost in promoting development.

Expansion also suffered from the character of Chinese economy itself. The colonization which the Mongols themselves had promoted had practically filled the market re-

[1] There is a discussion of this type of process in my *Manchuria, Cradle of Conflict*.

quirements both for the Mongol territories in Manchuria and for export down the Liao valley to the sea. Chinese agriculture, being based on hand labor and small holdings, is to a large extent agriculture for the support of the farming families themselves. It requires markets close at hand for the sale of the small individual surpluses it produces. Within China, therefore, agriculture is associated with the comparatively large city populations that are scattered all through the provinces. On the Frontier, it depends on Mongol and Chinese caravans to distribute grain among the Mongols. Grain cannot be shipped over long distances back into China, by the methods of transport native to the Chinese economy, because of the high cost of cart or caravan transport in a populated country without free pastures for grazing. Even the change from official prohibition to official encouragement, therefore, did not rapidly increase the rate of immigration into Manchuria, in default of cities to take up the surplus of agricultural produce.

Colonization, therefore, while it continued to break down the integrity of the Mongols, was unsatisfactory in complementing the higher aims of Chinese policy, until it received a fresh impetus from the Western pressure which had already contributed to the reversal of Frontier policies. This came in the form of railways, for which the important dates in Manchuria are the opening of the Chinese Eastern Railway in 1903, by the Russians, the Japanese reorganization in 1907 of the South Manchuria Railway (begun by the Russians in 1896) and the completion of the British-financed railway from Peking through Shanhaikuan to

Mukden, also in 1907.[2] These railways gave colonization a dynamic expansive character which had previously been lacking, by making possible the export of grain over much greater distances, and the settlement of Chinese far beyond what had previously been their economic range.

The modern history of Chinese colonization is a history of railways, backed up by modern arms; and as Manchuria has a far greater railway mileage than any part of China, the Manchurian Mongols have been the chief sufferers. The ascendancy of China in Mongolia, in itself a radically new thing in history, has depended primarily on the pressure of "foreign imperialism" which forced railway development on China. It has been emphasized by international policy toward China, as the successor of the Manchu Empire.

When the Manchu Empire was destroyed by revolution in China, the Chinese Republic fell heir to the later colonization policy of the Empire. Neither the Mongols nor the other Frontier peoples, however, as has already been pointed out, accepted the defeat of the Manchus in China as conferring on China a title to the outer dominions of the Empire. The legal approach to the establishment of a Republic coextensive with the old Empire was therefore by way of a federation of the constituent parts of the Empire— a procedure approved by the foreign Powers which virtually exercised a power of supervision over the affairs of China.[3] The groups nominally participating in the formation of the Republic were the five "races"—Chinese, Man-

[2] See also below, pp. 284-286.
[3] See also the chapter "China and the Barbarians" (by the present writer) in *Empire in the East*.

chus, Mongols, Tibetans and Moslems, whose union was symbolized in a five-colored flag. The inclusion of the Moslems as a race was a concession to the Moslems of Kansu and Chinese Turkistan, who are either Central Asian Turks or strongly differentiated, by their partly Central Asian descent, from the Chinese.

This formula was enunciated for the purpose of conciliating the non-Chinese races, and forestalling nationalist and separatist movements like that of Outer Mongolia, and for the sake of prestige and foreign recognition. Naturally, however, there was inherent in the Chinese majority a tendency to abandon the attitude of conciliation as the position of China itself improved, through railway expansion in Manchuria and Mongolia, through the acquisition by the Chinese of military equipment which the other races could not obtain, and through international recognition of China as the sovereign nation within the Republic. Pressure on Mongol territory and tribal organization adjacent to Chinese population was increased by the extension of provincial government. The establishment of "regular" provinces in Manchuria under the Empire was followed under the Republic by the creation of "Special Administrative Areas" reaching up into the western belt of Inner Mongolia, from Jehol to the Ordos bend of the Yellow River, and linked with the Chinese provinces immediately to the south of them.

This process was brought to a final stage in 1929, the year in which China, under the Kuomintang, attained its maximum success in nationalism, in its policies abroad, in

Manchuria and in frontier expansionism generally. In this year all of Inner Mongolia not already allotted to the provinces of Manchuria was organized into "regular" Chinese provinces by the conversion of the "Special Administrative Areas" into the new provinces of Jehol (Josoto and Jo-oda Leagues and the former Imperial Hunting Park); Chahar (the majority of the Chahar Mongols and all of Silingol League); and Suiyüan (the Suiyüan Tumets, the four westernmost Banners of the Chahar Mongols, Olanchab League and the Mongols of the Ordos or Yeghe Jo League). The provinces of Ninghsia (taking in the Alakshan and Ejen-ni Gol or Edsin Gol Mongols) and of Ch'inghai (taking in the Kokonor and Tsaidam regions, inhabited by Mongols, border Tibetans and Moslems) were formed at the same time. From this year onward, Chinese official maps have revealed no Mongolia except Outer Mongolia, and from the externals of Chinese policy it would be impossible to detect, without special knowledge, the important Mongol interests within Manchuria and along the rest of the Inner Mongolian frontier.

Under this arrangement Mongols not yet reached by the active advance of Chinese colonization remained in practice under the administration of their own princes. The Chinese policy was to uphold the authority of the princes in such regions, but at the same time to keep up the demand, year by year, for new cessions of Mongol land to be colonized. As fast as the land was taken over, it was brought under "normal" provincial administration, and Mongols who remained within such territory were removed from the jurisdiction of their princes. The division of all Inner Mongolian territories among Chinese provinces, pending the final application of colonization methods, was designed to hinder the Mongols in acting as a solid racial group, and to prevent the Mongol question from being discussed as a whole, in direct negotiation between the Central Government and representatives of all the Mongols, without the intervention of provincial interests.

During this period the supposedly "federative" principle of the original Republic disappeared. The Kuomintang, or *Chinese* Nationalist Party, during the phase of its greatest power, from 1927 to 1931, discarded the five-barred flag symbolizing a union of races, and undertook to impose Chinese standards on all Mongols, Tibetans and Moslems under its control or within reach of its propaganda, with the intention of transforming them all, whether they liked it or not, into Chinese-speaking, Chinese-thinking Chinese. As for the Manchus, they no longer offered a genuine racial problem, although the pronounced regionalism of Manchuria, which did offer a major political problem, might justly be considered a transvalued form of what had once been a Manchu racial problem.

The open subordination of Mongol to Chinese interests, however, began even before Chinese pressure had reached its highest intensity. In about 1914 or 1915 Chinese officials in charge of colonization began to establish precedents for a legal theory that Mongol land did not belong to a Mongol nation or race, nor to any Mongol tribe, nor yet to the "sovereign" princes of the Mongols, but to the Chinese nation. The increasing feeling of helplessness among the Mongols, especially in Manchuria, had led to a great increase of Mongol agriculture. The Mongols not only resigned themselves to living on the Chinese level, but hoped, by bringing the land under cultivation and occupying it themselves, to check the Chinese advance. In promoting colonization, therefore, and especially in keeping open the margin of profit for colonization commissioners, it was necessary to find legal grounds for evicting the Mongols.

In settling down to agriculture of their own accord, the Mongols had necessarily to secure the transfer of land from the tribal domain to private ownership, through their own authorities. This was done by means of what were called "prince's land deeds." In order to prevent the Mongols from settling down and forestalling Chinese colonization, it was necessary to deny the validity of these deeds. In 1914-15, therefore, the Chinese began to assert the principle that these Mongol land deeds were not valid unless they were ratified at the time of issue by the provincial government which nominally controlled the affairs of the Mongol territory in question. The Mongols responded by predating all "prince's land deeds" to 1913 or 1914—that is, to the period of conveniently vague legal standards between the inauguration of the Republic and the initiation of the new Chinese policy. It was therefore necessary to go still further, by applying the new interdiction retrospectively.

This was done by casting back to the edicts of 1748, when

the Mongol princes had been made responsible for checking Chinese colonization.[4] In order to confirm this respon-
sibility, the princes had been forbidden to allot land for
cultivation to either Chinese or Mongols, without the confirmation of the authorities who supervised Mongol affairs
on behalf of the Imperial Government. On the strength
of this law, all Mongol land settlement that had not passed
through the hands of the Chinese land-commissioners was
declared illegal. Now the decrees in question had plainly
been intended to *stop* Chinese colonization and *prevent* the
spread of agriculture among the Mongols themselves. To
construe them afresh as establishing the legal principle that
Mongol land does not belong to the Mongols but to the
(Chinese) State, and to apply this principle for the purpose
of expropriating land from the Mongols, whether or not
already farmed, and preventing the Mongols from saving
themselves by taking up agriculture, appears to me to be a
masterly example of legal chicane and historical cynicism.

The shamelessness of the new policy was emphasized by
the fact that it was not applied in Mongol lands which
had already been colonized by Chinese on terms of perpetual rental to the Mongols, although they could equally
have been voided by appeal to the old Manchu decrees
which declared that Government officials would not be
responsible for payment of the rents.[5] In such regions, however, strong vested interests had in fact grown up. The
Chinese officials collected the rents, deducted a percentage
for themselves, and paid over the rest to the Mongols. Their

[4] See above, p. 79.   [5] See below, p. 199.

influence was enough to assure the continuation of the practice.

It was under the stimulus of the great land booms of 1916-19 and 1926-28 that the new land laws were most savagely enforced. In the first of these periods, Manchuria flourished through the supply of foodstuffs and raw produce to the warring nations of the world. In the second, the Chinese expansionist policy of railway-building to offset the economic advantages in Manchuria of Russia and Japan —especially Japan—brought about a spectacular rise in the value of farm lands and farm products; especially as it coincided with an inexhaustible supply of colonists driven out of China by famine and civil war, whose lack of capital enslaved them to the land magnates.

The great and rapid profits to be made from development by colonization made Chinese capital available in plenty.[6] The Chinese believed that the Mongols of Inner Mongolia could not possibly rebel with success. It was already evident that Inner and Outer Mongolia had missed the great historic opportunity of making common cause, during the Chinese Revolution of 1911. Wherever new railways had pushed into Inner Mongolia, the added mobility given to Chinese troops had offset the old superiority of the Mongols in war. Inner Mongolia was cut off from the supply of arms. The easy money to be made by evicting Mongols from their lands made it inevitable that they should be handled ruthlessly.

[6] For the interlocking of the official classes, the grain trusts, the railway interests, and so forth, see my *Manchuria, Cradle of Conflict*.

THE MONGOLS OF MANCHURIA

An astonishing proportion of the "virgin prairies" colonized by the Chinese during the Manchurian expansion which appeared so miraculous to the outside world, consisted of land already cultivated by the Mongols, often for a generation or more. It was they who had developed it from virgin prairie to successful cultivation. It was land that had been Mongol for centuries. They had acquired it in private ownership by formal and regular agreement, duly paid for and registered with the officials of their own people. They were told, however, that the soil of Mongolia did not belong to the Mongols. It belonged to the Chinese nation, and title of private possession could only be granted by the Chinese Government. "Officially," therefore, the land which they had paid for and had been cultivating was virgin prairie and part of the public domain. They must either buy it all over again from the land-commissioners in charge of surveying the "wilderness," or—get out.

This practice was the foundation of enormous fortunes made by Chinese officials—including every provincial governor in Manchuria—and the speculators working with them. It was indeed the provincial officials who were mainly responsible for the advance, because it was they who made the largest profits. The Central Government of China has usually, though not always, been more far-sighted and more benevolent in its handling of minority races, but it is regularly handicapped by lack of authority in the provinces. The Central Government has frequently laid emphasis on the necessity for introducing agriculture among the Mongols, in order to develop their civilization; it is the provincial officials who will neither leave the Mongols alone as nomads nor permit them to colonize on an equality with Chinese.

The officials who promoted colonization in territories belonging to the Mongols of Manchuria were able to allot to themselves, at the price of undeveloped land, holdings which they were immediately able to sell or lease at the price ruling for developed land. Even such Mongols as were able to buy back their own land were able to do so only at great sacrifice; for the Mongols, never having trusted Chinese banks, habitually invested their profits either in fresh lands or in cattle. They could not sell part of their land in order to buy back another part, because their title to the whole was not recognized; and when they tried to raise money on their livestock under conditions of forced sale, prices fell to a fifth of the true value. It seemed as though the Chinese were indeed destined to colonize right up to Siberia, as had been prophesied for them by so many Western observers, and as though the doom of the Mongols were ineluctable.

Chapter V

MONGOL REBELLIONS

ALL through the turn from the decadence of the Empire to the intensification of Chinese pressure under the Republic, stimulated by the Western, the un-Chinese dynamics of railway expansion and superior arms, there was a progressive demoralization of the Mongols, and notably of the Mongols in Manchuria, on whom railways and colonization bore hardest. Something has been said already of the distortion of Mongol social forms, and the false emphasis given to the position of the princes. The Manchu tendency to transform the princes from leaders of tribes into sovereigns of petty states was modified still further under Chinese ascendancy. While the Chinese practice denied the ownership of Mongol land by either tribes or princes, it backed up the *social* authority of the princes by treating them almost as if they were "owners" of the Mongol people.

The interest of the princes was thus detached from that of the people. Many of them, not feeling strong enough to resist the Chinese policy, tried to get what they could out of defeat by associating themselves with the officials, in order to get a share of the profits on land transactions. Many of them succeeded in getting grants of what had once been their own tribal land, and thus transformed themselves into wealthy landlords; but some of them resented this kind of capitulation, and endeavored to rally the Mongols to resistance and to create a Mongol cause. For this reason, there has probably not been a single rebellion in the last forty years that has not included princely leaders.

The separation of the princely interest from the tribal interest brought about a further demoralization. The common Mongols, like the princes, were divided. One group, believing that defeatism was unnecessary, urged resistance to Mongol princes and Chinese officials alike. Another, believing that Mongol power had vanished and that the Mongol tradition was doomed, wanted only to settle down to agriculture like the Chinese, and on an equality with the Chinese. This explains why Chinese republicanism and revolutionary feeling have never, in actual practice, been cordial to progressive movements among the Mongols. The practical interests of Frontier officials demanded that princes be treated as autocrats and used as agents in colonization, and therefore that the common Mongols be kept ignorant, economically helpless, and completely under the power of the princes. It was inevitable that even when the conversion of Mongols into farmers was announced as one of the aims of colonization, the practical execution of colonizing projects should result in the eviction of Mongols in favor of Chinese.

From the first of these groups there sprang the Young Mongols of the present day, among whom social feeling is more important than political theory. They believe that the Mongols are still numerous enough, rich enough in lands and strong enough in position to survive, if properly led. They believe that if the princes cannot lead them, then the princes must go. In support of this "revolutionary" idea they cite the old tribal tradition that the prince's title does not rest on heredity alone, but on heredity conditioned by tribal choice and consent. This tradition is undoubtedly genuine, and is one of the first principles of tribal organization, though it was much weakened by neglect during more than two centuries of easy social conditions under the Manchu alliance and the privileges it conferred.

The Mongols have never had succession by primogeniture. Their principle is that the most worthy of the sons or nephews (on the male side) of a deceased prince should succeed, and that the choice should be made by a council of the princely clan, composed of brothers and cousins and uncles (on the male side) of the deceased prince; aided by distinguished tribal representatives who are not members of the actual princely clan. Furthermore, if a prince is not satisfactory he may be deposed by a similar council, which may be called either at the instance of the clan or of the tribe. This right of appointment and deposition was made subject, under the Empire, to Imperial approval. It now rests, theoretically, with the Chinese Republic--which in spite of its Republican theories has actually subdivided tribes and created new princes—but the Mongols have never forgotten that the right rested originally with them. It can therefore be claimed (as in Outer Mongolia, where all princes have been deposed, it has been claimed) that the underlying sovereignty is that of the tribe, and that the prince, in the final analysis, is only the leader of the tribe. It follows, from this interpretation, that on the fall of the Empire the "sovereignty of choice" did not pass to the Chinese Republic but reverted to the Mongol people.

From the second group there developed the defeatist Mongols, demanding no rights, but only the opportunity of surviving among the Chinese colonists, and resigned to the adoption of Chinese ways. This group, if only it had been treated with fairness by the officials in charge of colonization, would have been a powerful instrument for turning all Inner Mongolia Chinese, extending Chinese influences and promoting the kind of peaceful absorption of the Mongols which would have made Inner Mongolia an integral part of China. The dominant interests in colonization, however, made it brutally plain that they had the power to take what they wanted. Agricultural, Chinese-speaking Mongols, well on the way to being transformed into Chinese, were so ruthlessly handled that they were thrice and again confirmed in the bitter knowledge that whenever it paid a sufficiently powerful group of provincial officials to take away from the Mongols something of what was still left to them, a pretext would be found and given the effect of law.

THE MONGOLS OF MANCHURIA

The only effective challenge to the new phase of Chinese ascendancy would have been a stout assertion of the values derived from Mongol history, and of the validity of the Mongol position as derived from this history, in face of and in spite of the "new" China and the "maritime" values which, by the supremacy of the Western Powers, were being made to overshadow Mongolia. In the same way, the only effective answer to the Chinese tactics of local advance, under the terms of local administrative procedure, would have been a general Mongol resistance based boldly on a claim to national independence. This the Mongols failed to see—largely because of the distortion of social organization, and the atrophy of tribal coördination, which had resulted from the habit of privilege and self-indulgence under the Manchu dynasty. They made, instead, the mistake of leaving the initiative to the Chinese, expressing their resistance only in the unemphatic form of local recalcitrance or the local evasion of local procedure. This reduced the conflict between the Mongol policy of adopting agriculture, and the Chinese policy of importing Chinese colonists and preventing the development of Mongol agriculture, to terms of local friction.

While the selfishness, the shortsightedness and the barefaced oppression inherent in their Frontier methods explain why recent Chinese colonization of Mongol territories, especially in Manchuria, has always been carried on under strong military protection, it is largely the political ineptitude of the Mongols which explains the lack of a coherent front among them. The great failure of the Mongols to unite in 1911 has already been discussed; but even this was only the major symptom of a decay which had really begun in the seventeenth century, when the Mongols had resigned the initiative, in higher policy, to the Manchus, and taken the easier way of a subsidized and privileged people. The interference with the natural growth of their social forms and institutions resulting from this abandonment of the initiative has crippled them to such an extent that they can now be formed afresh, as a national entity, only by thoroughgoing revolution from within or by firm control from without.

Chinese colonization means the complete extinction of the Mongols, and this is the primary explanation of the numerous Mongol rebellions, from 1891 to 1930. Some of these rebellions were declared, by their leaders, to aim at local autonomy, or the restoration of the Manchu Empire, or the unification of Inner and Outer Mongolia; but every one of them was made inevitable by the increasing pressure of Chinese colonization, the increasing arrogance of Chinese procedure and the increasing despair of the Mongols, which broke out in the bitter feeling that it was better to die like warriors than like cattle. Yet it was the lack, among the Mongols themselves, of the power to grow and create that accounted for the essential aimlessness of these outbreaks.

The subject of Mongol rebellions is of obvious importance in the study of Chinese colonization history; yet nothing like an adequate account of them is anywhere available. They occur in regions that are not frequently traversed by outside observers, and quite beyond the reach of newspapers. The frontier hides them like a veil. Their importance, like their patriotic and nationalist character, is naturally minimized by the Chinese provincial authorities, who refer to them as "outbreaks of banditry," and nothing beyond this ironic echo is ever heard of them. It is, perhaps, a kind of retribution that risings against the Japanese in Manchukuo should in later years have been called "outbreaks of Chinese banditry," in order to deny them the attention of the world.

As early as 1891 [1] there was a rebellion in Jehol province, where the Chinese, who had come in first as tenants, had grown so in power that they began to dominate the Mongols. In this early rebellion, as in so many that followed it, one of the Mongol leaders was of princely rank, although the rebellion was partly caused by the feeling that the princes were betraying the Mongol people in order to save their own financial interests. On the side of the Chinese, the trouble was made more violent by the activities of the Chin Tan Society,[2] one of the great secret societies of China.

Although this rising occurred before the end of the Manchu dynasty, the Imperial policy had already altered so definitely, becoming "Chinese" instead of "Frontier" or "Manchu" in type, that the forces of "law and order" were on the side of the Chinese. Many Mongol villages were de-

[1] In this brief account I omit references to Mongol rebellions west of "Eastern Inner Mongolia."

[2] Binsteed. The name of the society, which is often baldly translated "Golden Pill Society," can better be rendered by some such equivalent as "Elixir of Life Society," or "Philosopher's Stone Society."

stroyed, the "palaces" of princes were burned, and several thousand Mongols are said to have been massacred. This was the beginning of a great migration of agricultural Mongols from Jehol—from the southern parts of Jo-oda League as well as from Josoto League—into the Jerim League territories, and especially into the western Banners of that League. The migration was kept up steadily by fresh contingents in later years, until, according to Mongols, there are now half a million Jehol Mongols in Jerim League.

In some of the districts of Jerim League these immigrants actually outnumber the local Mongols. Being farmers, a great many of them took up land under "prince's land deeds," either as independent holders or as tenants of Mongols of the district. Thus they were again among the principal sufferers when the Chinese, denying the validity of such deeds, began afresh the expropriation of settled Mongol lands by force, in the land-grabbing days of 1916-19 and 1926-31.

Between this time and the Chinese Revolution two more important Mongol rebellions broke out, both in Fengt'ien province—one among the Suruk Mongols, in a region of long-established Mongol agriculture, near the Willow Palisade and the Peking-Mukden Railway, in the Changwu district, and one near T'aonan, where dispossessed Mongols from Jehol were threatened by Chinese colonization in their new settlements.

In this period also the whole Manchurian situation was changed by the Sino-Japanese War of 1894-95, the Boxer Rising of 1900 and the Russo-Japanese War of 1904-5.

THE MONGOLS OF MANCHURIA

The Russians, having helped China in the negotiations after the Sino-Japanese War, edged into a position of advantage in Manchuria and began the building of the Chinese Eastern Railway in 1897. It is said by the Mongols that the Mongol leaders of that time were overawed by the presence of Russian troops along the projected line of the railway, across the Barga territory, the lower Nonni valley and the northern part of Jerim League, and that this prevented the early organization of an autonomy movement among the Mongols of Manchuria. It was only natural that the Mongols should be cowed, for the Chinese policy in Manchuria was being backed by Russia against Japan, although the Russians were also encroaching directly on China. So far as the Manchurian Mongols were concerned, Russia and China were allied powers.

The Russians increased their military occupation of Manchuria during the Boxer Rising of 1900, and prolonged it afterwards. For these reasons there was a very early tendency among the Mongols of Manchuria to look on the Japanese as a people whò might, by breaking down the power of Russia and China, relieve the pressure on the Mongols. When the Russo-Japanese War began, many Mongols took service as irregulars in the pay of the Japanese. These were chiefly the malcontent, dispossessed, landless Mongols. Their leaders, and their hatred of Chinese colonization, became well known at this time to Chang Tso-lin and one of the most important of his lieutenants, Wu Chün-sheng, who also were serving as Japanese auxiliaries. This General Wu had been in contact with Mongols along the frontier from his youth onward, and it is even said that at one time he had powerful friendships among the Mongols, because of having saved the village of a princess from a bandit siege. He later became Governor of Heilungchiang, and was killed by the same bomb that killed Chang Tso-lin, his leader and "sworn-brother" of a lifetime. He was popularly known as Wu of the Big Tongue, because of an impediment in his speech. Like Chang Tso-lin he had been at different times a bandit and a soldier in the Imperial service before the Revolution.

After the war Chang Tso-lin and his principal associates, using the influence of their Japanese connections (or so it is commonly believed) secured commissions in the Chinese (Imperial) regular forces, and thus at the beginning of the Revolution were able to seize the control of Manchuria. The Mongol leaders who had also served Japan, being less adroit as politicians and also handicapped by the old administrative system which kept Mongols out of the ordinary military and administrative services, were unable to improve their position permanently. Some of them were alternately officers of Mongol militia and leaders of bandits. Nor did the position of the Mongols as a whole improve. The Japanese were busy consolidating their influence among politicians, and while they did their best to keep up their connections with the Mongols, they were forced by considerations of world policy to limit their activities in Manchuria. They could not launch an active Mongol policy without first taking open control of Manchuria. Chang Tso-lin and his personal followers, on the other hand, hav-

ing realized through Frontier experience and personal contact with the Mongols what great power the Mongols
might have if only they were unified and well led, were
constantly on the watch against Mongol risings.

In 1911-12, when the Chinese Revolution overthrew the
Manchu dynasty, the Barga Mongols, west of the Hsingan
range in Heilungchiang province, declared for separation
from China and Manchuria, and union with Outer Mongolia. Eventually, with Russia acting as intermediary, Barga
reverted to the supervisory control of Heilungchiang province, but with enough autonomy in local affairs to placate
its Mongol tribes. Although Russia was at this very time
working to detach Outer Mongolia from Chinese control, it did not suit Russian policy to have Barga united
with Outer Mongolia. The Chinese Eastern Railway ran
right across Barga, and as China had an interest in the
railway, this would have confirmed Chinese connections
with Outer Mongolia just when Russia was anxious to
emphasize the lack of any such connections.

From 1911 to 1913 not only Barga, but all Inner Mongolia was in turmoil. Among the Mongols of Manchuria
the center of revolt was west of T'aonan, in the Jasakto
Khan and Tusiye Gung Banners, both of the Khorchin
tribe, in Jerim League. This rising was led by Otai, Prince
of Jasakto Khan Banner. The Chinese transcription of his
name is Wu-t'ai, and in fact he was probably named after
the Wu-t'ai Shan, a group of five holy mountains in northern Shansi province, which is an important center of Mongol pilgrimages. The most important Living Buddha in

Jerim League was also implicated. His temple or monastery, known as Gegen Sume (written form, Gegegen Sume), or Temple of the Luminous One, is about twenty miles west of T'aoan, on the T'ao River.

At the same time an expeditionary force, divided into five columns, was dispatched from Outer Mongolia to bring Inner Mongolia over to the cause of unity and independence. Two of these columns were under the command of Inner Mongolian leaders who, after being at the head of earlier rebellions, and serving with the Japanese as auxiliaries against the Russians, had been jockeyed out of the race for power and position which followed the restoration of Chinese authority in Manchuria, and had left in disgust for Outer Mongolia.

The rebellion in Manchuria was put down with appalling savagery by the General Wu Chün-sheng who has already been mentioned. The Mongols, though badly armed, fought stubbornly, but were helpless because too many of them were settled farmers and thus lacked the traditional advantage of mobility in fighting against the Chinese. The forces of General Wu, avoiding direct encounter as far as possible, set themselves to the destruction of Mongol villages and crops. "The people who had not taken part in the independence movement, thinking that because they were not involved there was no need to flee, were taken by surprise when the troops attacking the Mongols arrived, and making no distinction between guilty and innocent, slaughtered and robbed at will. Women and children were not spared. The houses of the people and the Duke's residence were all burned down, and all their cattle confiscated." [8]

The expeditionary forces from Urga, though not unsuccessful, were futile. After defeating the Chinese in every encounter, notably in the region north of Kalgan, they returned to Outer Mongolia with quantities of loot, of which arms and equipment were the most important part, but without having organized any sort of conquest. The Chinese, after the defeat of their troops, which were the pick of their army at the time, newly trained on Western lines and furnished with new arms and equipment, resorted to negotiation. One of the Kharchin princes of Jehol, who was then in the Central Government Bureau of Mongol and Tibetan affairs, conducted the negotiations, which led to the withdrawal of the Outer Mongolian troops. He was aided by the fact that many Kharchin Mongols, old rebels from Inner Mongolia, were serving with the Outer Mongolian forces, and through them he approached the Outer Mongolian leaders. Several of this prince's followers and agents were ennobled by the Chinese (Republican) Government for their services, and the fact has been remembered against the Kharchin Mongols, by other Mongols, to this day. As for the Kharchins, they have since that time controlled the most powerful political and careerist clique within the Bureau of Mongol and Tibetan Affairs. The clique is now headed by a Kharchin Mongol whose Chinese name is Wu Ho-ling.

[8] *Hsingan Report* (an official Chinese publication), in an account of Tusiye Gung Banner.

THE MONGOLS OF MANCHURIA

The failure of Inner and Outer Mongolia to unite in 1911-12 had serious consequences. The Jebtsun Damba Khotokhto, or Urga Living Buddha, was then so commanding a figure that he could easily be made a kind of sovereign. He was the primate, so to speak, of the religious hierarchy throughout Mongolia, and by adding temporal authority to his religious primacy it was possible to create a personal sovereign, replacing the Manchu Emperor, for the time being, and out of the reach of quarrels over precedence among the hereditary Mongol princes. When he died, in 1923, the new form of government in Outer Mongolia had already been prepared, under the cover of the last year or two of his rule, and the transfer to the present Republic was made with considerable skill. No successor to the title of Jebtsun Damba Khotokhto was appointed, and the succession to this religious "incarnation" was declared at an end.

Moreover there has been a growth, in later years, of intelligent and powerful factions among the Mongols which do not believe in either a pontiff or an Emperor, and there is now no obvious single personality within the Mongol organization suitable to be raised to the office of personal sovereign. The only religious personality who would be an adequate substitute for the Urga Living Buddha is the Panch'an Lama (called Banchin Bogda by the Mongols), who has for ten years been an exile from Tibet. Certain of the princes of Inner Mongolia have undoubtedly considered the plan of making him a new pontiff of all Mongolia; but the Panch'an Lama has personally been drawing heavy

122

subsidies from the Nanking Government, and is moreover anxious to return to Tibet. The recent death of the Dalai Lama of Lhasa, creating a new political situation in Tibet, means that the Panch'an Lama personally, and his Tibetan followers also, will certainly be more interested in the possibility of a return to Tibet than in the serious risks of a Mongolian career. This leaves only P'u Yi, the legitimist heir of the Manchu Empire and now the Sovereign of Manchukuo, as a suitable person to restore Mongol unity under an Imperial system—but he also, though connected in one way with the Mongol tradition in Mongol affairs, has external connections which would involve alien intervention if he were restored as the sovereign of all the Mongols.

Actually, the failure to carry through a union of Inner and Outer Mongolia in 1911-12 must also have been influenced by the policies of Russia and Japan, who at that time, and largely because of the Chinese Revolution, were endeavoring to come to a new understanding about the balance of continental power in Northeastern Asia. Outer Mongolia was the natural limit, at least temporarily, of Russian policy, as can be seen from the Russian attitude toward Barga, which has already been discussed. "By the secret treaty between Russia and Japan of 1912, Mongolia was divided into two spheres of interest, the Peking meridian being the dividing line between the Russian and Japanese spheres. In the 1915 Twenty-One Demands, the Japanese requirements with regard to Eastern Inner Mongolia were in keeping with this delineation of spheres of interest." [4] The Peking meridian, it should be pointed out, coincides approximately with the historic western frontiers of the different groups of Manchurian Mongols.

Nevertheless, Inner Mongolian resistance to Chinese encroachment was not yet at an end. Risings continued to break out, which might appear to be historically unimportant, mere rebellions of despair, but which kept alive among the Eastern Mongols the feelings of nationalism and racial separatism. In 1916, when the death of Yüan Shih-k'ai promised an interval of indecision and weakness among the Chinese, and also as a result of rumors of the restoration of a monarchical form of government just before Yüan Shih-k'ai died, the Mongols rose again on the fringe of colonization west of the Mukden-Ch'angch'ün-Harbin line of railway expansion. One of their stoutest leaders, Babojab, occupied for a time the important town of Chengchiat'ün, or Liaoyüan.

The disorders continued into the following year, and spread even farther, as the result of the attempt, under Chang Hsün, to restore the Manchu Emperor in Peking. In this year the Barga Mongols fought another of their semi-successful rebellions, staving off Chinese encroachment for the time, but failing to win complete recognition and permanent settlement of their claims. In this year also (1917) Babojab appeared again, in alliance with the Manchu Prince Su, fighting for the restoration of the

[4] Sokolsky; but Sokolsky, like other writers, appears to believe that "Eastern Inner Mongolia" consists of Jehol and Barga, and to be ignorant of the fact that there are also Mongols in Fengt'ien, Kirin and Heilungchiang proper, east of the Hsingan range.

Manchu Empire, in a movement linked with the attempt of Chang Hsün to restore the Emperor in Peking,

This was Babojab's last campaign; he was killed in action near Linhsi, in Jehol province. He had organized the Changwu rebellion,[5] before the Chinese Revolution, had taken part in every subsequent rebellion, had served with the Japanese as an auxiliary against the Russians in 1904-5, and had led one of the Outer Mongolian columns which advanced on Inner Mongolia in 1912-13. His name is kept alive in many ballads about the "Thirteen Companies" that had made up his following ever since the Changwu rising. With him there ended a definite period in the rebellions of the Eastern Mongols, although the flame of his last campaign flickered on into 1918, in a local rising in the T'aonan-T'aoan region.

In 1919 there began an unrest of different character, affecting both Outer and Inner Mongolia. This was the year in which a congress of Mongol revolutionaries met in Siberia, to form and proclaim an All-Mongolian Government. It was also the year in which General Hsü Shu-tseng, "Little" Hsu, took advantage of the fall of the Russian Empire to invade Outer Mongolia. The expedition, entering Outer Mongolia on the pretext of defending the Mongols against the spread of disorder from Siberia, was allowed to reach Urga without opposition. It then seized the person of the Jebtsun Damba Khotokhto and coerced the Mongols into signing away the degree of autonomy which they had won in 1911-12; an act which permanently em-

[5] See p. 223.

bittered Outer Mongolia against China, making future negotiation impossible for years.

A party of White (anti-Bolshevik) Russians, Mongols and Tibetans then raided into Urga, seized the Jebtsun Damba Khotokhto from the Chinese, and started a rising which defeated and slaughtered almost the whole of the Chinese expeditionary force. It set up a new independent Outer Mongolian Government, under the Jebtsun Damba Khotokhto, which failed because of the savagery of the anti-Bolshevik Russians under the "Mad Baron" Ungern-Sternberg. The revolutionary Mongols came into power, supported by the armies of the Russian Revolution. The Russians appeared as the saviors of the Mongols, and treated them so wisely that the Revolutionary Government in Outer Mongolia has continued to rely on Russia ever since; the most statesmanlike action of the Russians being the withdrawal of their troops after the establishment of the new Government. Outer Mongolia reverted to something like its old form of independence, but under definite commitment to internal social revolution and in close association with the Soviet Union, while Inner Mongolia relapsed into its uneasy dependence on China. From the All-Mongolian Revolutionary Congress of 1919 may be dated the admission, by the most dynamic group among the Mongols, of the futility of mere resistance as a method of preserving the integrity of Mongol territory and the Mongol people. What "revolution" really means among the Mongols is open-eyed admission of the fact that independence cannot be maintained without the creation of social forms adequate to the life of a modern nation in the modern world.

In the history of Inner Mongolia also the long record of defeat was to a certain extent balanced by the more vigorous growth of a political faculty, which had hitherto been the fatal point of Mongol weakness. The forces of rebellion began to swing from blind antagonism and the defense of threatened territory to political maturity and constructive policy. The feeling that many of the princes were playing both the Mongol and the Chinese game, alternately heading the Mongol resistance and taking a cash profit on Chinese colonization, allowed a few anti-aristocratic leaders to emerge and gain prestige. This in turn permitted a radical reconsideration of the old Mongol ideology. The old tradition that a bad prince could be, and ought to be, deposed in favor of a new prince, was constructively interpreted to allow the idea of throwing the leadership of the Mongols open to all men of talent, irrespective of birth.

Many Mongols believe that the fighting and organizing leaders of Inner Mongolia, though they lost ground steadily to the Chinese, were instrumental in preparing the way for revolution in Outer Mongolia, where the development of political thinking was actually later, because Outer Mongolia did not come under severe pressure until 1919. Some of the best of the Inner Mongolian leaders took refuge from time to time in Outer Mongolia, where they rose to positions of authority and prepared the way for the ideology of revolution. The fact that many of these early democratic leaders among the Mongols were aristocrats by birth is to my mind a proof of the continuing vitality of the race, and a disproof of the common belief that they have degenerated beyond all hope of recovery as a vigorous nation.

From 1919 onward, as Outer Mongolia began to gain ground under revolutionary control, while Inner Mongolia continued to lose ground before the Chinese, the princes, as a caste, lost prestige, and the Young Mongols began to emerge as a more and more coherent party, supported by many young men of aristocratic birth. Between the failure of the princes on one side to organize a more hopeful policy than intermittent, negative resistance, and the failure of Outer Mongolia on the other side (owing mainly to considerations of international policy, and especially reluctance to challenge Japanese interests in Manchuria) to organize a workable union of all the Mongols, the quasi-revolutionary Young Mongol party came actually to look for support in China.

They were forced to work for some way of settling Inner Mongolian questions by agreement, in order to put an end to the bloody process of encroachment followed by despairing rebellion, followed again by repression. Thus they arrived at a policy of substituting local autonomy for independence, of working for a breathing space that would give the Mongols a chance of developing their own lands, instead of handing them over to the Chinese to be developed, and of replacing the rule of the princes by a gradual development of democratic forms. In this they were encouraged by the teachings of Sun Yat-sen, the founder of the Chinese Kuomintang, which allowed the principle of local self-determination and local self-government for racial minorities.

From this movement there developed in 1925 the Inner Mongolian Kuomintang, founded at Kalgan but organized chiefly by Manchurian Mongols, among them several young men of princely family. They were pledged to the destruction of militarism (which was not a Mongol but a Chinese phenomenon), to curtailment of the powers of princes and aristocracy, to regional autonomy for the Mongols, and to relief from the pressure of colonization and the process of turning Mongol territorial units into Chinese administrative units. They even raised a force of Mongol cavalry—also recruited in the main from Manchurian Mongols—which in 1926 fought on the side of Feng Yü-hsiang against Chang Tso-lin. These troops accompanied Feng on his retreat into Kansu. In 1927, when the Chinese Kuomintang drove out the Communist faction within the party, and Feng returned from temporary retirement in Russia, the Mongol Kuomintang went through a similar "cleansing," and most of the leaders who had Communist affiliations fled either to Outer Mongolia or to Russia.

When, in the same year, Feng Yü-hsiang decided to break off his Russian connections and to adhere, at least for a while, to Chiang K'ai-shek, and so joined in the march of the Nationalists on Peking, his Mongol troops took part in the campaign, serving in provinces as remote from Mongolia as Honan and Shantung. After the triumphant "Nationalist Unification" of China under the

Kuomintang, symbolized by changing the name of Peking (Pei-ching, Northern Capital) to Peiping (Pei-p'ing, Northern Peace or Pacification of the North), and removing the capital to Nanking (Nan-ching, Southern Capital), the Young Mongols hoped to be allowed to reform and reorganize Inner Mongolia on Kuomintang lines, on a basis of federation with the Chinese Kuomintang, but with a recognized regional standing.

They were disappointed. The Chinese Kuomintang, made confident by victory, was primarily interested in strengthening the northwestern frontier (Kansu, Western Mongolia west of Inner Mongolia proper, and Chinese Turkistan) and in bringing over the Manchurian provinces, including Jehol, under the Young Marshal Chang Hsüeh-liang, to recognition of and alliance with the Nanking Government. Nor could the Kuomintang disregard the vested interest in colonization and land-dealing of the officials in the northern and Manchurian provinces; who, though they had come to terms with the Kuomintang, were flatly opposed to any measures giving the Mongols increased control over Mongol affairs.

Nor, again, was the highly centralized organization of the Kuomintang itself hospitable to the idea of a semi-independent Inner Mongolian Kuomintang. The original Inner Mongolian Kuomintang was therefore dissolved, and representatives for Mongol regions were appointed by the Central (Chinese) Kuomintang. They were not even necessarily Mongols, though some of the more subservient Mongol politicians were retained. A number of Cantonese and other Southerners, with no knowledge of Mongolia and no sympathy for Mongol aspirations, were at the same time appointed to the Central Government Bureau of Mongol and Tibetan Affairs. The Mongol policy of the Kuomintang became essentially the old Chinese policy of exterminating the Mongols, or forcing them to turn into Chinese, as fast as possible.

The Young Mongols, after this disappointment, lost prestige among their own followers, and irredentist Mongol patriotism fell back into the old hopeless condition of sporadic rebellion and frontier banditry. Mongols who had anything to lose, played for safety, while those who had lost everything became bandits, roving free companies like the famous "Thirteen Companies," almost as hostile to their own princes and aristocracy as they were to the Chinese. Mongol bandits, it should be pointed out, simply do not exist in Mongol territory under free Mongol administration. They are found only in regions where the administration has been taken over or interfered with by the Chinese, and where the Mongols are victims of unfair political and economic discrimination.

No more organized Mongol rebellions occurred in Manchuria until 1928, when the Barga Mongols, under threat of colonization and the extension of Chinese political control, rose once again and again were half-successful. The Manchurian authorities, afraid of risking a campaign against them, settled by negotiation. One of the leaders fled to Urga. One, named Merse, was taken over into the following of Marshal Chang Hsüeh-liang, where he continued to work as best he could in the Mongol interest, urging recognition of Mongol rights and a fair settlement that would permanently guarantee the Mongols in possession of the lands remaining to them. His later policy was to work for local self-government, but not for total independence. Other leaders of the rising, it is said, were seized after the crisis was over and judicially murdered.

Merse, who was perhaps better known under his Chinese name of Kuo Tao-fu, was a man of about thirty, of extraordinary intellectual brilliance and immense personal courage. He had a fluent command not only of his own Daghor dialect (he was a Hailar Daghor, of aristocratic family) and of Mongol, but of Manchu, Russian and Chinese. He had been prominent in the original Inner Mongolian Kuomintang, and he wrote, probably, the most frank attacks on Chinese policy that have ever been printed in Chinese by a Mongol. One of his articles, translated from a Chinese periodical called *Progress,* was reprinted in *Pacific Affairs,* but without any mention of the author's Mongol nationality. In 1929, when the Manchurian provinces were preparing to send delegates to the Kyoto Conference of the Institute of Pacific Relations, he published in Chinese a valuable pamphlet on "The Mongol Question." [6]

When Merse nominally entered the service of the Young Marshal, he became in reality a political hostage. He was at first allowed to establish a Normal School for Mongols at Mukden, but when it was found that it was his intention

[6] For this and the previous reference, see Bibliography.

to teach the pupils Chinese, English and other subjects primarily for the purpose of making them better Mongols and future leaders of their people, he was removed from the presidency of the school, and a Chinese appointed, to ensure that the school should be used for the purpose of converting Mongols into Chinese. He was then made Mongol Secretary to the Young Marshal, but continued to speak as boldly as ever in criticism of policies toward the Mongols. Immediately after the Japanese intervention of 1931, he fled from surveillance in Peiping, and reached Hailar. Then he disappeared, and it is believed by Mongols that he was seized and murdered by Su Ping-wen, in command of the Chinese forces at Hailar, who with Ma Chan-shan was one of the last Chinese generals to hold out against the Japanese occupation of Manchuria, and was driven out finally into Siberia. It is possible, however, that Merse escaped to Outer Mongolia or Siberia.

While the Barga Mongols managed, or almost managed, to hold their own, the other Mongols of Manchuria continued to lose ground. The last of their risings was in 1930, when a great tract of land in Darkhan Wang Banner, in Jerim League, north of T'ungliao, in Fengt'ien province, was thrown open for colonization, and a new *hsien* or Chinese county established, under the name of Liaopei. The Mongols of the country were almost all settled farmers, but the old ruling against the legality of their title-deeds was cited, and they were evicted. It is asserted by the Mongols that the land-companies exploiting this new colonization territory were the financial agents of personal followers of Chang Hsüeh-liang, and that the Young Marshal himself was financially interested in the exploitation of the region. Very few Mongols were able to buy back their expropriated land.

The Prince of the Banner, being an absentee who divided his time between Mukden and Peiping, and being in addition related by marriage to the family of Chang Hsüeh-liang, was in an awkward position. The chief military official of the Banner therefore went to Mukden, where he had the temerity to appear before the local Kuomintang, to plead for the evicted Mongols. He was imprisoned, but later released, whereupon he led a savage uprising of the desperate Mongols. It was put down with more than equal savagery. Troops and artillery were called out in such force, and the insurgents pressed so closely, that other Mongols dared not aid them. Several thousand people, with all their women and children, were forced out of their villages and driven away westward, without provisions for the winter and without even cattle to support them as nomads. Their leader was killed in action, but the last "bandits" left over from this "pacification" had not yet been cleared away when the Japanese struck at Mukden, on the 18th of September, 1931.

Chapter VI

THE MONGOLS UNDER MANCHUKUO

JAPAN, in creating Manchukuo, has founded a continental empire in Asia which is none the less an empire for being free of the title of Japanese sovereignty. The symbol of this empire is the Great Wall of China, for it is along the Great Wall that its destiny must be worked out. China and Russia are the natural empires of Asia; a mainland empire based on the islands of Japan can only be artificial, in the sense that the British Empire, for instance, is artificial. When the Powers of the Western world succeeded at the Washington Conference of 1921 in making Japan consent to a radical cutting down of Japanese expansion in China and Manchuria, it seemed as if the future lay between China and Russia. It seemed as if these two nations must approach each other, absorbing or dividing between them the immense domains of Manchuria, Mongolia and Chinese Turkistan until, along a continuous land frontier of more than three thousand miles, the greatest Asiatic nation and the greatest Western nation should stand face to face, and a momentous new chapter of history be opened.

The action of Japan in 1931 shattered this mirror of history, and when the fragments are pieced together again we do not know what images will be reflected in them; but we can divine something of their general order. From 1895, after defeating China, Japan had been working for a place on the mainland of Asia, but had been kept in check by the other nations of the world, which leagued together in various combinations to prevent final success. In 1931 Japan at last broke through the half-concealed, half-acknowledged cordon of restraint, and made good the ambition of nearly forty years.

Yet, because the "man-made" position of Japan in Manchukuo inevitably conflicts with the "natural" positions of China and Russia, Japan cannot halt at the present frontiers of Manchuria and declare a limit to the historical changes implicit in the creation of Manchukuo. It is impossible to make the Great Wall frontier the vital frontier between China and Manchukuo only; if the Great Wall is to become once more a significant frontier, then the change must be made to apply to the whole length of the frontier. It cannot be limited simply to the eastern end. This means that what has been begun in Manchuria must be fulfilled, not in China as most people suppose, but in Mongolia, because Mongolia is now the key to the frontier positions of Manchukuo, China and Russia alike. Even a direct extension of the influence of Manchukuo into China cannot be made good, permanently, unless it is based on Mongolia.

Japan has accepted the challenge of the future by creating, within Manchukuo, the autonomous Mongol province of Hsingan, occupying the whole western frontier. If Manchukuo be considered a buffer state, then Hsingan is the buffer province of the buffer state. Following the axis of the main Hsingan range, which runs from the Amur basin southward all the way into Jehol province, the autonomous Mongol region of Hsingan borders both on Western Inner Mongolia, still under Chinese control, and on Outer Mongolia. Whoever controls the Mongols of the Hsingan range can therefore exercise an influence on both Inner and Outer Mongolia that cannot be exercised from any other region.

The Mongols, until the action of Japan in 1931 altered the whole complexion of Mongol affairs, were divided between Outer Mongolia, revolutionary but independent, and Inner Mongolia, conservative but in subjection. The outlying Mongols of the west, especially in Chinese Turkistan, were too isolated for independent action; their fate depended on that of Inner and Outer Mongolia. It is obvious that Japanese plans laid down in advance for dealing with any emergency that might call for intervention in Manchuria, must have included specific plans for dealing with the Mongols. Indeed the Japanese had long kept in touch with anti-Chinese Mongol leaders, although the contact had not been effective, because no support of the Mongols could be effective without direct intervention. A few Japanese adventurers, however, had actually served with Mongol insurrectionists, and attempts had been made to improve the pastoral economy of the Mongol regions in Manchuria, through the experiment stations of the South Manchuria Railway.

The Mongols of Manchuria needed reorganization and a concerted leadership. The size and strategic position of the remaining Mongol territory in Manchuria give the Mongols a strength disproportionate to their numbers, which are probably not more than two million. Their new province of Hsingan is not only the largest in Manchukuo, but is also the territory most remote from immediate Japanese influence and most inaccessible to strong intervention, so that the Mongols can either be invaluable as allies or extremely difficult to deal with if they are suspicious. Many of the Manchurian Mongols believe that Outer Mongolia is essentially an independent nation, though admittedly under strong Russian influence. Any constructive Japanese policy must therefore be able to compare favorably with the essentially generous policy of the Soviet Union toward Outer Mongolia.

If the Mongols of Manchuria should be antagonized by Japan, they could infinitely increase the difficulty of handling the frontier problems of Manchukuo. If, on the other hand, they are won over to Japanese policies, they can be made the most effective possible screen between the Japanese and Russian spheres of influence. At the same time, by attracting the sympathy of the Mongols who are still under Chinese domination, they can extend the influence and prestige of Japan and Manchukuo far out on the frontier between China and Inner Mongolia, thus cutting off the Chinese approach to the *terra irredenta*, and choking communication between China and any anti-Japanese movement in Manchukuo.

The ambition of certain Japanese is not even limited to Manchurian Mongolia; they believe that, like the Manchus (and working from much the same terrain) they can build up a continental power including all Mongolia, which would give them an enormous leverage in any policy toward either Russia or China. There are also Mongols who believe that by means of a Japanese alliance the revolutionary Government in Outer Mongolia can be overthrown and a united Mongolia created, restoring the old position and prestige of the hereditary princes. So much for Japan: but indeed there is grave question how far Japanese policy toward the Mongols may be considered optional, and how far it may have to be considered compulsory. It was impossible for Japan to undertake the control of Manchukuo without setting in motion a far-reaching Mongol policy; and with that policy once set in motion, there is no telling how far Japan may be forced to follow it up, thus being drawn deeper and deeper into Mongolia, and toward the frontier of Siberia, relegating Vladivostok to a secondary position and creating a wholly new tension between Japan and Russia.

As for the Mongols, they have been faced for a generation by the blank alternative of Russia or China; but the action of Japan has broken this opposition and instituted a triple balance of power. If, say the Mongols who believe in the dour Turkish way of defiance to all comers, the

Mongols fall back on themselves as did the Turks under Kemal, and set Russians, Japanese and Chinese all against each other, then they may yet retrieve a truly Mongol Mongolia; but for this they need a leader who will seem like Chingghis Bogda returning out of history, and at the same time be as modern as Kemal, the savior of the Turks, and no leader of this caliber is yet evident.

It is much more likely, in view of the character of recent Mongol history and events, that the first impetus toward a categorical change in the real situation of Mongolia will come from the outside—either from the revolutionary inspiration of the Soviet Union or from a dynamic reconstruction of monarchical principles in Manchukuo. In this respect Japan was at first handicapped by the necessarily anomalous position of Manchukuo. P'u Yi, as Chief Executive of Manchukuo, meant nothing to either Mongols or Chinese. As a sovereign, he may come to mean a great deal.

To the Mongols especially the recognition, as Sovereign of Manchukuo, of the legitimate heir of the Manchu overlords of Mongolia has a real meaning. It is also as nearly as possible a guarantee of good faith, in that it makes much more difficult the future annexation of Manchukuo. It is even a kind of hint that if the Mongols outside of Manchuria should offer allegiance to P'u Yi, it might be possible to create a "Mengkukuo" or Mongol State, ruled like Manchukuo by P'u Yi, and affiliated like Manchukuo with Japan, but not actually part of Manchukuo—an arrangement quite comprehensible to the Mongols, in view

of the character of the former Manchu Empire. All depends, however, on whether the reconstruction of a system
of Imperial overlord, ruling princes, and tribal loyalties,
combined with an intelligent policy of adaptation to the
modern world, is positively and creatively carried out, or
is merely a negative device for checking the growth of Mongol national life. Few Mongols have any working knowledge of world affairs, so that in the first instance the relative prestige of Japan and the Soviet Union will be almost
a decisive factor. Many Mongols, however, as is natural
among a people with their quality of tradition (though
this is not recognized by writers who treat the Mongols,
whether in periods of conquest or in periods of decline, as
mere barbarians) have a genuine instinct for statesman-
ship. So soon as the relative *working* values of Outer Mongolia and Manchurian Mongolia can be tested in comparison, therefore, it cannot be doubted that the Mongols
will correctly decide between the positive and constructive, as against the merely negative and defensive.

It is now possible to discuss, against the foreground of
current events as well as against the background of history,
the special characteristics of Hsingan province. Theoretically, it is a kind of national reservation, within which the
Mongols may govern themselves. Its highest officials do
not deal with the various ministries, as do the Chinese
provinces of Manchukuo, but are in direct communication
with the Privy Council. It has its allotment of Japanese
advisors, as do the other provinces, but they exercise a less

minute control, for the Mongol position is virtually one of alliance.

The province has its own troops, and is free of garrisons of the Manchukuo army. The civil administration and military organization are either in the hands of Mongols, or promised to them for the future. The titles, honors and prerogatives of hereditary princes are recognized locally, within the tribe, but over and above the tribal organization there is a provincial administration, the officials of which are in part elected by the tribal organizations and in part appointed by the Manchukuo Government. The headquarters of this provincial representation, or supervision, are not within the province, but at Hsinching, the national capital—which again is in keeping with the special standing of the Mongols, approximating to alliance. The province has no capital of its own. T'ungliao has been mentioned as a possible future capital, but T'ungliao is the center of an "island" of Chinese settlement and development, and is perhaps more likely to remain a detached, separately administered part of Fengt'ien province.

Internally, Hsingan is divided into four sub-provinces: the Northern (Barga), the Eastern (Nonni valley), the Southern (Jerim League) and the Western (Jo-oda League). The whole of Josoto League has been left out. Each of the sub-provinces therefore coincides in part with pre-existing Mongol boundaries. Geographically, it is plain that two major considerations have governed the delimitation of the frontiers. As far as possible, all true Mongol territory, in which the majority of the population is still

Mongol, has been reserved for the Mongols; but where advanced railway exploitation conflicts with Mongol claims, the Mongols have been forced to resign the territory to the Chinese provinces of Manchukuo; although the Mongols may remain in it if they wish. The interests of such Mongols are supervized by local Mongol Bureaus, which are organized according to the original tribal affiliation.

The province as a whole therefore lies to the west of the region of major railway development. The Chinese Eastern Railway crosses it in the north, from Manchuli to the station called Chingghis Khan, where the Hsingan Wall intersects the railway line. Farther south, there is a short line extending from T'aoan northwest into Hsingan province. This line was originally intended to run to the small trading town of Solun, and eventually to cross the Hsingan range and the Barga plains to the Siberian frontier. It was hoped to get the line across the mountains without tunneling. Such a line would have been of strategic importance under the Chinese administration of Manchuria, as it would have given China, for the first time, a flank approach to Outer Mongolia, and would have formed an inner line of communication with regard to the Chinese Eastern. The original project was based on the most ambitious government-support'ed colonization plan in Manchuria, and this would have to be abandoned if Mongol wishes were consulted. The problem of developing Mongol economy to the point where railways can be made to pay without the support of Chinese colonization is one which will test the ability of the Japanese in the handling of Manchukuo.

Still farther south, portions of the Chengchiat'ün-T'ungliao and Tahushan-T'ungliao railways run west and north respectively into Hsingan province, meeting at T'ungliao. The major regions left out of the Mongol province are Josoto League and about half of the Jo-oda League, in Jehol, the eastern half of the Nonni valley and the eastern part of Jerim. The important regions lost by the Jerim League Mongols lie to the east of the Ssup'ingkai-T'aonan-Angangchi railway system. They contain a heavy percentage of Mongol population, as do all the regions in which the Mongols have been constrained to resign their separatist claims; but although these Mongols are for the most part definitely Mongol in feeling, the regions themselves are destined to an agricultural and industrial future, and Mongol interests have therefore been subordinated to those of Chinese and Japanese. The "lost" territories of the Manchurian Mongols, in their relation to the autonomous territory, can be seen from the map. The details of historical boundaries, present boundaries, tribal affiliation and so forth will be discussed in the sections devoted to the major Mongol tribal divisions and their component Banners.

Chapter VII

MONGOL TRIBES, LEAGUES AND BANNERS

BEFORE considering in detail the present organization of the Mongols in Manchuria, it is necessary to define the terms used for Mongol tribal units and administrative divisions;[1] especially as the term "tribe" has been used somewhat loosely in the foregoing pages.

The tribe, considered as an ethnic unit, like the Khorchin or Gorlos tribes of Manchuria, is an *aimak*. (The Khalkhas, who form the majority of the Mongols in Outer Mongolia, are properly speaking one *aimak*, but have long been divided into four *aimak*, the fifth *aimak* of Outer Mongolia being composed chiefly of Western Mongols, related to the Ölöts of Chinese Turkistan and tribally differentiated from the Khalkhas.) The *aimak* when expanded to the scale of a nation, especially if it has absorbed other *aimak* in the process, becomes an *olos*. The Ölöts, originally an

[1] See also the article "Mongolia," by the present writer, in the *China Year Book*, editions of 1933 and 1934, in which are listed not only the tribes and banners of the Mongols in Manchuria, but all Mongol tribes and banners having anything to do with China.

aimak, attained at one time the standing of an *olos.* It was the break up of this *olos* which eventually brought the Ölöts under the Manchu Empire, in the eighteenth century.

The tribal following of a ruling prince—the tribal unit, that is, which the Manchus, by defining territorial boundaries, converted into something resembling a petty state, or principality—is the *hoshio.* (The written form is *hoshigo,* and the commonest Chinese transliteration is *ho-shao.* The word sometimes appears in English, through the influence of the Russian transliteration, as *hoshun.*) An *aimak* may sometimes consist of only one *hoshio,* or it may contain several *hoshio,* and they may all occupy contiguous territories or they may be at some distance from each other. The Aro-Khorchin *hoshio* in Jo-oda League, for instance, is detached from the six Khorchin *hoshio* in Jerim League.

The term *hoshio* is commonly rendered in English as Banner; but this in fact is not a translation of the Mongol term, but of the Chinese word *ch'i.* The original term has a variety of meanings, such as "point"; "the spur of a hill"; "the iron-shod point of a (wooden) ploughshare," and so forth; the Chinese term is presumably a rendering of a special sense, probably with a military connotation, such as "the 'portion' of followers or fighting men allotted to a chief." The Chinese term *ch'i* and the English term Banner are both unfortunate, in that they do not distinguish between Mongol and Manchu Banners.

The Manchu Banner has no tribal significance, although it is possible that the Banner system was derived from an original tribal federation. The Manchu Banner organization, even before the conquest of China, was a *regimental* formation. There were at first four and then eight, while at a later time certain "palace Banners" were added, which were not primarily military and had a lower social standing. The eight-banner organization, as the Manchu armies increased before the conquest of China, was expanded by adding a Chinese and a Mongol "battalion" to each Banner, so that there were in reality twenty-four Banners. Four of these triple Banners, making twelve in all, were "brigaded" as a Right Wing, and four as a Left Wing.

After the Conquest, the Manchu Banners, or regiments, were still further diversified by the requirements of garrison establishment. A complete cadre of eight Banners, each with its Manchu, Mongol and Chinese "battalions," was retained at Peking, while the "palace Banners" were added. Parallel Banner formations were maintained at Mukden, Kirin and so forth; some had a complete cadre of eight, some had more than eight but less than sixteen, some had less than eight, and some had and some did not have Mongol or Chinese "battalions." Mongol Banners, forming "battalions" of the Manchu Banner regiments, had no tribal function; they consisted of Mongols recruited from the tribes, and thereby detached from their native tribal organizations to form hereditary professional troops.

Nor was there any ethnic connection between, say, a Manchu of the All-White Banner of Peking and a Manchu of the All-White Banner of Kirin. There did arise a kind of secondary hereditary connection between Man-

chu families and Manchu Banners in each garrison center, but this grew out of a fiction. All Manchus, legally,
were liable to be drafted for Banner service; their legal
status was that of hereditary professional soldiers. Actually,
in Peking, for instance, only a certain number were assigned to a Banner payroll in each year; the rest were
hsien san, or "unappointed," "unattached." Since Banner
pay included family allowances, however, all the sons of a
Manchu drawing pay from a particular Banner would
consider themselves affiliated to that Banner, unless,
through the system of yearly military tests, they were assigned to a different Banner; and even so, as the Peking
Manchus developed into a social caste that was in some
ways a leisure class and in some ways an unemployed
class, living on Government subsidies, there developed a
system of nepotism by which the descendants of a Banner soldier were continually reappointed to the same Banner, in order to keep the clan name on the payrolls.

The Mongol Banner proper, or *hoshio,* was quite different. Undoubtedly its origin may be traced to the personal
followings of individual chiefs, the followers of a group of
related chiefs forming the larger body known as a tribe.
This primary conception of the personal following went
through a whole series of modifications, first in the course
of independent Mongol history and later under the influence of the Manchus. In Mongol history, before the Manchu Empire, two opposite influences were at work: the
unification of hordes of personal followers, under petty
leaders, by great leaders, and the splitting up of these con-

glomerate "tribes," again under petty leaders, after the death of a great leader. "Tribes" of this kind broke up and formed afresh in a strikingly fluid way, as illustrated by tribal history between the death of Yisugei, father of Chingghis, and the time when Chingghis himself was old enough to begin his career; for instance:

"In this time, because the brothers [Chingghis and his brothers, that is] were all small, little by little all the tribes [aimak] under them, judging that the Taijigot tribe was the powerful one, revolted and dispersed. When the body-servant, Holjan by name, who followed the T'aitsu [Chingghis] was also about to revolt and go, the T'aitsu went to him and took him by the sleeve and drew him back, letting the tears fall from his eyes, and entreated him, weeping; but Holjan said—'The water of the deep lake is dry, and the rock of the firm peak already shattered; what business have you to stay me?'; and jerking his arm he made him let go; he led all the rest in revolting and going." [2]

New tribes could be formed out of remnants of defeated and scattered tribes, if a suitable leader came forward. Thus, on the fall of the Liao dynasty, which had originated in Manchuria, a prince of the Imperial clan broke away, worked along the Inner Mongolian border all the way westward into Chinese Turkistan, and founded a new "dynasty" or kingdom on the borders of Chinese Turkistan and Siberia, known as the Khara-Khitai. This new tribal power could not possibly have been recruited in the main

[2] *Gughe Sodor.*

from the Khitan or Khitai (plural form, Khitat) of Manchuria; it must have been based on a personal following
of soldier-adventurers, picked up from peoples all the way
between Manchuria and Turkistan. Yet it is spoken of as
if it were a branch of the Khitan people who founded the
Liao Empire. The chief differentiation is in the style of
Khara-Khitai, the word *khara,* black, having the connotation of "common," or "ordinary"—the Non-Imperial
Liao, that is.

In studying the Mongol tribal grouping of our own
time, the policy of the Manchu Empire must constantly
be borne in mind; the insistence on territorial frontiers,
in order to stop the "snowball" processes of Mongol tribal
warfare, and the strict regulation of the counter-process of
breaking up into ever-smaller units.

The Mongol system of blood inheritance modified by
clan choice and tribal acquiescence has already been mentioned, and also the Manchu assumption of the prerogative
of confirming princes in their succession. Owing to this
intervention there are now two main classes among the
Mongol princes: those with sovereign titles and those with
honorary titles. There are cadet branches of certain princely
families with hereditary titles of honor, usually dating back
to some especially distinguished military service rendered
to the Manchus, or to intermarriage with the Manchu Imperial House. Only one prince in each Banner is recognized as the ruling prince. He holds a seal of office in
confirmation of his appointment, and consequently the
princes who have only titles of honor are called "sealless"

princes. If a ruling prince should be deposed, a successor may be sometimes appointed, not from his immediate family but from among the "sealless" princes of cadet branches of the same family. Sometimes, in recent years, because the rigidity of the system has not been kept up under the Chinese overlord Government, the office of ruling prince has actually been held in rotation by different related princes within the Banner.

There is also, in many Banners, a difference between practice and theory. It often happens that in one Banner there may be several princes who would, if the Mongols had been free of the overlord Government, have succeeded to the rule of a portion of the tribe. These princes exercise, in practice, a kind of rule over their own subjects, and are not interfered with by the ruling prince of the Banner; but the overlord Government recognizes only one ruling prince, and therefore if it has official business with the "sealless" prince, it is transacted not with him direct, but through the office of the ruling prince.

This phenomenon of princes recognized by their own people as virtually independent is especially common among the Manchurian Mongols, because of the great number of princes who were granted special titles as a result of intermarriage with the Manchu Imperial House. It has been given an added emphasis in recent years because of the tendency among the Manchurian Mongols to divide up the tribal heritage under private ownership, through "prince's land deeds" registered with the tribal authorities. When the land is divided in this way, the adherents of a "sealless" prince tend to settle in a group, which confirms their social cohesion.

All princes do not have the same title: the title by which a prince is known is generally derived from a title of honor conferred under the Manchu Empire. A prince is not, for example, addressed as Prince Altan Dorji, or Prince Golden Thunderbolt, which would be his personal name, but as Darkhan Wang, Independent Prince, by his title of honor. There are no satisfactory translations of many of these titles, and thus it happens that some ruling princes are called "prince" (*wang;* the Mongols use the Chinese word), while others are called "duke" (Chinese *kung,* Mongol *gung*).

In addition to making the Banner system more rigid than it had formerly been, the Manchus introduced a totally new administrative category, designed to weaken the tribal cohesion of the Mongols. This was the *chigolgan* or "gathering," for which the Chinese term is *meng* and the English "league." The officials of a League are partly elected from within the League and partly appointed by the overlord Government, and the purpose of the system is to make the tribes and Banners check and balance each other, by having the affairs of each tribe come to some extent under the supervision of officials from other tribes. The League usually included several tribes, and in some cases different Banners of the same tribe came under different Leagues.

In Outer Mongolia, where the Manchu overlordship was later in being recognized, and in practice never so powerful as in Inner Mongolia, the League system was never established, the *aimak* functioning instead of it. Even in Inner Mongolia, several groups never came within a League. The most important of these groups in Manchuria is that of the Barga Mongols, but here the tribal mixture, and the semi-Manchu style of organization, made a League supererogatory.

Finally, some mention must be made of the Mongols who have no hereditary princes at all, such as the Chahars, north of Kalgan, and the Barga Mongols within Manchuria. In Chahar the absence of hereditary princes is due to the fact that the Chahars were one of the few tribes actually conquered by the Manchus, who deposed their princes and substituted a special Banner system which is a compromise between the Mongol or sub-tribal Banner and the Manchu regimental Banner. The Banners of Chahar are military in organization, with appointive officials, but they are assigned to permanent territorial stations, like the Mongol Banners proper.

The Banners of Barga are comparable to those of Chahar. They came under Manchu influence at an early period, and were organized on the Manchu system, without princes, but each Banner is also a tribal unit. There are also in Barga aristocratic families which have hereditary titles; but they are not hereditary rulers of their tribes, although accepted as natural leaders and always represented among the tribal officials.

Within what is usually considered Manchuria Proper— the Three Eastern Provinces of Fengt'ien (known for a while, under the Kuomintang, as Liaoning) Kirin and

Heilungchiang, there are the Jerim League, Barga, and certain other groups. In Jehol, which from the time it was made a province, in 1929, formed a fourth province of Manchuria, and was later included within Manchukuo by a Japanese campaign of occupation, there are the Leagues of Josoto and Jo-oda. The different Leagues and Banners of the Manchurian Mongols have now to be considered in their relation to Manchukuo, to the old provinces of Manchuria, and to the newly created province of Hsingan.

Chapter VIII

THE NORTHERN OR BARGA DIVISION OF HSINGAN

BARGA has always been recognized as a separate administrative district. Its eastern and southeastern frontier is the watershed of the main Hsingan range; on the south and west it borders Outer Mongolia, and on the north Siberia. Although by this definition all of the old province of Heilungchiang west of the Hsingan range belongs to Barga, a useful distinction can be made between "Mongol" Barga in the center and south, and "wilderness" Barga in the north. There is, on some of the Japanese maps, a line running from Mergen, on the Nonni, westward across the Hsingan to the Gan River (Chinese transliteration, Ken). Here it almost joins an ancient frontier wall popularly known as the Wall of Chingghis, though it is more likely to date from the Chin dynasty and to be a part of the same defensive system as the Hsingan Wall than to be a work of the Mongols.

This would indicate a tribal boundary cutting off the Barga group of tribes from the northern triangle of territory between the Hsingan range and the Argun River; and it is probably correct. (The name Argun is rendered as E-erh-k'o-na by the Chinese. It is probably from the Mongol word *urghen,* broad, though it has also been explained as "twisting."[1]) Miss Lindgren marks "Orochon and Manegri" as the tribes of this triangle, and they are Tungus tribes which are distinct from the Mongolized Tungus included within the Barga group of tribes. The whole of the country west of the Hsingan is, however, included within the northern division of Hsingan province. The territory is about 75,000 square miles in area, with a population, according to a Russian estimate, of about 50,000.[2] In 1808 the population was 4,769 families, numbering 29,713 people in all.[3] The Chinese administrative name for the territory is Hu-lun-pei-erh (Khulunbuir) from the names of two lakes. (The modern Mongol spellings are *khulun,* possibly from *khulen,* the wild ass, though the wild ass is not now found in this region, and *boir,* possibly from the word for a bull camel.) The name Barga comes from the tribal name Bargo, often pronounced Barokh in the vernacular. It is a very old tribal name[4] and is found in place names as far east as Kirin. The Chinese transliteration is Pa-erh-hu.

The Chinese name of the province of Heilungchiang is taken from their name for the Amur, Black Dragon River. The name Amur itself is from the Mongol *amor,* peace. The Manchu name of the river is Sakhaliyan, "black," from

[1] Lindgren, in *Geog. Journ.*
[2] *North Manchuria.*
[3] *Unofficial Record of Heilungchiang.*
[4] Lindgren, *loc. cit.*

which is derived the name of the Island of Saghalin. The Chinese name Hsingan, Rising Peace, is merely a transliteration of the Mongol word *khingghan*, "an abrupt-sided mountain."

The history of the present tribal distribution in Barga began in the seventeenth century. While the Manchus were building up their power to the point where they could conquer China, the early Russian Cossack adventurers were raiding into the Amur wilderness. This produced a confused tribal movement of Mongols and Tungus in the Amur-Hsingan region, some of the tribes accepting the Russians as the new great power, while others withdrew before them and offered allegiance to the Manchus, hoping for support against the newcomers. After the conquest of China, the Manchus made a strong effort to rectify the frontier situation, and after attacking such Russian outposts as Albasin, succeeded finally in 1689, under the terms of the Treaty of Nerchinsk, in setting their frontier at the watershed of the streams falling into the Amur from the north (not the Amur itself, as at present).[5]

The first step of the Manchus in creating a buffer system of tribes was to raise troops in the Nonni region, move them across the Hsingan, and quarter them in the Barga country. It is to be supposed that the indigenous tribes were expected to group themselves around the nucleus offered by this garrison. Undoubtedly, the garrison establishment was able to link up with tribes of Mongol type in the

---

[5] See also Baddeley's full account, from Russian sources.

Barga plains,[6] but it is probable that it also had the effect of splitting apart the Tungus groups in the mountains and forested country. Thus, at the present time, there is an un-Mongolized, "wilderness" type of Tungus to be found north of the line of the Gan River and Chingghis Khan Wall, and another group, largely Mongolized, south of the line of the Chinese Eastern Railway, on the western slopes of the Hsingan.

The original garrison establishment occupied the territory still known as Old Barga. It was recruited in eight military Banners, in the Manchu style, from tribes that were not identical with the Manchus in race, but were in part related to the Manchus. Lands were then allotted to each Banner, so that while they remained regimental in organization, like Manchu Banners, they also took on a tribal character like that of Mongol Banners.

The Banners of Barga are thus comparable to the Banners of the Chahar Mongols; hence the old usage of speaking of the Chahars as the Inner Eight Banners and of the Barga tribes as the Outer Eight Banners; although, with the addition of further Banners, this usage really became inappropriate. (There are, in all, twelve Chahar Banners; but as four of these are Imperial Herdsmen, the phrase Inner Eight Banners must have been meant to apply to the eight "military" or "regimental" Banners, which were designated by colors, on the Manchu system.)

The Old Barga establishment was recruited in the first

---

[6] But note also the movement of Mongol tribes *away* from this region, like the Aro-Khorchin. See page 271.

instance from two groups; the Solons and the group which, very confusingly, is known specifically in the Chinese records as "Old Barga." The tribal affinities of the Solons will be discussed in the next chapter, dealing with the Nonni tribes. The "Old Barga" (Chinese Ch'en Pa-erh-hu) are apparently the "Chipchins" referred to by Binsteed, Lindgren and other writers. According to Lindgren, they came from the Nonni; according to Binsteed, they came first from Khalkha (Outer Mongolia) to Tsitsihar, and in 1732, together with the Solons, were moved from Tsitsihar to Barga "for being troublesome." According to a mimeographed MS. by a contemporary Mongol scholar,[7] the Solons were moved to Barga in the reign of Ch'ien Lung (1736-1796), while the "Old Barga" or Chipchins came from the Imperial Hunting Park, in Jehol, and were moved to Barga during the reigns of Yung Cheng and Ch'ien Lung (1723-1736; 1736-1796). Thus they began their migration before the Solons, and independently of them. They are, according to this authority, tribally related to the Buriats, and must therefore have migrated into Jehol from the north, before being moved back from Jehol to the north. The attribution, to the Chipchins, of an ethnic relation to the Buriats is probably correct. The name Chipchin itself is perhaps from the word *chabchima,* vernacular *chabchin,* meaning "cut off," "a remnant."

The Solons and "Old Barga"—Chipchin-Buriats were joined by a contingent of Ölöts, who were also placed in the Old Barga territory. The written form of Ölöt is

[7] For this reference, as for Binsteed and Lindgren, see Bibliography.

Ughelet, probably meaning "tall." The Ölöts were the creators of the Western Mongol Empire which ruled in Chinese Turkistan, invaded Tibet and nearly conquered Khalkha or Outer Mongolia; they were the last Mongols to come within the Manchu Empire. The Ölöts of Barga are said by Binsteed to have been captured by the Manchus in 1732, in the course of their wars with the Western Mongols. This dates them to the reign of Yung Cheng. According to the Mongol authority just cited, they were moved to Barga in the next reign, that of Ch'ien Lung, and contain two tribal elements, the "New" and the "Old." The "New" Ölöts were troops of the Jungar Confederation, or later Ölöt Empire. The "Old" Ölöts are not true Ölöts at all, but "are of the Khirghiz tribe, of the same race as the Oriyangghai"—that is to say, Central Asian Turks, who had been incorporated within the Ölöt Empire. "They are different in language from the Mongols. Having served as troops under Amorsana [a Khan of the Jungar Confederation] they followed the 'New' Ölöts in moving to this region." [8] Originally organized as one Banner, they now form two.

The next historical development was the addition of the territory of New Barga to the territory of Old Barga. The tribes of this territory, called Hsin Pa-erh-hu or New Barga by the Chinese, can more conveniently and less confusingly be called New Buriat. (The Mongol written form is Buriyet, vernacular Böriyat.) According to Binsteed, these tribes migrated from Northern Outer Mongolia about 1735; so

[8] Mimeograph MS.

that the dates 1732 and 1735 distinguish the formation of Old and New Barga. According to the Mongol authority already quoted, the migration went on during the reigns of K'ang Hsi, Yung Cheng and Ch'ien Lung (1662-1723; 1723-1736; 1736-1796) so that the movement began well before the date set by Binsteed, whose sources are chiefly Russian. This discrepancy may perhaps be accounted for if it is assumed that the migration began and went on for some time before official notice was taken of it.

The terms New Barga and Old Barga now have little significance, but they are of historical interest. New Barga lies to the west of Old Barga, and this could easily account for the fact that it was organized later by the Manchus, although on the whole its tribes probably entered their present territory earlier than the tribes of Old Barga.

This early and important migration of Buriats into New Barga is to be explained, I believe, by the determination of the Siberian frontier under the Treaty of Nerchinsk in 1689. The delimitation then confirmed brought the present Siberian Buriats of the Baikal and Trans-Baikal region under the Russians. I assume that some of the Buriats held pastures to the south of the new frontier, in the northern fringe of Outer Mongolia; that they were afraid of being included with the Siberian Buriats by the Russians, and that therefore they began to move eastward to get into touch with the Manchus, who were beginning to penetrate into and organize the Barga region, though they were not yet able to take a strong line in Outer Mongolia. When the Manchus had completed their frontier establishment in

Barga, the territories of Old and New Barga covered the middle and south (the open plains country) of the territory now administratively known as Barga. It is evident that no serious attempt was made to bring under strict control the scattered forest-roving Tungus groups of the northern wilderness triangle and the western slopes of the Hsingan range.

The eight-banner cadre of Barga was officially replaced in the last year of the Empire (1911), by an organization of seventeen Banners, designated as follows:[9]

Old Barga

    East Wing 4 Solon Banners (Bordered Yellow; All White; Bordered Red; Bordered Blue).
               1 Ölöt Banner (Bordered Yellow; attached as supernumerary to this Wing).
    West Wing 2 Solon Banners (All Yellow; All Red).
               2 Chipchin Banners (All Blue; Bordered White).

New Barga

    East Wing 4 Banners of Buriats (Bordered White; Bordered Yellow; All White; All Blue).
    West Wing 4 Banners of Buriats (All Yellow; All Red; Bordered Blue; Bordered Red).

It can be seen from this listing that the Manchu-style regimentation was not superseded, but expanded into a double eight-banner formation, with one supernumerary Ölöt Banner. The list of Banners here given has been ar-

[9] Mimeograph MS.

rived at by a comparison of the Mongol authority already quoted with Binsteed and the Japanese maps, and as none of the sources has complete details, there may be one or two errors in the attribution of Banners to their proper Wings.

In the twenty-one years of the Chinese Republic that followed, the Manchu-style Banner system fell almost completely into desuetude, while the number of tribal-territorial units was increased from seventeen to twenty-one. This was done by:

(a) Dividing the original Ölöt Banner into two Banners, according to the racial differentiation which has already been noted.
(b) Organizing the Mongolized Oronchon as a Banner.
(c) Forming two new Buriat Banners which may for convenience be called Old and New Refugee Buriat Banners.

Of these four extra Banners, the Ölöts need no further discussion.

The Mongolized Oronchon are of special interest. It is probable that they have held their present lands, on the western slopes of the Hsingan, south of the Chinese Eastern Railway, at least since the seventeenth century. Like the Solons, they are of old Tungusic stock. They are probably the only truly indigenous group that has yet been mentioned in Barga; yet according to the available lists of Banners and tribes it is plain that they have only been formally organized as a Banner within the last twenty

years. This political backwardness is a Tungus characteristic, and it may be due to their original distribution in forest regions, in small groups almost out of touch with each
other. The Manchus, for instance, who derive from the
Tungus stock, were so late in reaching the status of a nation that by the time organic unity had been created their
tribal components had become comparatively unimportant,
and they had already been heavily affected by Chinese influences. The same thing was true of the Nüchen or Chin,
also of Tungusic stock, who preceded the Manchus as an
Imperial power.

Generally speaking the "tribe," among Tungus who still
live under forest conditions, would seem to be recognized
simply as a larger category of kinship; it is less real to
them than the clan, which in practice is their major social
unit. It is probable that all Tungus were once reindeer
nomads, and it may be that the crucial change which
turned Tungus groups like the Nüchen-Chin and Manchus
toward evolution into tribes and nations was the destruction of the cultural and social economy of reindeer nomadic
life, either through moving south of the natural range of
reindeer, or through catastrophic loss of the reindeer from
some such cause as plague. The now strongly Mongolized,
horse-using, herd-owning Solons of Barga, for instance, are
hardly to be compared with the "wild" and still character-
istically Tungusic Solons of the eastern forested slopes of
the Hsingan.

It seems likely that the Oronchon group now being discussed were for generations so wild and fleeting a forest people that, though their kinship with the Manchus was always officially recognized, it was pointless to impose a formal organization on them. Individuals were freely recruited into the Manchu military service, but for the rest they were left to themselves. Thirty or forty years ago they lost their reindeer through plague,[10] and though attempts were made to obtain fresh reindeer stock from Siberia, they have ever since been rapidly "turning Mongol," and are now sufficiently "tribal" to be organized in the modern Mongol style on a tribal-territorial basis.

The last of the regular Banners of Barga to be considered are those of the Refugee Buriats, as they may most conveniently be called, to avoid confusion with the groups called Old and New Pa-erh-hu by the Chinese. These Banners are described in the following terms by the Mongol authority already cited:

"Buriats [Chinese transliteration, Pu-li-ya-t'e]: One Banner. They came as refugees after the confusion between Red and White in Russia [the Revolution]. To these must be added a Banner who are descendants of the Mongol Kucheng Khan, who ruled in Russian territory in the Ming period (1368-1644). Under the reigns of K'ang Hsi and Ch'ien Lung (1662-1723; 1736-1796; the reign of Yung Cheng coming in between) they were encroached on by Russian troops, and therefore moved from Lake Baikal to this region." [11] (It is worth noting that here, as generally with Mongols, the wording implies that a whole tribe are

[10] Lindgren.   [11] Mimeograph MS.

"descendants" of a prince. But see also below, under Mong-goljin Tumets.)

The wording here is obscure. The heading gives one Banner, the description gives two Banners, but puts the newly arrived refugees before those of the seventeenth and eighteenth centuries. It will be remembered that the eight Banners of New Barga are also Buriats, but that they came from Outer Mongolia, south of what is now the Siberian frontier, whereas the seventeenth and eighteenth century refugees here described came from north of the frontier. I infer that the "Siberian" or "old" refugees migrated to Barga at the same time as the eight "Outer Mongolian" Buriat Banners of New Barga, but were at first simply attached to this larger group, and were only given separate Banner status at the same time as the modern refugees from Siberia.

This author is often obscure. He mentions, for instance, that there are now twenty-one Banners in Barga, whereas the most recent Chinese Government lists I have seen [12] content themselves with a long-obsolete eight-Banner grouping; but from the sectional headings that he gives it would be impossible to enumerate the twenty-one Banners without expert knowledge. Nevertheless he is an author to be respected, and where he differs from other sources he differs usually in being more detailed and precise, indicating that he has not been satisfied with recapitulating the standard Chinese records, but has gone

[12] *Mongol Ten-Day Journal,* 10 Oct., 1931; this in turn appears to be based on a *Table of Mongol Leagues and Banners* published at Nanking in the previous year.

either to written Mongol records or to local Mongol spoken tradition.

There are yet two groups in Barga to be noted; the Hailar Daghors and the Tungusic tribes of the northern triangle.

Of these the Daghors are the more important. Their ethnic affinities will be discussed in the chapter dealing with the Nonni tribes. Most of them live in one or two villages a few miles west of Hailar. They are organized as one *hsieh-ling,* this being the Chinese term for one of the subdivisions of a Manchu military Banner. The first Hailar Daghors entered Barga with the original organization, by the Manchus, of Old Barga. By virtue of their high standing with the Manchus they held many important military positions. Daghor officials despatched on service to Barga from the Daghor communities in the Nonni valley in later years also tended to settle permanently; but as the higher official business of Barga was regularly referred to Heilungchiang province, and as Tsitsihar, the capital of Heilungchiang, stands in the original country of the Daghors, the outlying Daghors of Hailar have never lost touch with the main body of their people in the Nonni valley.

By virtue of their energy, capability and inherited tradition of official service, the Daghors have always tended to monopolize high official appointments in Barga. At the present time they dominate the tribal affairs of the whole region. The Governor of the Barga division of Hsingan province comes of one of the most distinguished Daghor families, and has the hereditary title of Duke. Almost all educated Daghors (and many of them are educated) can read and write Manchu, which by reason largely of the Daghor tradition is still the language of all official documents in Barga. Few of them, however, can speak it as a living language.

All Daghors preserve their own language, which is one of special interest because it stands between the related languages of Mongol and Manchu. Educated Daghors also know Mongol, most of them study Chinese, and many of them know Russian as well. It is said that the only Mongol who ever studied in America was a Daghor, and numbers of them have gone to Russia or Japan for their higher education. They dominate the politics of Barga to such an extent that the leaders of all parties are Daghors—the extreme conservatives, those who have long worked for a limited regional autonomy, those who believe in Republican Revolution, and those who favor Communism and union with Outer Mongolia. They have contributed some of the most capable leaders of the Young Mongol movement. As a class they are brave, patriotic and progressive.

The Tungus tribes of the northern triangle of Barga, finally, are of interest historically and ethnically, but have never formed part of the tribal complex of Barga proper. They are marked on Lindgren's ethnographic sketch map as "Manegir and Orochon." [13] The *Unofficial Record of Heilungchiang* gives *Mo-no-ho-erh,* which is plainly a rendering of Managir or Manegir (Russian form, Manegri), as a *clan* name among the Birar, a Tungus group compara-

[13] For this and the next two references, see Bibliography.

ble to the Orochon. The name is also listed among the Amur Tungus tribes in *Turanians and Pan-Turanianism.*

The name Orochon occurs also as Oronchon and Oroch, and in other forms, among the scattered and confused Tungus groups that are found from the Amur to the Ussuri. I use the form Oronchon, following the usage of Chinese and Mongols.

These groups were loosely classed as "New Manchus," like all similar groups racially akin to the Manchus, from whom troops were recruited after the original consolidation of the "Old Manchus" in Kirin; but they were practically left alone so far as formal government was concerned. Thus while geographical Barga included the whole of Heilungchiang province west of the Hsingan, political and governmental Barga extended only as far north, roughly, as the line of the Gan River and Chingghis Khan Wall.

Besides these tribesmen there are a few recently-immigrated Reindeer Tungus from Siberia in the northern triangle, who were visited by Lindgren and described in the article already quoted. There are also groups of Russian exiles about the Gan River, in the "Three Rivers" district, and numbers of small river-bank settlements of Chinese along the Argun River, most of whom came upstream along the Amur; but they are not numerous or important enough for separate discussion within the limits of a study of Mongol Manchuria.

Chapter IX

THE EASTERN OR NONNI DIVISION OF HSINGAN AND THE LOST MONGOL TERRITORIES ASSOCIATED WITH IT

THE name Nonni is a rendering, presumably affected by the Russian pronunciation, of the name of the river which the Daghors call Non. The Chinese version is *nen*, also read *nun: Nen-chiang*, the river Nen.

While the Barga territory has been retained intact as part of the autonomous Mongol province within Manchukuo, the actual boundaries of the Nonni valley territory must be considered in relation to its much wider historical frontiers. The sub-province as now constituted is bounded on the north by the Ilkhuri Alin range, thus excluding a number of small Tungusic groups between the Ilkhuri Alin and the Amur. (The Ilkhuri Alin, which like the main Hsingan is not distinctively marked on the accompanying maps, forms the watershed between the northwestern headwaters of the Nonni and the Amur valley. It is also a bridge from the main or Great Hsingan, between the Nonni valley and the Barga country, to the Little

Hsingan, northeast of the Nonni. The name Ilkhuri Alin appears to be Manchu, *alin* being "mountains.")

On the east, the Nonni division of Hsingan is bounded by the northwestern headwaters of the Nonni from the Ilkhuri Alin to Nenchiang city, or Mergen, and by the main stream of the Nonni from Mergen to the Hsingan Wall. The frontier then follows the Hsingan Wall south-westward all the way to the headwaters of the T'ao or Tor. The main Hsingan forms the whole westerly frontier, dividing the Nonni territory from the Barga country.

This excludes, on the northeast, the old garrison cantonments of Aigun or Heilungchiangch'eng (Heilungchiang Town), and on the east and in the Tsitsihar region a very large proportion of the important Daghor group. It is ironical that while the virility and political sense of the Daghors, and their prestige among the Mongols, must have been a factor in determining the inclusion of the largely non-Mongol Nonni valley region within Hsingan province, other considerations have obviously made it necessary to exclude from the sub-province the most important areas of Daghor population. The Nonni valley is a commanding line of approach to the Amur and the Siberian frontier. Railways leading north are already being constructed on the eastern side of the valley, and for the consolidation of the Amur frontier railway expansion and colonization must be pushed forward at a rate which would not accord with the general policy of a Mongol province.

Historically, however, the Nonni region as a natural geographical unit extends eastward from the Nonni itself to the system of minor rivers which flow together to form the Hulan River, falling into the Sungari near Harbin. (The name Hulan is probably a Chinese adaptation of some Manchu or other non-Chinese name. The name Sungari, adapted in Chinese as Sunghua-chiang, Fir-flower River, is from the Manchu Songgari, the name of the Milky Way. The name Harbin is possibly from the Mongol verb *harbomoi,* vernacular *harbona,* "to shoot with arrows" and, possibly, "to spear fish.")

The great plain between the Nonni and the Hulan was undoubtedly, at the end of the sixteenth century, before the emergence of the Manchus as a political nation, a vortex which powerfully affected race-movements in Manchuria. It was a debatable ground between the Mongol stock and the Tungusic stock. Here Mongols met tribes of Manchu type and here, at a later period, there was established a graduated series of Manchu-Tungus elements, ranging from the Old Manchu walled cities of the upper Sungari, with their quasi-Chinese culture, through different classes of New Manchus to the "wild" Tungus of the forested mountains, the tribal raw material of the whole Manchu nation.

The Mongols, coming into this plains country from the west or southwest, established their tribal frontiers well to the northeast of what is now the line of the Chinese Eastern Railway. Beyond the frontier of Mongols living under Mongol organization were Mongols who had begun to coalesce with the Tungus, and Tungus who had come out of the encircling mountains and begun to merge with the Mongols.

When the Manchus, at the beginning of the seventeenth century, had become a solid political power making perceptible headway against the Chinese, they dealt with the Mongols as tribal or sub-tribal units, taking them over Banner by Banner under their own leaders. The Mongols thus retained their own social and political organization almost intact. The Tungus groups beyond the periphery of the old Manchu city-states, first united by Nurhachih, could not be enlisted in the same way as the Mongols, because their tribal divisions and organization were not definite enough. Their kinship with the Manchus in race and language being however obvious and recognized from the beginning, they could best be organized by direct enlistment into the Manchu regimental Banners.

For this the Manchu Banner system was well suited. As the Manchus extended their control and government northward into the terrain of their Tungusic kinsmen, all that was necessary was to expand the Banner organization, which in itself was capable of indefinite multiplication. Each town that was made the center of a new administrative district became the garrison headquarters of a new regimental group of eight Banners. The men who enlisted in these Banners, and their families in the adjoining districts, automatically became New Manchus. Men from remote tribal groups in the hills and forests could also enlist in the Manchu Banners, and indeed were always especially valued by the Manchus; but the status of New Manchus hardly affected the families and relatives of such men, living beyond the scope of regular government administration.

The organization of Banner garrisons in North Manchuria did not on the whole clarify or stabilize the lines of "tribal" or "racial" division among the peoples it affected. Under the uniform surface of the eight-banner regimental cadres the distinctions between what we must, for want of a good term, call "race" or "tribe" were extraordinarily fluid. Distinctions were in fact as often social or cultural as "tribal." Most of the older written material that we have is Chinese, the work of men who had a superficial knowledge of local nomenclature but little insight into the character of tribal processes. Yet it is possible to discern, under the confusion of names and tribal attributions, that several processes were constantly at work.

Groups might break away from a tribe until nothing but a clan was left. Conversely, a clan might gather strength and numbers until it swelled into a tribe. One and the same people might be known in one place or at one time by a place name, and in other places or at other times by a clan name or general tribal name. Groups of different provenance could come together under a single name. A people of single origin, established in the same place for generations, might split into two parts, one of which retained the old way of life and with it the old name, while the other changed from a hunting to a pastoral economy and

later to agriculture, changing its name and "tribal" standing each time.

These processes are still going on, especially among
groups of the Tungusic stock, and changes of dialect or
language go on concurrently. They are less important and
less rapid among groups of Mongol stock, because processes of tribal modification began to be standardized among
the Mongols not long after the time of Chingghis; indeed,
they had already a recognizable pattern before his time.
Under the Manchu dynasty, therefore, Mongol processes
became on the whole simply more rigid, and in certain respects distorted.

This type of differentiation and re-differentiation covers
an extraordinary range of names, which cannot here be
pursued into all its ramifications. To do so would make
it necessary to take up the whole tribal question of the
Amur, Sungari and Ussuri valleys. The reader may be
referred to *Turanians and Pan-Turanianism* for lists (not
complete, however) of these tribes, and for bibliographical
references; to Baddeley, who is invaluable for the seventeenth century and the record of relations between Russians and Manchus, and also has an excellent bibliography;
and to Shirokogoroff for the special study of the Tungus.
In a study of the Mongols of Manchuria it is enough to
establish the historical importance of the Manchu-Tungus
groups, the position of the Daghors as a link between
Manchus and Mongols, the type of gradation between city-
Manchus of the south and the Tungusic "raw material"

of the north, and the modes of tribal mutation within the Tungusic series of peoples.[1]

In the region stretching from the Hulan and Nonni valleys northward and westward to the Amur and the Great Hsingan massif, the spread of Manchu control was in the main a problem of instituting the uniform Manchu system while allowing for the cultural variety of the peoples brought under control, who ranged from agricultural villagers to forest hunters and nomads. There was, it is clear, no general conquest. The military problem was not internal but external. Before the Manchus had fully established their administration, they came into conflict with the Russians on the Amur. By the time that the Russian frontier question had been settled, in 1689, the double pressure of Manchus and Russians had brought about a great deal of tribal shifting. Some of the indigenous groups attaching themselves to the Russians and others to the Manchus.

Even the Daghors, who on the whole were the mainstay of the Manchu Amur frontier, were affected by this type of cleavage, and Daghor villages are found to this day on the Russian side of the Amur.[2] This tribal confusion was made worse by the fact that the Russian frontier was nominally set at the watershed north of the Amur, while in prac-

---

[1] See also *The Gold Tribe, "Fishskin Tatars" of the Lower Sungari*, by the present writer.

[2] See also Baddeley, for early Russian accounts of Daghor villages and strongholds near the Amur, and for mention of Gantimur (Gangtemur, Steel-Iron) the Daghor chief who went over to the Russians, and one of whose descendants was at Port Arthur.

tice the Russian influence continued to penetrate to the Amur itself.

On the Manchu side, all North Manchuria, from Hulan north to the Amur and west into Barga, was regarded as a frontier "tribal" province. Its military officials ranked above the civil, and eight-banner cadres were maintained at Hulan, Tsitsihar, Mergen and Aigun, and in Buteha and Barga. (The northeastern frontier, approached from the lower Sungari, was handled separately.) The senior general had his headquarters first at Aigun or Heilung-chiang Town, for which reason the whole province came to be known as Heilungchiang; but after the settlement of the Russian frontier conflict, headquarters were moved to Tsitsihar, for the sake of better communications with Kirin and Mukden, and the capital has remained ever since at Tsitsihar.

By the end of the nineteenth century the Banner population of Hulan had been overwhelmed by incoming Chinese colonists, and the practical frontier between "civilians" (Chinese) and Bannermen had shifted westward to a line about midway between the Hulan and Nonni valleys. The Hulan region need no longer be considered in a survey of tribal questions.

Within the Banner organizations in the Nonni valley, the main racial elements were not coördinated with the Banners in a "battalion" system, as in Peking and Kirin. The most important racial groups were associated with "companies" within the Banner "regiments."

The following figures, which are probably a rough guide

to racial proportions, are taken from the *Unofficial Record of Heilungchiang*. This work, the preface to which is dated 1810, may be considered reliable for the period before the major influx of Chinese. The list given, however, refers not to the "companies" themselves, but to the company-commanders. Owing to the fact that an unspecified number of these commissions were hereditary, it may well have been that some of the "companies" existed only on paper.

The eight Banners of Tsitsihar listed forty company commanders, distributed as follows:

Manchu	16
Chinese Bannermen (Han Chün)	4
Solon	4
Daghor	14
Pa-erh-hu	2

The Chinese Bannermen were mostly of Shantung derivation, and were drafted to this region from Kirin.

The Pa-erh-hu here mentioned were mostly of the stock listed above, in the chapter on Barga, as Chipchins or Old Pa-erh-hu. When, having been moved from Jehol to the Nonni, the main body of them were drafted to the Hailar country, a number remained behind in the Manchu-style regimental Banners. A few New Pa-erh-hu, of the Buriat group from North Mongolia, also remained in these Banners.

Of the four Solon company commanders it is said that later, owing to the small number of Solons available, the posts were filled by Daghors.

The eight Banners of Mergen listed seventeen company-commanders, distributed as follows:

Chinese Bannermen (Han Chün)....... 2
Solon 10
Daghor 5

The eight Banners of Aigun listed twenty company commanders, distributed as follows:

Manchu 10
Chinese Bannermen (Han Chün)....... 2
Solon 1
Daghor 7

(In the Aigun list, as printed in the original source, the Manchu company commanders are given as sixteen, but this from the context is evidently a misprint for ten.)

The racial distribution in the eight Banners of Buteha is not indicated. These Banners had a special standing, and will be discussed later.

The population figures given by the work just quoted, taken from a census of 1808, are as follows:

Eight Banners of Tsitsihar... 9702 families or 48,311 in all
Eight Banners of Mergen.... 1855 " " 7,969 " "
Eight Banners of Aigun..... 4199 " " 19,388 " "
Eight Banners of Buteha.... 4033 " " 18,933 " "
Eight Banners of Hulan..... 1659 " " 11,914 " "

These figures indicate that the average family in Hulan numbered over 7—probably because, even at this date, settlement had proceeded so far that the proportion of women to men was higher. In Tsitsihar the number was approximately 5 to the family; in Mergen, where it is reasonable to assume that the proportion of unmarried troops was higher, the family averaged about 4; in Aigun about 4½; and in Buteha, where the population was almost entirely "tribal" about 4½ also—the average nomad family being smaller than that of the settled agricultural family.

The Manchus of the Nonni, like those of Kirin, have become so largely Chinese that they are of little importance in the affairs of the Mongol or "tribal" province of Hsingan, though like the Kirin Manchus, and also the old frontier Chinese, they are still important within Manchuria by virtue of their historical and regional tradition. There are, however, still a very few Manchu-speaking villages in the upper Nonni valley.

The Chinese Bannermen, naturally, like the Manchus, must now be reckoned with the general Chinese Frontier group. With them may be classed the people of the old "road-settlements" organized by the Manchus, which maintained posts and transport between Tsitsihar and the Amur. They were Chinese who ranked as "government settlers." The Chinese slave classes have also been absorbed into the general Frontier group. They were usually criminal or political exiles, were much used by wealthy Manchus and Daghors right up to the Revolution in 1911, and were bought, sold and given as presents at will.

Within the last ten years, finally, there has been a great influx of "raw," non-frontier colonists from China proper, especially Shantung. They now form over half the total population, and the fall in standards of living, increase of banditry and concentration of wealth in the hands of a small group of Chinese officials (dominated by the military) which they caused have roused the intense resentment of the older classes in the population.

The Daghors now rank ahead of the Manchus in importance. They number, according to their own estimates, at least a hundred thousand. They are wealthy, though not so wealthy as they used to be before land speculation and grain trusts brought in a lower standard of living. Like the Daghors of Hailar, they are progressive and at the same time tenacious of their language and racial tradition. Their ability as politicians and administrators has done much to preserve them from absorption by the Chinese; but the invasion of their ancient territories, in the last ten years of Chinese rule, by Chinese of low economic standing, made their superior position much more insecure than it had been.

They are distributed all along the Nonni valley from Tsitsihar to Mergen (a town whose name appears to be from the Mongol word for "wise"; its Chinese name is Nenchiang or Nonni River Town). Their main concentration is between these two towns, and on the east side of the river, outside of the autonomous province. They are found also about Aigun and Taheiho (a Chinese name, meaning Great Black River) on the Amur, and even in villages on the Russian side of the Amur. There has hardly been time as yet to tell whether there will be any strong tendency among the Daghors to migrate within the frontiers of Hsingan province. The Governor of the Nonni division of Hsingan is a Daghor of the older generation, from Mergen, with the interesting personal name of Oronchon. He has a son educated in Japan.

According to the Mongol authority already quoted, the Daghors are "descendants" of Habto Hasar, a brother of Chingghis Khan; that is to say, they are descendants of his followers. This means that they are related to the general stock of the Mongols of Jerim League, the largest of all the Mongol groups in Manchuria. Pushing up the Nonni and over to the Amur valley, into the ancient country of the Tungus, and representing perhaps the Mongol overlordship over the forest tribes, they took over and assimilated with themselves a great many Tungus followers. The racial fusion was accompanied by a linguistic fusion, so that the Daghor language is intermediate between the Mongol and the Tungus-Manchu branches of the same general linguistic group. According to the Daghors [3] themselves, the Mongol elements in their language are archaic, indicating that their migration was relatively early. It may date to the end-period of Mongol expansion into Manchuria; perhaps the fourteenth century.

In the reign of T'ien Ming (1616-1627; this was the reign-style assumed by Nurhachih when, after his earlier conquests, he declared himself Emperor, thus openly announcing his pretensions to the rule of China and "all under

[3] Personal statements made to me by Merse, Oronchon and other Daghors.

Heaven") the main concentration of the Daghors was in the Amur valley rather than along the Nonni. A Daghor chief of that time came over voluntarily to the Manchus, and as the effective power of the Manchus had not yet reached the Amur, this gave the Daghors a high standing. As Russian pressure later increased, some of the Daghors turned from the Manchus to the Russians, and this led to an expedition against the "recalcitrant" Daghors which the records claim was successful, and which must in fact have been partly successful, though some of the Daghors did remain under the Russians. After the Treaty of Nerchinsk in 1689 the main body of the Daghors withdrew into the Nonni valley, where they are now distributed. It is from the "voluntary" enlistment under the Manchus that the name Daghor is derived, according to the Daghors themselves and to Mongols also. The name is traced to the Mongol verb *dagomoi,* vernacular *dagana,* "to follow," "to accompany," the connotation being that of a "feudatory" relationship. The name is most commonly rendered as Ta-hu-li by the Chinese, and also as Ta-hu-erh, and frequently appears in English as Daur, through the influence of the Russian pronunciation.

The fragmentary groups of "wild" Tungusic type have now to be considered, and I believe that they can best be understood by reference to the history of the Daghors. It is probable that as the Daghors moved up the Nonni and into the Amur valley they acted as a wedge of militant horse-riders driven into the ancient reindeer country. It is likely that some of the Tungus groups, as a result of this cultural invasion, lost their reindeer economy without being able to make a full transition to the Daghor way of life. Thus there was formed a number of groups of general ethnic uniformity, but weak in tribal structure. They had lost their reindeer but had acquired few horses, and such horses as they had were used for transport, not kept grazing in herds, since the country itself, being forested and mountainous, was not adapted to a pastoral economy. Each group ranged along a series of semi-permanent clearings in the forest, but continued to live mainly by hunting. The range of each group was roughly determined by the configuration of the valleys running from the main watershed of the Hsingan range to the west bank of the Nonni.

These groups were loosely organized as the eight Banners of Buteha. Their military duties were insignificant. The name Buteha (Manchu *butkha,* "hunting") was not tribal, though it came gradually to be used almost in a tribal way, blanketing the clan and tribal names of the groups it covered. The term Buteha, in the proper use, covers the whole "hunting wilderness" from the west bank of the Nonni to the Hsingan watershed. All the tribes and clans within this region were affiliated to the Buteha Banners, which were divided in the usual way into an East and a West Wing. Their special function was to collect the Imperial "hunters' tribute," of which an interesting account is given by Baddeley. They were scattered out of sight and reach of regular officials except during the periodic assemblies, at the edge of the wilderness, when they turned over their "tribute" of sables, received their largesse from the Emperor, and traded for the drink and trash which the merchants of civilization have always offered to "savages." Their families and camps, being remote from the garrisons in which occasional individuals enlisted (being specially favored on account of their marksmanship and their repute as "bold savages"), were little affected by their nominal rating as "Banner people" or New Manchus.

On one of the Japanese maps of the region several "Banners" are marked, in Chinese characters, which I have not been able to identify from Chinese sources. They are, from north to south, "Na-wen," "Pa-yen," "Mo-li-ta-wa," "A-jung" and "Hsi-cha-ka-erh." All apply to the Buteha wilderness, where the population is undoubtedly of Tungus, not of Mongol type; yet the names, under the distortion of the Chinese rendering, appear to be partly from a language of Mongol type. This can only mean that they are names applied to local groups by the Daghors; and this is borne out by the fact that one of the groups evidently has another name by which it calls itself.

Na-wen can be identified with Non, the original Daghor name (said to mean "younger sister") of the Nonni River. This name is placed beside the largest northwestern headwater stream of the Nonni, and is thus easily accounted for.

Pa-yen can only be from the word *bayan,* used in both Mongol and Manchu, meaning "wealthy." It is a common type of place-name and personal or clan or tribal name. This group, I am told by a Daghor informant, call themselves Khongkhor.[4] "They speak with us Daghors in our own language," according to my informant, "but among themselves they have a speech of their own which we cannot understand."

Mo-li-ta-wa I suppose to be a Daghor name, meaning Winding Pass; the Mongol form would be *moroi daba* and the Manchu form *morihan daban*.

A-jung, in which the syllable conventionally romanized *jung* is pronounced, approximately, *rung*, can be referred to the Mongol *aro*, "rear," "north."

Hsi-cha-ka-erh is plainly the Mongol word *khijagar*, "frontier," "outlying."

All of these are probably groups that have been differentiated of late years from the Birar, Orochon and forest Solon "tribes" of the Buteha wilderness, and I have therefore arbitrarily, but perhaps not incorrectly, associated them on the map with the East and West Wings of Buteha.

In dealing with names like Birar, Solon and Oronchon or Orochon, it is necessary to refer constantly to the facile mutation between clan and tribe among Tungus groups, and to the effect of cultural changes. There is a mention of the Birar in the *Unofficial Record of Heilungchiang* as having four petty officials, of a rank inferior to company-commander, in the Manchu banner system. The name Birar is widely distributed along the Amur valley. It evidently derives from the Manchu word *bira*, "a small stream," and seems to be a name frequently applied by

---

[4] There is a slightly different sound-value in the two o's of this name. Shirokogoroff derives it from a Daghor word meaning "wild." Compare Mongol *khong-khor*, "deep," "hollow," "hidden away."

Tungus groups to other Tungus groups. It is probable that there are "Birar" elements (the Chinese rendering is Pi-la-erh), among such modern groups as the Na-wen or Non who have just been discussed.

The Solons of the Nonni are ethnically related to the Solons of Barga, but the two groups have diverged widely from each other. The term Solon (rendered So-lun by the Chinese) on the Barga side of the Hsingan means a people of Tungus extraction, now closely assimilated to the Mongols and having a tribal-territorial organization like that of the Mongols. In the Nonni valley, however, a Solon meant first a New Manchu, enlisted in the Manchu military Banners; but in modern times the tendency is more and more to use the term Solon for "wild" forest hunters, and the term Orochon or Oronchon for comparatively well-organized tribal groups of the same general stock.

I think it is possible to discern the historical processes of change in these connotations. When the organized New Manchu Solons were drafted in large numbers to Barga, they left behind them other Solons divided between the military Banners of Tsitsihar, Mergen and Aigun and the hunting Banners of Buteha. Those in the military Banners were assimilated by the Manchus and Daghors, while those in the Buteha wilderness remained ethnically distinct, though weakly organized. Those on the Barga side of the Hsingan also developed away from the "raw" Tungus condition, and thus the Buteha Solons became isolated. Because they were the most conspicuous "wild" people in the Buteha forests, the name Solon tended to spread over all the people of that wilderness, and has now become, in the Nonni valley, a generic term for unorganized forest groups.

In the last ten years of Chinese rule in Manchuria, colonists began to cross the Nonni and clear the Buteha wilderness; and at a somewhat earlier period the Mongols pushed them away from their southernmost range, near the headwaters of the T'ao or Tor, where the Solon name is still preserved in the Chinese name of the little town of Solun. The Solons at first resisted the Chinese advance, until troops were brought in. After a good deal of fighting, the front of the Chinese advance was cleared. The Solons are now much diminished in numbers and demoralized by the drink obtained from Chinese traders. The majority of them are in the southern extension of the old Buteha wilderness, in the district marked on the Japanese map as Khijagar.

The term Orochon or Oronchon has had an opposite history. On the northwestern side of the Hsingan-Ilkhuri Alin, where the reindeer culture survived, the term Oronchon tends to be used generically of all reindeer nomads; only the Mongolized Oronchon in the south, detached from the northern triangle of Barga, have tended to become "tribal." On the Nonni side of the Hsingan-Ilkhuri Alin, where the reindeer culture disappeared or was destroyed at a comparatively early date, and where the term Solon came to be used generically of forest nomads, the term Oronchon came to be applied to the more recognizably New Manchu type of Tungus.

Of the Oronchon of the Nonni valley the *Unofficial Record of Heilungchiang* says that they are related to the Solon and Daghor, but nearer to the Solon. It also says that the Birar are "of the same kind" as the Oronchon. This is probably a fair identification of their standing in the graduated series between Manchu and "raw" Tungus. The same source makes an interesting distinction between two kinds of Oronchon, which illustrates the manner in which, within the Manchu-Tungus complex, economic and social differences tended to serve as quasi-tribal differentiations. The Oronchon who served as Banner troops a hundred years ago were known as "mounted" Oronchon (Manchu *moringga,* rendered in the text as *mo-ling-a*). Those who lived as sable hunters in the Buteha wilderness were known as "walking" or "foot" Oronchon (Manchu *yafahan,* transliterated *ya-fa-han* in the text). Many of them, it is stated, enlisted as troops—with the implication that in so doing they changed their status. This perhaps explains the later tendency for Oronchon to become a term for a people of a status comparable to that of the Daghors, while the "wild" Oronchon became merged in the Solon category.

The only true Mongol group in the Nonni valley are the Yeghe Minggan, or Great Thousand. This has every appearance of being a clan name. They are also known as the Mannai Ölöt; this name is probably to be referred to the Mongol term *manglai* or *mangnai,* "the front"; "the middle of the forehead"; also, "an advance guard." They are, by origin, Ölöts or Western Mongols, of the sub-tribe called Höit. They were followers of Amorsana (Tranquil Mind), one of the later Khans of the Jungar (East Wing) confederation of the Ölöts, and were transported from the borders of Jungaria or Northern Chinese Turkistan in the reign of Ch'ien Lung.[5] They differ from the Ölöts of Barga in having a line of hereditary princes. The tribal lands alotted to them, south and southwest of Tsitsihar, have been swamped by Chinese colonists, and are not included in Hsingan province.

In conclusion, it may be said of the Nonni division of Hsingan that it is a synthetic political product. Its present boundaries are pushed well back from its historical frontiers, and include little but forest wilderness. Within this wilderness it is still possible to halt Chinese colonization and give the indigenous people time to adapt themselves. The kind of autonomy allowed to these people, and the kind of steps taken for their economic rehabilitation will largely determine whether such valuable elements as the Daghors will move within the autonomous area and take an active part in its development.

[5] Mimeograph MS. This author confirms that Yeghe Minggan is a clan name.

Chapter X

THE SOUTHERN OR JERIM LEAGUE DIVISION OF HSINGAN AND THE LOST MONGOL TERRITORIES ASSOCIATED WITH IT

THE name Jerim is said to come from a Mongol word meaning "loyal." The Chinese transcription is Cheli-mu. Originally a distinct part of Manchuria, it was gradually brought within the provinces of Fengt'ien, Kirin and Heilungchiang.

The Mongols of Jerim are historically important because, as the most easterly of the Mongols, they were the first to come into contact with the Manchus. It was with them that the Manchus made the first of the series of alliances that led eventually to the defeat of the Chahars and the domination of Inner Mongolia, protecting the flank of the Manchus during the conquest of China, and eventually making it possible to extend Manchu influence all over Mongolia.

All of the princes of the Jerim tribes are descended from Habto Hasar, a brother of Chingghis Khan. (It will be remembered that the Daghors are also said to be descended from followers of Habto Hasar.) Under the later Manchu

dynasty, the first step in subordinating Jerim to the provinces of Manchuria was accomplished. The six Banners
of the Khorchin tribe were placed under the supervision of
Fengt'ien. (The name Fengt'ien means, By the Command
of Heaven. The name Liaoning, which was used for a
while under the Kuomintang, means Peace of Liao, referring to the Liao valley. Since the foundation of Manchukuo
the name Fengt'ien, with its Imperial connotation, has been
restored.)

One of the two Banners of the Gorlos tribe came under
Kirin; the other Gorlos Banner, together with the tribes
of Jalaid and Durbet, each of one Banner, came under
Heilungchiang. (The name Heilungchiang has already
been discussed. The name Kirin, transliterated Chi-lin by
the Chinese, is of Manchu origin.)

The Jerim League territory within Hsingan province is
far smaller than its historical territory. It has been pointed
out before that the needs of the railway systems and the
extent to which Chinese colonization has already displaced
the Mongols have evidently been the main considerations
in determining the new frontier lines. The general differences between the old and new frontiers can be seen from
the map; particular differences can best be discussed under
the headings of the various Banners.

THE JALAID TRIBE

One Banner

The Chinese transcription is Cha-lai-t'e. Originally a part
of the Khorchin tribe, the Jalaid split off at about the be-

ginning of the seventeenth century. The Banner joined the Manchus in 1624. Its original territory measured 400 by 60 *li*, or roughly 133 by 20 miles.[1] It lies southwest of Tsitsihar and on the west of the lower Nonni. Rather more than half of the Banner has been excluded from Hsingan province. The colonized southerly half is crossed by the T'aonan-Angangch'i Railway, and the town of T'ailai stands in its old territory. The name T'ailai is probably from the Mongol *tariya*, "farming." Colonization has been going on only for twenty years or so. The first agricultural development was due to Mongols from Jehol province, who had been displaced by Chinese pressure. There are many of these agricultural Mongols within the part of the Banner which has been included in Hsingan province. Until the formation of Hsingan province the entire Banner came under the control of Heilungchiang province.

THE DURBET TRIBE

One Banner

The Mongol name is from the plural form of the numeral *durben*, "four." There are several Durbet tribes among the Mongols, not necessarily related to each other. The Chinese transcription is Tu-erh-po-t'e. Like the Jalaid, this tribe was formerly a part of the Khorchin. It joined the Manchus in 1624, at the same time as the Jalaid. Its original territory measured 240 by 170 *li*, or about 80 by 57 miles.

---

[1] *Mongol Pastures*. This work, the standard Chinese authority on the Mongols, does not deal with the tribes of Barga or the Nonni. In discussing the Mongols of Jerim League and of Josoto and Jo-oda Leagues in Jehol, I have consulted it throughout.

It lies southeast of Tsitsihar and on the east of the Nonni.
The Chinese Eastern Railway runs through the middle of
it. The whole Banner has been excluded from Hsingan
province, and remains within Heilungchiang. Colonization
rapidly followed the building of the railway, and the Banner is now heavily colonized, the rich agricultural county
of Anda being part of its original territory, as are the
counties of Lintien and T'aik'ang (misprinted Ch'ungk'ang
on the Japanese map). The Mongols who remain are agricultural villagers, but have not lost their language or national feeling. (The name Anda is probably from the Mongol *anda,* "a sworn brother." Lintien is Forest Domain, and
T'aik'ang is Prosperous Repose, an "auspicious" name of a
kind often chosen in colonization regions to celebrate the
"beginnings of civilization." T'ailai, already mentioned, is
a name of this kind, but is at the same time probably a
phonetic rendering of a Mongol name.)

THE GORLOS TRIBE

The Chinese rendering is Kuo-erh-lo-ssu. The two Banners are differentiated as North and South. Originally an
independent tribe, with princes of their own, the Gorlos
were conquered by Habto Hasar, brother of Chingghis and
founder of the line from which derive the princes of Jerim
League. The present princes of Gorlos are therefore also
descended from Habto Hasar. The tribe itself may be partly
of non-Mongol origin, related to the Nüchen people and
therefore to the Manchus. These two Banners also joined
the Manchus in 1624. The size of the original territory of

the whole tribe is given in the *Mongol Pastures* as 660 by 450 *li*, or approximately 220 by 150 miles.

North Gorlos

or, in Mongol, Aro Gorlos, the smaller of the two Banners, is bounded on the northeast by the Hulan region, on the southeast by the Sungari, on the southwest by the Nonni and on the northwest by Durbet. The easternmost corner of the Banner reaches almost to Harbin. The Chinese Eastern Railway crosses the Banner, and as the territory is fertile, colonization has been heavy, though not so heavy as in South Gorlos.

The Mongols are agricultural, wealthy and progressive. They retain a good deal of livestock. They are strongly Mongol in feeling and have not lost their language. Although the whole Banner has been divided into *hsien* or Chinese counties, the Mongols retain an organization of their own, headed by their prince (who has actually the title of duke). Where Mongol villages are grouped together they keep up a kind of militia, as a defense against bandits. They draw important revenues from lands leased to the Chinese before the modern period of expropriating colonization. The whole Banner has been excluded from Hsingan province and remains within Heilungchiang, against the will of the Mongols themselves.

The Banner contains the counties of Chaotung, Chaochou and Talai. (Chaotung, Foundation of the East; Chaochou, Foundation of a Department; Talai, Great Reward—

and perhaps also a phonetic rendering of the Mongol *tariya*, "farming.")

South Gorlos

or, in Mongol, Emune Gorlos, is enclosed on the north by the Sungari and on the east by the Willow Palisade. On the south and west it borders with different Khorchin Banners and in the northwest it is contiguous for a short distance with North Gorlos. The city of Ch'angch'ün, Long Spring (the spring of the year, not a spring of water), now Capital of Manchukuo under the name of Hsinching or New Capital, stands on territory taken from South Gorlos.

The South Manchuria Railway and part of the Hsinching-Kirin line run through this territory. In the east, such Mongols as remain have been almost entirely absorbed by the Chinese, and many have lost their language. In the southwest, colonization has been less overwhelming and the Mongols, though agricultural, retain their organization and separate identity.

Colonization had begun by the second half of the seventeenth century, when in the reign of K'ang Hsi (1662-1723), urgent measures were taken to support the Amur frontier against the Russians.[2] At this period the transport of food for the troops was a serious problem. It was gradually solved by the development of agriculture in the rich country held in the great bend of the Sungari, between the end of the Willow Palisade and the site of the modern Harbin, and near the borders of South and North Gorlos. Here the

[2] *Gazetteer of Kirin, chüan* 1.

198

districts of Shuangch'engp'u (Settlement of Two Cities), Ashihho (modern Ach'eng or City of A—the original name being from a non-Chinese language, probably Manchu), Petuna (Chinese Potuna; perhaps from the Mongol *budune,* the name of a kind of partridge; now re-named Fuyühsien, from the name of a tribe of ancient times) and so forth, were settled. Although this region was assigned to the Manchus for settlement,[3] the general increase of agriculture by these methods encouraged the spread of unofficial colonization. The Banner of South Gorlos extended so far to the east that the line of communication with the new districts lay right across it, so that penetration by Chinese was inevitable.

Ch'angch'ün is mentioned in 1800 as a district settled by Chinese, who had evidently been there for some time, under the jurisdiction of special officials. Efforts were made to restrain the spread of the Chinese, and Mongols who leased lands to the Chinese were warned that the Chinese officials would not help them to collect their rents. Nevertheless this became the standard procedure. It was impossible to stop the Chinese from coming in, because Mongols were making money out of leasing land to them. Investigations at intervals revealed increasing numbers.[4] In 1814 there is mention of trouble about the boundaries between Mongol lands and the lands allotted to the post-stations along the great road running through Gorlos, and reference is made to the fact that this had already been discussed

[3] *Loc. cit., chüan* 1 & 2.
[4] *Ta Ch'ing Hui Tien,* Li Fan Yüan 17, *chüan* 742; also Hu Pu 14, *chüan* 141.

with the Mongol princes in 1766.[5] This interpenetration of Mongol districts by the settled garrisons of the post-stations was a further aid to the nominally illegal entry of Chinese. The consequence has been that the few Mongols remaining in the eastern districts of South Gorlos are comparable to the old Kirin Manchu landlord classes; they have to a great extent lost their language and distinctive customs. Some of their aristocratic families have made capital out of their Mongol connections by acting as negotiators between Chinese officials and the Mongols—the fact that they are nominally eligible for Mongol official positions, while largely Chinese in personal outlook, making them very handy to the Chinese policy.

South Gorlos, like North Gorlos, has been entirely excluded from Hsingan province. The Chinese counties now formed within the Banner are Ch'angch'ün and Tehui, which have long been settled, and the newer counties of Nungan, Ch'angling and Ch'ienan. (Ch'angch'ün has already been listed. Tehui is Virtue and Humanity. Nungan is Agriculture and Peace—a typical colonization name. Ch'angling is The Long Ridge—a merely descriptive place-name. Ch'ienan is Stable and Peaceful.)

THE KHORCHIN TRIBE

The Mongol name may perhaps be connected with the word *khorcha*, "sharp." The Chinese phonetic rendering is K'o-erh-ch'in. The original territory of the six Banners together measured 2100 by 870 *li*, or about 700 by 290 miles.

[5] *Gazetteer of Kirin, chüan 2.*

THE MONGOLS OF MANCHURIA

The six Banners of this tribe are divided into two Wings, East and West, and these two Wings are made to include the whole of Jerim League, by reckoning the two Banners of Jalaid and Durbet as attached to Khorchin West Wing and the two Banners of Gorlos as attached to Khorchin East Wing. Except on the extreme southeastern fringe of their territory, these Mongols were affected by Chinese colonization much later than were the Gorlos Mongols. Having known much less of the old, spontaneous and profitable form of colonization, and much more of the modern, exploitational and bitterly resented form, the Khorchin Mongols are violently anti-Chinese and intensely nationalistic in feeling. The six Banners, taken from southeast to northwest, are as follows:

Khorchin East Wing South Banner

The Mongol terms may also be interpreted as Left Wing, Front Banner. Popularly known as Bintu Wang Banner, either from the title of honor of the ruling princes, or from the personal name of a former prince. The Chinese transliteration is Pint'u, misprinted Pinkuo on some of the Japanese maps. The date at which the Banner adhered to the Manchus is not recorded in the *Mongol Pastures;* but in 1635 the prince of this Banner joined the Manchus in fighting against the Ming dynasty in China. The Banner reaches the Willow Palisade on the southeast and Jehol province on the southwest. The region was therefore of critical importance in preparing the Manchu offensive against China, and in 1636 the Manchus built a stronghold in it to command the route leading into Manchuria from Shanhaikuan. The railway from Tahushan (Great Tiger Mountain) to T'ungliao runs through this Banner. In its former territory there stand the important town and county of Changwu (Military Display; a garrison name). To the southeast of Changwu were certain Imperial pasture lands, apparently set aside from the territory of this Banner, which will be discussed separately.

Colonization began early. In 1784 the supervision of Chinese colonists in Khorchin territory, and of traders "wandering" in Bintu Wang Banner, was entrusted to the officials of T'iehling (The Iron Range), across the Willow Palisade from Mongol territory.[6] Binsteed states that at the time of the Chinese Revolution the land in the south had all been colonized, the poorer land in the north remaining in Mongol possession. The situation has changed little in the last twenty years, and in drawing the limits of Hsingan province rather less than half the Banner has been retained within the autonomous Mongol country.

Khorchin East Wing North Banner

or Left Wing Rear Banner. Popularly known as Bo Wang Banner or Prince Bo's Banner, from the Chinese abbreviation (using the first syllable only) of the personal name of a former prince. The Chinese transliteration is Po Wang. In the time of Nurhachih, founder of the Manchu dynasty, the prince of this Banner supported the

---

[6] *Ta Ch'ing Hui Tien*, Li Fan Yüan 17, *chüan* 742. The reference to Bintu Wang Banner is also given in *Mongol Pastures*.

Yehonala against the Manchus. He was defeated, and in 1617, the year after Nurhachih assumed the style of Emperor, under the reign-name of T'ien Ming, joined the Manchus, being the first of all the Mongol princes to do so.

This territory lies north of the Banner previously described, and like it reaches to the Willow Palisade on the east. It covers the strategic approach to Mongol territory from the direction of Mukden and the lower Liao valley, which explains its early relations with the Manchus.

Colonization is mentioned in 1812 [7] and again in the following year, by which time evidently the eastern corner of the Banner, between the Liao and the Willow Palisade, had been well settled by Chinese. These tenant-colonists were placed under special officials, and half their ground-rentals were to be paid to the ruling prince and half divided among the Mongols of the Banner, "according to the custom in Gorlos." Further colonization is mentioned in 1832, when it was ordered that boundary marks be set up and a line of trees planted (like the Willow Palisade) defining the boundary between Chinese and Mongols. At this time the Mongols had already begun to take up agriculture themselves, for fifty-seven Mongol villages are mentioned as left within the Chinese area, each with its own small territory marked out. The beginnings of Mongol agriculture in this Banner must however be dated even earlier, by two hundred years, for in 1632 there is mentioned a community of Kharchins (who must have moved from what is now

[7] *Ta Ch'ing Hui Tien*, Li Fan Yüan 17, *chüan* 742, where the references under both 1812 and 1813 are to be found; in *Mongol Pastures* only the second is given.

Jehol) in the neighborhood of Fak'umen.[8] This town, the name of which is possibly corrupted from the Manchu *fako*,[9] "a wall," "a barrier" (the syllable *men* is the Chinese for "gate") stands astride the Willow Palisade. It was for generations one of the chief "portals" of the Willow Palisade, through which all communication between Chinese and Mongols was supposed to pass.

It must have been from Fak'umen and Ch'angt'u, both standing at the edge of the old Chinese Pale, that the earliest Chinese colonization spread into Mongol territory. Ch'angt'u, Prosperous Quarter, is a typical "auspicious" name. Both towns are now the center of counties. The *hsien* or county of K'angp'ing, Reposeful Plain, was added in 1880,[10] on the old post-road (known also as the Tribute Road, because the princes traveled by it on their way to Peking) running from Fak'umen through the Khorchin and other Jerim League territories up to the Nonni. Other important towns are T'ungchiangk'ou, River Junction, where the Liao goes through the Willow Palisades, and Pamiench'eng, Eight-sided City, on the Ssup'ingkai-T'aonan Railway, which cuts across a corner of the Banner.

According to Binsteed, four-fifths of the Banner had been colonized by the time of the Chinese Revolution, and

[8] Both dates from *Mongol Pastures*.

[9] This derivation was suggested to me by Merse, the Daghor leader. He also maintained that the Manchu *fako* is etymologically connected with the Mongol *bogomta*, "a fortification"—mutations between *b* in Mongol and *f* or *w* in Manchu being common, with the Daghor language as an intermediate stage. The Mongol name for the Great Wall is *bogomta kherem*, vernacular *boomt kherem*, "fortified wall."

[10] Date from *Northeastern Year Book*.

the Mongols of the eastern part had "become Chinese." Binsteed, however, sometimes uses the word "colonized" with reference to land settled by Mongols. According to the Mongols themselves, rather less than half the Banner has been definitely occupied by Chinese, and this is borne out by the fact that slightly more than half has been retained in the autonomous province. Most of the Mongols of the Banner are settled farmers, but there is a good deal of poor land, in the west, which is used for pasture. Some of the Mongols in the oldest zone of Chinese penetration, in the east, have lost their language, but all Mongols to the west of the present line of Chinese colonization retain their language and a strong national consciousness.

The most famous prince of this Banner was Sankolinsin, to use the form in which his name was written by contemporary foreigners, who learned it through the Chinese transcription. The original Mongol name is Senggerinchin. He commanded Mongol levies against the T'aip'ing rebels (1850-1864) in the Yangtze valley, and against the French and British who took Peking in 1860-1, and was killed finally in action against a minor body of rebels in North China. He was known to the British troops as Sam Collinson. His son and successor rose even higher in the Manchu service, and was finally given a Court appointment, according to the standard practice of keeping any prince who grew too powerful or popular at Peking, in order that his heirs might grow up to the city life of sophisticated Manchus and lose touch with tribal life and affairs. It is from the Chinese abbreviation of the name of the son of Senggerinchin that the Banner is still known as Po Wang or Bo Wang Banner.

The present hereditary prince, a pathetic opium smoker who is an example of the success of the Manchu policy, lives in Peiping. He has been deposed by Manchukuo. The new prince is a member of the same clan. He is popularly known as Bao T'ungling—Bao or Pao being the Chinese abbreviation of Borjighit, the clan name of direct male descendants of brothers of Chingghis Khan, and *t'ungling,* an old-style military rank still used by commanders of troops in Mongol regions. This chief has had a long career as an anti-Chinese nationalist and "bandit" leader. He is popular among Mongols who are both nationalist and conservative, but not considered modern enough in mind and outlook by younger Mongols.

Khorchin East Wing Center Banner

or Left Wing Center Banner. Popularly known as Darkhan Wang Banner (Chinese form, Ta-erh-han) or Banner of the Independent Prince, from the hereditary title of honor of its ruling line. This is the largest and perhaps the most important of all the Khorchin Banners. Although known as Center Banner, it lies north of both the other Khorchin Banners of this Wing; the term Central therefore refers to the fact that the two Gorlos Banners were attached to Khorchin East Wing, thus placing Darkhan Wang Banner in the center. Its territory runs westward from the Willow Palisade all the way to the western frontier of Manchuria, and thus it is the linking Banner between Fengt'ien province (Willow Palisade) Kirin province (South Gorlos Banner) Jehol province (Naiman and East Jarod Banners) and Chahar province (East Ujumuchin Banner of Silingol, nominally under Chahar).

I cannot find the exact date at which this Banner joined the Manchus; but in 1636 it was an ally of the Manchus in the attack on the Chahar Mongols, and from about that time the ruling family intermarried with the Imperial House and was treated with such special honor that it must have been considered the most important of the Eastern Mongol allies. In 1840 it is recorded that in this Banner alone there were two thousand people related to the Manchu Imperial clan. Besides the ruling family, there are five cadet branches of the same family (six according to Binsteed, but this appears to be a mistake) each headed by a "sealless" prince, so that the Banner is sometimes referred to as the Six Princely Houses of Darkhan. Although in its relations with the Manchus, and later with the Chinese Republic, the Banner has always been treated as a unit, within the Banner itself each of the "sealless" princes has his own followers and territories.

In this Banner also "spontaneous" colonization began early near the Willow Palisade. Chinese merchants within the Banner were placed under the supervision of the officials at K'aiyüan (Opening of the Plain; formerly known as Sunchiat'ai, Post of the Sun Family; a "pioneer" name) within the Chinese Pale, in 1784. According to Binsteed, "unassisted" Chinese colonization was moving northwestward at the time of the Chinese Revolution. In recent years colonization has been rapid, as the whole eastern extension of the Banner is accessible from the Tahushan-T'ungliao and Ssup'ingkai-T'aonan Railways, which cross it. There are now five Chinese-colonized counties within the Banner. The oldest is Huaite, founded in 1877, adjoining the South Gorlos boundary. It was formerly known as Pachiatzu, Eight Families, a "pioneer" name. Huaite means Cherishing Virtue. This kind of change, from a "pioneer" to an "auspicious" name is a common phenomenon; it often marks the passing of the frontier phase and the establishment of permanent Chinese conditions.

Liaoyüan or Sources of the Liao, formerly Chengchiat'ün or Village of the Cheng Family, near the junction of the headwater streams of the Liao, is a comparatively old Chinese settlement which was made a county town in 1913. In 1914 Lishu or Pear Tree, near the Willow Palisade, was made the center of a new county. This town is mentioned in the *Mongol Pastures*, under the dates of 1762 and "the period of K'ang Hsi" (1662-1723) in connection with the system of allotting certain sections of Mongol land for cultivation in order to provide the Mongols with grain reserves against the contingency of famine years. The system applied to Jerim League and to the Leagues of Josoto and Jo-oda.

T'ungliao, on the Shira Muren (sometimes transliterated by the Chinese as Hsi-la-mu-lun and sometimes translated as Huang Ho or Yellow River), the main headstream of the Liao, was made the center of a county in 1918. The original settlement was known as Payint'ala or Payint'ailai, a corruption possibly of the Mongol term *bayan tala,* "rich plain," but more probably of *bayan tariya,* "rich cultivation." The name T'ungliao means Communication with, or Penetration of, the Liao. The term Liao here refers not to the Liao River itself, but the ancient regional name of Liao Hsi, West of the Liao, the antithesis of Liaotung, East of the Liao, which was the Chinese Pale. This county is an "island" of Chinese colonization surrounded by Mongols. It is proposed to make it a detached part of Fengt'ien province, enclosed within Hsingan province, but its final status has perhaps not yet been determined. The Mongols do not like the idea of such an enclave, and some Mongols would like to make it the capital of their province. It is said also that the Chinese of the region do not like to be surrounded by independent Mongols, and that many of them have abandoned their holdings and left, in fear of Mongol reprisals for the oppression of many years.

Shuangshan, or Two Mountains, was the last Chinese county to be added in Darkhan Wang Banner, in 1929.[11] The attempt to found still another county north of T'ungliao, to be called Liaopei or North of Liao, which provoked the Mongol rising of 1930 and has under Manchukuo been abandoned, has already been mentioned, in the discussion of Mongol rebellions.

Considering that regions developed by railways have in general been excluded from Mongol control, the Mongols of this Banner have been lucky. A great part of the

[11] This date, and the one above, are both taken from *Northeastern Year Book.*

Tah...shan-T'ungliao and Liaoyüan-T'ungliao railways run through their territory, meeting at T'ungliao; but the only lands that they have lost are those on the easterly side of the Ssup'ingkai-Liaoyüan-T'aonan line of railways, in addition to the T'ungliao "island." (The name of Ssup'ingkai, an important railway junction though not the center of a separate county, means Four Level Streets. The term *kai*, which is the common local pronunciation of *chieh*, "a street," is frequently used in Manchuria for "a village."

This concludes the list of the Khorchin East Wing Banners. The three Banners of the West Wing have lost almost as much territory through Chinese colonization, but the impact of the Chinese has been more recent, and the Mongols in consequence are even more Mongol in character and feeling. Although many of the Mongols in the West Wing Banners have taken up agriculture (partly through the immigration of Kharchins and other Mongols from Jehol) the traditional pastoral economy still survives in the back-country, away from the railways and the Chinese.

Khorchin West Wing Center Banner

or Right Wing Center Banner. Popularly known as Tosiyato Wang Banner (Chinese form, T'u-shih-yeh-t'u) from the hereditary title of honor of the ruling prince. The Banner joined the Manchus in 1626, and is considered the senior Banner of the Wing, as Darkhan Wang Banner is considered the senior Banner of East Wing. Its position is not "central," and the designation of Center Banner may perhaps derive either from a former central position, or from its seniority. The title Tosiyato appears to mean "one who has been commissioned with a charge or office."

The territory is roughly oblong, and runs from a point near the Ssup'ingkai-T'aonan Railway and midway between Liaoyüan and T'aonan northwestward to the borders of Manchuria, where it touches East Ujumuchin Banner of Silingol League. A large part of the trade of East Ujumuchin passes through this Banner and that next to be considered.

Colonization dates only from the first development of the T'aonan-T'aoan region, in the 1890's; and this Banner at first was only lightly affected, being on the outskirts of the region developed. The major impact of colonization came with the increase of railway expansion in the last ten years of Chinese rule.

Two Chinese counties have been formed, both in the region economically tributary to the Ssup'ingkai-T'aonan Railway. T'uch'üan, Gushing Springs, is part of the T'aonan district; it was organized in 1908 and reorganized in 1914 under its present name. Tanyu, at the southeastern end of the Banner, was first organized in 1912 and reorganized in 1917. (The characters used in this place-name are curious; but the name does not sound like a corruption of a Mongol word. Tanyu would read Gall Elm; possibly the character *tan* is used in substitution for another, also read *tan,* which in turn is used sometimes in place of a character read *t'an;* in which case the meaning might be Spreading Elm. See Giles, characters 10,629, 10,625 and 10,694.)

Only about a quarter of the Banner has been excluded from Hsingan province. In the territory remaining in Mongol possession, the arable land is comparatively poor in quality, and the total of pasture is probably greater than that under plough.

Khorchin West Wing South Banner

or Right Wing Front Banner. Popularly known as Jasakto Khan Banner (Chinese form, Cha-sa-k'e-t'u), from the hereditary title of honor of the prince, meaning, roughly, Prince of the Realm, or Sovereign Prince. This Banner also joined the Manchus in 1626. The Banner was little affected by colonization until the modern period, but in the last forty years has lost about half its territory. The Tor River, called T'ao or T'ao-erh by the Chinese, runs through this Banner.

The following districts have been detached and made into Chinese counties: K'ait'ung (1904) on the Ssup'ingkai-T'aonan Railway; T'aoan, now the junction point of the T'aonan-Angangch'i and T'aoan-Solun Railways (organized in 1904 and reorganized in 1914); and T'aonan, which was organized in 1905 and reorganized in 1913. The name of K'ait'ung is probably reminiscent of the phrases *k'ai huang,* "to colonize the wilderness," and *chiao-t'ung,* "communications"; the name of the original settlement was Ch'ichingtzu, Seven Wells. T'aoan means Peace of T'ao, referring to the T'ao River district. It was formerly known as Paich'engtzu, White City, perhaps from ruins in the vicinity; and before that as Chingan, Tranquillity and

Peace. Both these names, in various spellings (such as Kingan, which has nothing to do with Khingan or Hsingan) are still found on maps. T'aonan means South of T'ao (the T'ao River). It was formerly known as Shuangliuchen, or Settlement of Two Streams, and as Sachikai, Street or Village of Sachi, from the days when it was a trading post known to the Mongols as Sajimodon, and called after a votive tree which is still standing, or was until recently.

When the Chinese colonists in the T'ao valley were first brought under official control, T'aoan was made the administrative center. Later it was shifted to T'aonan, 20 miles away, and T'aonan is now the most populous Chinese city of the region. The Chinese had begun to settle some years before 1900, long before their presence was officially recognized and supported by the Government, and during this interim period there was much disorder, bloodshed and "Mongol banditry." Prince Otai of this Banner was a leader in the renewed effort to shake off the Chinese after the Revolution, as has been described in the chapter on Mongol rebellions.

In 1929 this Banner, and the one next to be considered, came under the influence of fresh Chinese activity, being within the scope of the great Hsingan Reclamation Project, which was designed to complete the Chinese colonization of this part of Jerim League, and to push a railway from T'aoan up to the town of Solun, over the Hsingan range to the point where Jerim League, Silingol League, Outer

Mongolia and Barga meet, and on across the Barga plain. This would have brought the Chinese to the edge of Outer Mongolia by a route that avoided the Gobi and at the same time outflanked both the Chinese Eastern Railway and the Japanese railway system in Manchuria, thus radically altering the Outer Mongolian situation for the first time since 1912, and forcing the issue of the relative positions of China, Russia and Japan in Northeastern Asia. There can be no doubt but that the rapid development of this project, and its prospects of success, had a great deal to do in bringing about the acute tension between China and Japan which made the Japanese Army demand intervention in 1931. The killing of Captain Nakamura, by troops of the Reclamation Army, one of the most important of the incidents that precipitated Japanese intervention, occurred in this Banner, at the present railhead of the T'aoan-Solun Railway, near Suo Kung Fu or She Kung Fu, Palace of the Duke She or Suo, the residence of a "sealless" prince of the Banner.

The Hsingan Reclamation Project, under the direction of General Tsou Tso-hua, senior officer of the Manchurian Artillery and an important member of the personal following of Marshal Chang Hsüeh-liang, was undoubtedly the most efficient enterprise in Chinese colonization that had ever been attempted. One of its proclaimed principles was favorable treatment for the Mongols; [12] it was definitely stated that an effort would be made to incorporate the Mongols in the Chinese colonization, instead of driving them out in front of the Chinese advance; and that the

[12] *Hsingan Monthly*, No. 1. 1930 (undated).

promotion of agriculture was not to exclude the pastoral interest as one of the economic resources of the region. Mongols assert, however, that favorable treatment of the Mongols was not evident in practice, owing to corruption among the lower officials and among officers of the military forces who wanted to seize good lands for themselves, and that in fact Mongols were evicted from their farms in the old way under the old pretexts. The Reclamation forces worked so effectively, by occupying the country with strong garrisons in advance of colonization, that revolt was impossible, although there was a great deal of "Mongol banditry"; but when Japanese intervention in 1931 broke up the Reclamation Project, the Mongols rose and drove out the remnants of the Reclamation Army.

According to the Reclamation authorities,[13] the Mongol population of the Banner (exclusive of Mongols under the jurisdiction of the counties of T'aoan, T'aonan and K'ait'ung) was rather more than 10,000 families, numbering over 25,000 people. Of these about 70 per cent were immigrant Mongols from Jehol, who thus outnumbered the native Mongols of the Banner. The immigrant Mongols were mainly agricultural and the native Mongols pastoral. About half the river valley lands were under Mongol cultivation.

In the northwest of this Banner, in the Hsingan foothills, there is an interesting community known as the Manchu-Mongols, who will be discussed separately.

About half of the Banner is now excluded from Hsingan province, the northwestern half being left to the Mongols.

[13] *Hsingan Report.*

Khorchin West Wing North Banner

or Right Wing Rear Banner; popularly known as Tusiye Gung Banner, or Supporting Duke Banner, from the title of honor of the prince. The Chinese rendering, instead of being a transliteration, as is usual, is a translation, so that it appears as Chen Kuo Kung—Duke Supporting the Nation (the Manchu Dynasty, that is). This Banner also joined the Manchus in 1626. The boundary between this Banner and the one last described is not given in full on the Japanese maps, and the boundary as I have drawn it cannot be taken as authoritative. The indications given in the *Mongol Pastures* are to the effect that it "straddles" the T'ao River; but this could only apply to the upper waters of the T'ao. It may mean, however, that the boundary comes down between the T'ao and its main tributary, and not as I have given it.

According to the account given in the *Hsingan Report*, this Banner must have suffered more, in the rebellion led by Prince Otai, than did the Prince's own Banner. Before the rising, there were rich people who numbered their sheep by the thousand and their horses and horned cattle by the hundred. When the rising had been put down by Wu of the Big Tongue there were none who had more than two hundred sheep and a score or so of horses and cattle. The Mongols of the Banner were thus forced to take up agriculture, for which reason agriculture is more advanced among them than in the neighboring Banners.

The population, according to the same source, is something over 5,000 families, totalling less than 20,000 people, and including about 70 per cent of immigrant Jehol Mongols. The figures, as given, would indicate that the average Mongol family in this Banner numbers nearly 4 people, as against 2½ to 3 people in Jasakto Wang Banner. As no reason is given, it is obvious that one series of figures is wrong—or perhaps both. The original Report does not claim that they are accurate, merely saying that they are taken from Mongol statements. I can only conjecture that the Mongols gave wrong returns, fearing that the figures would be used for purposes of taxation. The Report supplements the figures by stating that the Mongol family "averages" from 4 or 5 to 7 or 8 persons.

Families averaging over 4 or 5, I may add, are likely to be found only among agricultural Mongols, where syphilis is much less prevalent than among the nomads. When Mongols are living under Mongol conditions, there is a great deal of sexual liberty. Women are not approximated to property as they are in agricultural nations, and the lack of hereditary landed possessions means that legitimacy was never forced into the same social prominence; except in the case of princely families, in which genealogy has always been important. Neither virginity before marriage nor chastity afterwards are strictly demanded by the standards of nomad Mongols. The spread of syphilis is therefore favored, and its incidence is appalling.

Agricultural Mongols are soon affected by Chinese standards—principally because they so fiercely resent being looked down on as "beast-like barbarians" by the Chinese.

The property standard also has its effect in making legitimate male heirs essential. Women are therefore placed under a strict code, the spread of syphilis is checked, and the Mongols begin to multiply as rapidly as the Chinese. Agricultural economy and the decrease of syphilis together account for the relatively heavy Mongol population in Manchuria as compared with Western Inner Mongolia and Outer Mongolia. It is worth pointing out that different methods are likely to bring about comparable results in Outer Mongolia. Instruction in sexual hygiene, and treatment for venereal disease, are promoted everywhere under Russian influence. It is probable therefore that within a generation the population of Outer Mongolia, which has long been almost stationary, and even perhaps slightly on the decrease, will begin to increase rapidly. This may not bring enlightenment to the people who blame the decline of the Mongols entirely on the Lama Church, because the Church is also being preached against in Outer Mongolia. It will, however, make it evident at last that the Mongols are not necessarily a decadent and dying people—and it will alter the whole racial question in the regions between Siberia and the Great Wall.

Tusiye Gung Banner, like Jasakto Khan Banner, has lost about half its territory to Chinese colonization, the northern half being reserved to Hsingan province. In the southern half, which is crossed by the T'aonan-Angangch'i Railway, the counties of Ankuang (1905) and Chentung (surveyed in 1908, colonized in 1909) have been formed. Ankuang, Peaceful and Broad, referring perhaps to a "broad and peaceful plain," was known formerly as Ch'akannao—evidently from *ch'a-kan-nao-po*, a corruption of the Mongol *chagan obo*, "white *obo*, or cairn." Chentung, Guarding the East, was formerly known as Hsienchiawop'u, Settlement of the Hsien Family.

This completes the survey of the Banners of Jerim League; but several minor groups have to be considered before passing on to the Mongols of Jehol province.

Chapter XI

THE IMPERIAL HERDSMEN OR SURUK MON-GOLS, THE SIBE (SIBEGE) MONGOLS AND THE MANCHU-MONGOLS

THE special groups that have now to be considered hardly affect the modern political, social or economic. problems of Manchuria, or the new Hsingan province, but are of importance historically and because they illustrate tribal processes and the modifications brought about by the Manchu organization of Manchuria.

The Imperial Herdsmen or Suruk Mongols

The Mongol term *suruk* means "a herd." The pastures of these Mongols were set aside from the southeastern corner of Bintu Wang Banner. They were divided between two *suruk* or herds, and were known as the Yanghsimu Pastures. This looks as though it were a Chinese corruption of a name formed from the Mongol word *yangjo*, meaning "form," or "fairness"—the Fair Pastures. The Mongol word itself is a corruption of the Chinese *yang-tzu*, "a sort," "a kind," through the vernacular usage meaning "shapely," "beautiful."

The two Suruk, East and West, were each divided into two Wings. In 1805 it is recorded that about 48,000 acres of the pasture lands were being cultivated, by the Mongols themselves. It was then decreed that the cultivation of about 19,000 acres of this total must be abandoned, because it "interfered with the pasture." The remaining 29,000 acres was redivided among the Mongols (under private ownership) at the rate of 8 acres to a man, with additional grants to the four Wing-commanders and other officials. The population was calculated at 3,530; but it is possible that this figure represents heads of families, not total population. It was further decreed "in perpetuity" that cultivation must not be extended beyond the limits then determined.[1]

Undoubtedly this decree, like others which attempted to limit the spread of agriculture, remained a dead letter. The chief interest of this particular decree is that it does not mention Chinese infiltration, and that it establishes the importance of agriculture in this Mongol region at the early date of 1805. It is, however, probable that the Suruk Mongols had been agricultural for nearly two centuries before this time. Their own tradition is that they came originally from the not distant Mongol regions of what is now Jehol province, and especially from the Monggoljin or Eastern Tumet Banner of Josoto League. I am inclined to think that they descend from small groups which came over to

[1] *Ta Ch'ing Hui Tien*, Hu Pu 10, *chüan* 137. The acreage figures are here calculated at the rate of 2 acres to 1 *shang*, that being the rate of equivalence used in *North Manchuria*, which in agricultural matters is exceptionally well informed; but land measures in China are variable, and the same authority also uses the estimate of 1.8 acres to 1 *shang*.

the Manchus before the general submission of the tribes from which they derived; that they were even then agricultural or half-agricultural, and that the most important reason for their migration into Bintu Wang Banner was the growing strength of the Manchu Government, which promised stable conditions under which they could farm in peace. The Imperial herds which they tended were never important in numbers; the tradition of the Suruk Mongols themselves is that these herds originally supplied the animals used for sacrifice at the Manchu Imperial Tombs near Mukden.

In 1902 the *hsien* or county of Changwu was formed out of these Imperial Pastures, being based on an original settlement called Hengtaotzu—a name meaning Crosswise Road, probably because it stood at a crossing of the Hsink'ai Ho or Newly Opened river, which flows into the lower Liao. The colonization caused an outbreak of "Mongol banditry" among the Herdsmen, who had already been alarmed by Chinese pressure. Out of these troubles emerged Babojab, one of the most famous Mongol leaders of his time, whose career has already been mentioned. Himself a Monggoljin or Eastern Tumet, of a tribe to whom the Herdsmen are traditionally related, and noted for its unruliness and anti-Chinese feeling, he raised among the Suruk Mongols the force that became known as the Thirteen Companies. Living off and on as bandits, and serving also at times in the Mongol militia, they drew recruits, in later years, from all over Eastern Mongolia. They were considered patriots by all Mongols, and their exploits are told in many ballads, which are still sung everywhere in Manchurian Mongolia.

When the Japanese occupied Manchuria in 1931, a son of Babojab, named Ganjurjab, called on the Mongols to rise against the Chinese and welcome the Japanese. (His name is taken from one of the scriptures of Lama Buddhism.) He had been brought up in Japan, and was so strongly Japanese in sympathy and policy that he became suspect to many of the Mongols. Quarrels among the younger Mongol leaders and indecision among the older men then broke up the initial move toward Mongol autonomy, and a few of the "soldier of fortune" type of leaders, developed through the years of rebellion, banditry and civil war, even started to negotiate with the anti-Japanese movement of the Chinese "Volunteers." It was the failure of the Mongols themselves to make a bold, united decision of any kind which forced the Japanese to take the initiative in organizing the Mongol affairs of Manchuria.

Of the Suruk Mongols of the present time, the people of the East Suruk have almost entirely been submerged in the Chinese population. Of the West Suruk about 3,000 people still preserve their language and racial integrity, though they have been "islanded" among the Chinese and have not been included in Hsingan province. Many other Suruk Mongols have migrated into Shiretu Khurie Lama Banner, which will be discussed later. The surviving Suruk Mongols incline decidedly to the Young Mongol type of nationalism. They have a high level of education in both Mongol and Chinese, and frequently manage, by going over into

Banners which preserve their Mongol organization, to obtain political and official posts.

The Sibe or Sibege Mongols

The name of this people is written in many ways in books of travel and so forth: Sibo and Sipo are perhaps the commonest forms. In older Chinese records they are called Hsi-pei, and a variety of characters and pronunciations occurs in later notices. The Mongol term is Sibege (written) or Sibe (vernacular) and the following appears to be the standard account of the name and tribe (if it may be called a tribe) among Mongols of the present day:[2]

The word *sibege* means "a gate," of a particular type to be seen all over Manchuria, with an extra top cross-bar, resembling the Japanese *torii*. The Manchu word is also *sibe*. When the Manchus confirmed the Willow Palisade as the frontier between Manchus and Chinese on the east and Mongols on the west, a number of "gates" were designated as the routes for trade and communication between Mongols and Chinese. Special guards at the gates were supposed to collect taxes on trade and to demand passes from Chinese traders and artisans entering Mongol country. Towns like Fak'umen, which has already been described, arose from the concentration of business at these points. A Mongol force was raised to guard the Mongol side of the barrier, and being on special duty, and in contact with the Chinese,

[2] Based in the main on conversations with a member of the princely family of North Gorlos, and checked so far as possible in conversations with other Mongols, and with a Sibe who is the "servitor" (hereditary body servant) of one of the "Sealless" princes of Darkhan Wang Banner.

these Mongols became detached from their tribes and formed a community of their own, known as "Gatemen," so to speak. They tended naturally to "turn Chinese" in the same way that the Kirin and Mukden Manchus did, became farmers and lost their language and national characteristics.

This Mongol account may be based on nothing more reliable than popular etymology. Chinese popular etymology, in a similar way, connects them with the Hsien-pei or Hsien-pi, a tribe of much earlier times. According to another account,[3] the Sibe themselves believed that they were akin to the Manchus in customs, but had been placed politically under the authority of the Khorchin Mongols. This account mentions that in Jasakto Khan Banner there is a ruined town known as Hsi-po City. In 1634, when a Manchu expedition was sent up to the Amur, it passed by this town. The Sibe must therefore have been posted along the Tribute Road, or military road from Fak'umen to the Nonni and Amur, as well as along the Willow Palisade. It is recorded in the same account that they were disorderly and openly robbed people, but that being under the Mongols, they could not be controlled—an interesting indication of the limitations of Manchu authority in Mongol territory.

Still another account is even more precise,[4] declaring that the Sibe and Kua-le-ch'a (Golcha or Gowalcha; compare the Manchu verb *gowaliyambi,* "to change," "to decline," "to dye or dye oneself") were tribes which, together with Bo Wang Banner of the Khorchin Mongols, fought against

[3] *Mongol Pastures.* [4] *Unofficial Record of Kirin, chüan* 3.

Nurhachih. After their defeat they were broken up and placed under the different Khorchin princes—presumably as a kind of subject or inferior people. Many of them later enlisted in the regimental Banners. This would make them a people remarkably similar to the Yehonala.

Their ancient center, according to this account, was in the Petuna region, now known as Fuyü or Fuyühsien. This, it may be pointed out, places them on the extreme outskirts of true Mongol population, and on the edge of the Gorlos rather than the Khorchin country, and strengthens their resemblance to the Yehonala type of tribe. In 1692 there were sixteen "companies" of Sibe in the Kirin cadre of eight Banners, and thirty "companies" of Sibe and ten of Golcha at Petuna. In 1699 a part of this Petuna contingent was removed to Mukden, the separate "companies" being discontinued. Thereafter the Sibe became "servitors"—hereditary body servants, of a standing higher than that of slaves—of princes living at the Capital, and no longer served as ordinary military Bannermen. The account concludes by saying that there is an unsubstantiated tradition, among the Golcha of Petuna, that the Emperor K'ang Hsi, when on a tour through Kirin province, pitied them for being under the Mongols, and ransomed them at the price of 80 *taels* (ounces) of silver for a family, appointing them to serve as Manchu-style Bannermen.

The Sibe now hardly exist as a community, except near Petuna, and even here they have become virtually Chinese in character. They do, however, survive in Chinese Turkistan. Being a permanently organized force of military reservists, during the first part of the Manchu Empire, they were easily called on for special duty. For this reason a number of them, together with Solon contingents, were drafted by the Manchus for service in Chinese Turkistan, where their descendants are still to be found, and where they still form a distinct ethnic and linguistic group.

The Manchu-Mongols

This group might well have been discussed under the heading of Jasakto Khan Banner, within which it holds a recognized territory; but it is worth separate treatment because of its peculiar interest in illustrating the processes of "change of race" which historically are of such importance in Manchuria.

The Manchu-Mongols have a special reserve of land in the northwest of Jasakto Khan Banner, with their own lama monastery and a Jalan or petty official of their own who is answerable to the Mongol prince. When I visited them in 1930 the headquarters of the Jalan were about 25 miles southwest of the town of Solun, on one of the headwater streams of the T'ao River. They were nomadic, but the rich people lived in semi-permanent camps and were beginning to build themselves houses. Their flocks were pastured at large, in the care of junior members of the families and of hired herdsmen. They had some land under cultivation at a distance, which was farmed for them by immigrant Mongols from Jehol; they did not grow grain for the market so much as for winter provision. The following account is condensed from the *Hsingan Report*.

THE MONGOLS OF MANCHURIA

In the reign of Ch'ien Lung (1736-1796) a Manchu Imperial Princess was given in marriage to the ruling Prince of this Banner. In her following were seven "slaves" who were later given Mongol wives. On the death of the Princess, the then Prince established them in their present territory. At the same time he gave them a kind of charter, exempting them from taxes and service, except for the expenses of the annual sacrifices at the tomb of the Princess. Of the seven families, two named Wang and one named Li came to the fore, acquiring wealth and dignity. They were later deprived of their charter of privilege by a trick, and now pay taxes and are called on for services like the other Mongols of the Banner, but retain their group identity and territorial position. In 1912 the well-known Prince Otai of Jasakto Khan Banner cheated them out of 330,000 *taels* (about 426,000 silver dollars) by pretending to sell them a tract of land which they later found had already been granted to somebody else. (This, however, may mean only that the land was seized from them by the provincial authorities on the usual pretext of the "prince's land deeds" not being valid.) They have increased to over a hundred families, numbering about a thousand people. On account of their strong territorial position and good organization, they have escaped banditry and political disturbance, and are unusually prosperous. In 1927 they attacked a troop of 70 or 80 bandits who in collusion with a Chinese official had captured three of their people by treachery. They killed over half of the bandits and besieged the rest in Solun

Town, in the quarters of their accomplice, the Chinese official, and forced them to give up the prisoners.

The Jalan or chief of the Manchu-Mongols owned in 1930 some 30,000 sheep, 1,500 or more horned cattle and over 1,000 horses, and there were three other families owning more than 10,000 sheep, 800 cows and 500 horses each. Even the poorest families had an average of about 100 sheep, 70 or 80 cows and a few riding horses. There were also "several tens" of other Mongols working as herders for them. Eight Chinese trading firms did business among them, "at a profit of several hundred per cent." Yet the popular belief that colonization creates a "higher standard of living" would introduce peasant life even in such regions as this!

The fact that this group is called Manchu-Mongol is, in my opinion, misleading. The original seven men were undoubtedly Chinese, and were called Manchu simply because they came as the servants of a Manchu princess. There is a tradition that they were artisans—a carpenter, a mason and so on—and artisans coming from Peking in the eighteenth century were not likely to be Manchus. The Peking Manchus of that time, being at the height of their prestige, were a leisured class who did not have to work as artisans. Furthermore, the surnames Wang and Li, given for three of the families, were not Chinese surnames that were commonly taken by Manchus during the period when they were at pains to distinguish themselves socially from the Chinese.

This group offers, therefore, a well-established and clearly

dated example of Chinese "turning Mongol." The numbers
are not important; the amount of Chinese blood in a hundred families descended from seven men of the eighteenth
century must be very small indeed. It is the process that is
important. It undoubtedly was common in the past, for
something of the same sort can still be seen in regions
where the Chinese penetrate among the Mongols in small
numbers. It is only the modern, sweeping process that re-
places Mongols with Chinese. The earlier process was for
Chinese to turn Mongol; and to raise their standard of living by so doing.

When Chinese come in contact with Mongols in such
small numbers that they do not bring with them the disastrous economic and social forms of landlordism and economic subjection to the land, they do not have to under-
live and drag down the Mongols, but are able to raise themselves to the Mongol level. A modern example of this type
of social-tribal-"racial" transformation is to be found in the
Barköl region of Chinese Turkistan, where in the mountains near the great caravan route from Kueihua to
Kuch'engtzu the so-called Erh-hun-tzu or Bastards are a
prosperous quasi-tribal group founded by Chinese who
have left the caravans and taken Mongol wives.[5]

It is the existence of these classes, incidentally, that accounts for such quaint Chinese legends as the story that
Shun Chih, the first Manchu Emperor to rule in China, was
born of a Chinese father.[6] In the *Mongol Pastures* there is

[5] *High Tartary.*
[6] There is an amusing version in *Annals and Memoirs of the Court of Peking.*

mentioned a comparable legend, to the effect that the princely families of both the Khorchin and the Kharchin Mongols are descended from a Shantung Chinese family of the name of Wang; but the story is dismissed as not worthy of belief.

Chapter XII

JEHOL PROVINCE

THE unnecessarily difficult name of Jehol is derived from the Chinese Je Ho, Hot River, through the French romanization, Je-ho-eul. This, however, is a rendering of a colloquial form (for which the standard romanization would be Je-ho-erh) and not of the standard form, Je-ho. The Mongols occasionally use the name Halon Oso (written form, Halagon Oso), which is a translation from the Chinese.

About four-fifths of the province, speaking roughly, were originally held by the Mongols of the Josoto and Jo-oda Leagues. The remaining fifth consisted of the Imperial Hunting Park, which itself had once been Mongol territory, and of the Lan River valley. (The name of the river is written with a character normally read *lo,* but in this case rendered as *lan* or *luan*, apparently by association with another character, meaning "turbulent water.")

The Imperial Hunting Park was set aside from territory originally belonging to the Kharchins of Josoto League, with smaller cessions from the All-Blue Banner of the Chahar Mongols and the Keshikten, Bairin and Ongniod Banners of Jo-oda League.[1] It was patrolled by military garrison settlements, recruited partly from Manchus and partly from Mongols. The *t'ing* or sub-prefecture of Weich'ang (Hunting Park) was founded in it in 1863, and converted into a county in 1914. The forests have been cut off, and the region made homogeneous with the Lan River valley. In the earlier period, when the Emperors actually hunted there, they had called in levies of Mongols, who provided horses and transport.

The Lan valley, sandwiched in between the All-Blue Banner of the Chahar Mongols on the west and the Kharchins on the east, and abutting to the south on the Great Wall, is a Chinese Pale closely corresponding to the region within the Willow Palisade in South Manchuria, and with the Lan River playing much the same part, economically, as the lower Liao River in South Manchuria. Its Chinese population probably dates in the main from Ming times (1368-1644). Both regions are Chinese, yet sundered from China, to a degree which the Westerner can hardly appreciate, by the Great Wall. Both, regionally and historically, have been identified with the territories beyond the Great Wall which for two thousand years have sent conquest after conquest into China to assert the power of the "Outer Barbarians." Both are therefore, in spite of their Chinese culture, associated more with the exercise of the power of

[1] Franke.

the Frontier over China than with the extension of Chinese power into the Frontier.

It can thus be seen that while Jehol and Manchuria are not necessarily identical, they are decidedly homogeneous. Whether Jehol, "historically," is or is not "an integral part" of Manchuria is a question merely for casuists. In so far as Jehol was not even separately organized as a province until 1929, and had until then been administratively handled for some time as an extension beyond the Great Wall of Chihli province, it cannot be recognized as an integral part of Manchuria. In so far as it was affiliated, from the time of its being made a separate province, to the Three Eastern Provinces, and governed thenceforth by a senior member of the Manchurian military-political group; and in so far as Manchuria and Jehol were from that time officially referred to as an organic group, known as the Four Eastern Provinces, it must be regarded as an integral part of Manchuria—of that Manchuria whose problems Japan undertook to handle by direct action in 1931.

In point of fact, the terms Jehol and Manchuria are both artificial. If historical function be taken as the determining value, then the two regions are not only homogeneous but indivisible. What is now called Manchuria was historically compounded out of a Manchu-inhabited region, a Mongol-inhabited region and a Chinese-inhabited region, which were politically fused in the seventeenth century into a regional power dominating China. Jehol was historically compounded out of a large Mongol-inhabited region and a very small Chinese-inhabited region; it was unmistakably integrated with Manchuria before the Manchu conquest of China, and from the seventeenth century onward shared the northeastern regional power which dominated China in the name of the Manchu dynasty. The tendency to separate it from Manchuria and associate it with China did not begin until after the Western impact on China had helped to reverse the direction of the historic forces of the Frontier, and to destroy the Manchu character of the dynasty.

The Mongols, historically and functionally, were the link between Jehol and Manchuria. The Mongols of Jehol began to join the Manchus only a little later—in some cases only a year or two—than the Mongols of Jerim League, and as part of the same movement, so that their relation to the Manchus was exactly the same. It was the later, artificial co-ordination of Jerim League with the provinces of Fengt'ien, Kirin and Heilungchiang, of Barga and the Nonni valley with Heilungchiang, and of the two Jehol Leagues with Chihli, which deliberately obscured the original structural solidarity of the Mongols of Manchuria and Jehol. The splitting up of the Mongols, moreover, was accomplished under two separate policies: the earlier Manchu policy which treated the Frontier as a power external to China and invested with power over China, but aimed at a division of power within the Frontier in order to leave initiative and higher control in Manchu hands; and the later Manchu-Chinese policy, which was designed to transfer power from the Frontier to China. It has already been pointed out that the final development of the later policy was the practice of treating the Mongols as if they *belonged* to China instead of being *partners* in the Manchu Empire, and that the Mongols themselves never concurred in this inversion of historical and legal interpretations.

In the light of Frontier history as a phenomenon *sui generis,* interlocking with the history of China but not a mere subordinate phase of history within China, which I have here and elsewhere [2] endeavored to present, it is obvious that the new interpretation was of capital significance. Yet even when it was given emphatic and "final" expression in 1929, by the formation of the provinces of Jehol, Chahar, Suiyüan, Ninghsia and Kokonor (Chinghai), each with a Mongol territory allotted to it for absorption, the significance was missed, in spite of its importance in the alignment of world power, because the world at large had never understood the history of either Manchus or Mongols, and had habitually misconstrued their relationship to each other and to China.

Within Jehol, there is a distinct tribal cleavage between the two Leagues of Jo-oda and Josoto. The Jo-oda Banners derive in the main from the same expansion, out of Outer Mongolia across the Hsingan into Manchuria, as the Jerim League Banners. The tribes of Josoto are different. The Kharchin Mongols not only belong to the major category of the Frontier, but within that category have the separate character of borderers. The Tumets of Josoto are also borderers, having migrated into Josoto from the similar border

[2] *Manchuria, Cradle of Conflict;* "China and the Barbarians," in *Empire in the East;* "Chinese Turkistan," in *The Open Court.*

region held by the Tumets of the Kueihua-Suiyüan sector.

Tribes like the Kharchin have a political tradition which links them as closely with China to the south as with the tribal affairs of the nomad Mongols to the north of them. Their country is not suited to sweeping migrations; the escarpment of the Mongolian plateau, which farther to the west is relatively distinct, here breaks down into confused hills with deep reëntrant valleys. It is probable that in this broken country the population as a whole has never been displaced and replaced, but that political change has been more important than migration, and that many races have met and fused. The significance, in this respect, of "Mongol" families of Chinese descent among the Kharchins may be cited afresh. It is almost certain that the Kharchins also derive in part from the Khitan and Nüchen peoples, who ruled under the Liao and Chin dynasties between the tenth and thirteenth centuries; of whom the Nüchen especially had Tungusic rather than Mongol affinities. It is beyond a doubt that the Kharchins were largely agricultural half a century before the Manchu conquest of China, and they may well have had a partly agricultural economy ever since the fourteenth century.

Manchu policy turned in the first instance on the strategic importance of Jehol, and especially of the southern mountain country of Josoto, which dominates both the Peking plain and the Shanhaikuan corridor between China and Manchuria. It was the adherence of Josoto League which finally placed the Manchus in position to develop their raids into China into a permanent occupation.

THE MONGOLS OF MANCHURIA

The mountains and the comparative poverty of the Josoto country discouraged trade in the past, just as they impede railway development in the present. Trade has always turned naturally to the narrow but easy Shanhaikuan passage. In strategy, on the other hand, the mountains have always dominated the coastal corridor. The Shanhaikuan passage is easily cut by military action and easily out-flanked by armies holding the Jehol hills and passes. It was for this reason that the Manchus confirmed the Chinese character of the small Chinese Pale in Southern Jehol, set apart the Hunting Park in order to separate the Kharchin and Chahar Mongols from each other by a wilderness, and built a summer Capital at Ch'engte (Complete Virtue) or Jehol City. It was advisable to keep a close check on the Mongols of Jehol, and to interpose a Chinese population between them and the actual line of the Great Wall. Full Manchu control of communication between Manchuria and China was essential. The extension of Chinese settlement to the north was equally opposed by the Manchus, because if the Chinese were to push through the mountains and reach the open country in Northern Jehol, they would upset the Mongol balance of power and the control over China established by the original Manchu-Mongol alliance. The decay of this old policy of safeguarding the Mongol character of the Mongols in Jehol and Manchuria, and the change in political conceptions from the theory of a Man-chu Empire *over* China to the theory of a Manchu Empire *in* China are therefore related phenomena.

In discussing the early forms of colonization in Jehol,

1748 was given as the year in which relative indifference to colonization among the Mongols was replaced by definite policies of control and restriction. The Jehol Banners that had then already been affected were the three Kharchin Banners and the Western Banner of the two Tumet Banners in Josoto League, and the Aokhan territory (then one Banner, now three) and the two Ongniod Banners in Jo-oda League. The Chinese, in other words, were already penetrating to the northern side of the mountain country, so that the balance of frontier populations was being disturbed. It should be pointed out that while the Manchu policy was in general a failure, owing partly to the Mongol drift toward evasion, it did succeed to a certain extent in limiting the area affected by Chinese penetration. From 1748 to the 1890's, when the modern forms of colonization began to gather momentum, while the number of Chinese in Jehol increased very greatly, the area affected increased relatively little.

This, undoubtedly, was because the Manchu interdictions were reinforced by the natural economic limitations of Chinese settlement, trade and transport under genuinely Chinese conditions. This bears out the importance of railways in extending the economic range of Chinese colonization. In Jerim League, in the forty years since colonization began to be energized by the building of railways, the area taken over by the Chinese has doubled and doubled again; and every major advance has been related to fresh railway construction. In Jehol, the increase in area has been relatively small; only about 50 per cent. Most of the increase, moreover, has not been effected by growth outward from the old zone of Chinese penetration, but from a separate movement of colonization coming in from the east, from Manchuria, and related directly to the economic energy of the Ssup'ingkai-Liaoyüan-T'ungliao and Tahushan-T'ungliao Railways. The main advance of the colonists has been up the Shira Muren valley, through K'ailu.

In Northern Jehol, therefore, colonization is distinctly "Manchurian" in type, and has resulted, as in Jerim League, in sweeping out the majority of the Mongols and leaving the rest in "islands," so that in Chinese districts there are Chinese only and in Mongol districts Mongols only. In Southern Jehol, the process has been one of multiplication of the Chinese population, intensifying the effect of the old interpenetration of Mongols by Chinese, and thus squeezing the life out of the insufficiently concentrated Mongol minority, and destroying its Mongol character and individuality. The economic and historical cleavage between Northern and Southern Jehol must therefore be made a point of reference in considering the separate Banners of the Leagues of Josoto and Jo-oda.

Chapter XIII

THE MONGOLS OF JOSOTO LEAGUE

THE name Josoto is said to derive from the name of a river.[1] The Chinese transliteration is Cho-so-t'u. The Mongol name may mean Clay River.

The League includes three tribal groups—the Kharchin, the Tumet and the Khalkha—and one independent Lama Banner of peculiar status. Of these the Kharchins may be regarded as indigenous; the Tumets came from the Suiyüan region at the beginning of the seventeenth century, and the Khalkhas from Outer Mongolia in the middle of the seventeenth century. The independent Lama Banner has a quasi-tribal organization. Its people, who may have been chiefly Tumets in the beginning, are now drawn from all the surrounding tribes.

The whole of Josoto League has been excluded from Hsingan province, and must therefore be reckoned a "lost" Mongol territory. The Mongols are in a hopeless minority among the Chinese, and there are no strategic reasons for

[1] Mimeograph MS.

243

creating a Mongol counterpoise to the Chinese population in this territory, as there are in the northern part of Jo-oda League. The old canons governing the relation of the Jehol mountains to the Shanhaikuan coastal corridor have been modified by the conditions of modern warfare, and will be further modified by railways running from T'ungliao to K'ailu and thence to Jehol City, and from Peip'iao to Jehol City.

THE KHARCHIN TRIBE

The name Kharchin, transcribed as K'a-la-ch'in or Ha-la-ch'in by the Chinese, is said by the Mongol authority quoted above to be derived from the name of a river, in which case it may perhaps be referred to the Mongol word *kharakchin,* "blackish." It may, on the other hand, be related to the root which appears in the verb *kharamoi,* vernacular *kharana,* "to look," "to watch," which would connect it with various words meaning "sentinels," "watchers," "herders," "custodians," and even "servitors." It is worth noting that there is a tradition [2] that the Kharchins were custodians of the granaries and treasures of the Yüan or Mongol dynasty ruling over China in the thirteenth and fourteenth centuries—which, again, would account for the early development of agriculture and a semi-settled economy among them. While the name, in modern Mongol usage, is written Kharchin, it is probable that Kharachin is an older form.

The original territory of the Kharchins extended from the Willow Palisade in the east, right across what later be-

[2] *Mongol Pastures.*

244

came the Imperial Hunting Park, to the All-Blue Banner of the Chahar Mongols, the easternmost Chahar Banner, its dimensions being 500 *li* from east to west and 450 *li* from north to south, or about 166 by 150 miles. The Kharchins formed a single Banner until after they entered the Manchu alliance, "at the beginning of the reign of Tien Ts'ung," who succeeded in 1627, and in 1635 changed his reign-style to Ch'ung Te, when he advanced his pretensions to the throne of China. The Kharchins, like the other Mongols of Jehol, joined the Manchus in the first instance in order to avoid submission to the Chahars, who were attempting to create a new united Mongol Empire.

The princes of the Kharchin are called by the Mongols Tabonang or Sons-in-law, because unlike the other princely families they are not descended from sons or brothers of Chingghis Khan, but from a chief of the Oriyanghan tribe, who married the daughter of Chingghis. The tribal name of Oriyanghan is still retained by the Kharchin princes as their clan name. I believe that the old Oriyanghan probably held the territory that is now held by the Kharchins, and also extended a good deal farther to the north; that they were either of Tungusic stock or were a mixture of Tungus and Mongol, and that they joined the Mongols of Chingghis by alliance, the marriage of their chief to the daughter of Chingghis binding the union. If this is true, then they had probably been in the first place connected with the Chin dynasty of the Nüchen Tatars, whom the Mongols conquered.

The name Oriyanghan appears in various forms, such as Oriyanghai or Oriyangghai and Oriyangghit (a plural form), and is commonly rendered Urianghai. In Chinese it is given as Wu-liang-hai, Wu-liang-han, and so forth, different sets of characters being used. The name is referred by Mongols to an old word *oi* (literary but no longer common in the vernacular) meaning "forest." As a tribal name it survives in the Altai region and in the Tangno-Oriyanghai (Tannu-Urianghai or Tannu-Tuva) territory, which was formerly a kind of outer ward of Outer Mongolia, and is now the Soviet Republic of Tannu-Tuva. (Tangno is from the Mongol *tangnai,* or *tanglai,* "midmost," "in the midst of," which is different from the ordinary word *domdado,* "middle.") As a clan name, Oriyanghai or Oriyanghan survives not only among the Kharchin aristocracy, but in the Silingol League, either in one of the Abaga Banners or in one of the Abaganar Banners. In this latter region I have passed near a quarter in which the name is apparently so general that Mongols met on the road speak of having come "from the Oriyanghai," or of events happening "among the Oriyanghai," instead of using the tribal-territorial Banner name.

It seems likely that all Oriyanghan tribes are of "forest" origin; but this does not necessarily mean that they are all of the same racial stock; although Turks, Tungus and Mongols are all of related stocks. The Altai-Oriyanghai and Tangno-Oriyanghai of the present day are certainly of a predominantly Turkish type. It seems more reasonable, as already suggested, to suppose that the Oriyanghan with whom we are here concerned have Tungus affinities.

Kharchin West Wing Banner

or Right Wing Banner. This is the senior Kharchin Banner. It lies northeast of Ch'engte or Jehol City. The Mongols have to a great extent turned Chinese; and as among all the Kharchins, the process of forgetting the Mongol language has been very much accelerated within the last fifteen years, so that the proportion of young people who do not speak Mongol is very much greater than that of mature people. This has been brought about largely by the increase of district schools and the spread of primary education under the Chinese Republic. Unless the Mongols can get education in Mongol, the language cannot compete with Chinese. In this respect there is a radical difference between Chinese and Russian policy. Mongols in Chinese schools either get no instruction or only very perfunctory instruction in Mongol. All "modern" and "political" teaching is in Chinese, although a good deal of propaganda is printed in Mongol. In Outer Mongolia, on the other hand, primary instruction is in Mongol, all education is Mongolized as far as possible, and Russian is taught only as a comparatively advanced subject.

Only one Chinese county town stands in the Banner territory, but all of the territory is within one or another Chinese county, reaching into the Banner from adjoining districts. The town in question is P'ingch'üan, or Flat Springs. It was made a county as long ago as 1778, and the settlement of Pakou or Eighth Valley which preceded it was organized in 1729. It is in the extreme south of the Banner territory, in the region first penetrated by the Chinese, and on the main trade route of Eastern Jehol.

Kharchin Center Banner

The prince is descended from a brother of Sobotai (Pearl), the original Prince of all the Kharchins, who joined the Manchus. This Banner was split off from the original Banner, which is now the West Wing Banner, in 1705, owing to increase in numbers. The territory of this Banner is enclosed within that of the West and East Wing Banners. The Mongols are the least Chinese of all the Kharchin Mongols. There is no county town within the Banner, but all of the territory is partitioned among different counties.

Kharchin East Wing Banner

or Left Wing Banner. It was formed in 1635, a few years after the Kharchins had joined the Manchus, by division of the original tribal territory. Its territory lies along the Willow Palisade, overlooking the coastal corridor that leads from Shanhaikuan into Manchuria, and the Taling Ho or Great Cold River flows through it. The Mongols are heavily submerged by the Chinese, and in the last few years the Mongol language has been losing ground rapidly. Mongol-speaking Mongols remain, however, and in the remoter villages men often speak little Chinese, while the women do not understand it at all. The important county town of

Lingyüan, Sources of the Ling, stands in this territory. It was made a county seat in 1914, but had been a sub-prefecture since 1738, and grew out of the earlier settlement of T'atzŭkou, Valley of the Pagodas.

THE TUMET TRIBE

The name Tumet is from the plural form of the Mongol word *tumen*, meaning "ten thousand," "an infinite number." The Chinese transcription is T'u-mu-t'e. These Tumets are tribally related to the Tumets of the Kueihua-Suiyüan region, whence they migrated at the beginning of the seventeenth century. They are comparable to the Kharchins in their tradition of being a special "borderer" people, and in having taken extensively to agriculture at an early date. It is quite likely that there are elements of ethnic and cultural continuity between the Tumets and the Ongut, that people of Central Asian affinity and Nestorian Christian religion who, in the thirteenth century, held a border state in the Suiyüan region, tributary to the Yüan dynasty of the Mongols, and whose princes have been associated with the legend of Prester John.[3]

The Tumets themselves were an important Frontier power in the sixteenth century. They were at their height under Anda, the Altan Khan or Golden Khan who built Kueihua; but thereafter were so pressed on by the Chahars that under a grandson of Anda part of the tribe migrated eastward and took up lands in the territory now known by their name, in Josoto League. The son of the prince who

[3] *Marco Polo*, ed. Yule & Cordier; also Pelliot, *Chrétiens d'Asie centrale.*

led the migration made common cause with the Kharchins, and in 1628 Kharchins and Tumets together asked for support from the Manchus against the Chahars. In 1634 the Manchus divided the migrated Tumets into three Banners, of which one, under the hereditary Tumet prince, is the West Wing Banner of to-day. The other two were a combination of Tumets and Kharchins, under Kharchin princes; in the following year one of the princes was deposed for some "crime"—probably of disloyalty to the Manchus, or of excessive ambition, and the two Banners were consolidated as one, now known as the Tumet East Wing or Monggoljin Banner.[4] According to the *Mongol Pastures,* the original territory of the present two Banners ran 460 *li* east and west by 310 *li* north and south, or about 153 by 103 miles.

Tumet West Wing Banner

or Right Wing Banner. The territory of this Banner lies along the Willow Palisade. These Tumets are considered by other Mongols to be even more "Chinese" than the Kharchins; but, as among the Kharchins, the Mongol language is preserved here and there, and numbers of well-to-do families preserve a literary knowledge of Mongol, because of its usefulness politically.

Only one county town stands in the Banner territory—the city of Ch'aoyang, Facing the Sun, formerly known as Santsot'a, or Three Pagodas. It was a sub-prefecture in 1738, and after various administrative changes was made a

---

[4] *Mongol Pastures.*

county town in 1914. A railway runs from Chinchou, Or-
nate Region, in Fengt'ien province, up to Peip'iao, North
Ticket (a name probably referring originally to a tax col-
lecting station) in the territory of this Banner. It serves a
bituminous coal field, the first recorded output of the mines
being 7,716 metric tons in 1921, rising to 509,872 metric tons
in 1930.[5] This railway is to be continued to Jehol City.

Tumet East Wing Banner

or Left Wing Banner. Popularly known as Monggoljin
Banner. This is an adjectival form, meaning "the Mongols,"
"the Mongol people," perhaps an indication that the neighboring Kharchins were not considered pure Mongols. The
prince of this Banner is of the same clan as the Kharchin
princes, as has been said, and therefore it might be expected, according to the standard Mongol usage, that it
would be called a Kharchin Banner; but it is officially a
Tumet Banner, because the majority of the people are
Tumet.

The Banner lies along the Willow Palisade, and formerly both the Shiretu Khurie Lama Banner and the small
Khalkha Banner in Josoto League were attached to it for
administrative purposes. The people of the Banner are the
most strongly Mongol in character and feeling of the
Tumet and Kharchin Banners. This is due in part to the
sandy and infertile soil, especially in the northern half of
the Banner, which attracted comparatively few Chinese
colonists; but it is mainly due to the Mongols themselves,

[5] *China Year Book*, 1931-2.

who are hardy, uncompromising and anti-Chinese. The Monggoljin bandits are known throughout Jehol province —which has been one of the best known bandit provinces— and have always been ready to join in any anti-Chinese rising. It will be remembered that the bandit-patriot Babo-jab was a Monggoljin Tumet by origin. Nevertheless the rule holds, in this Banner as elsewhere, that regions under full Mongol control are free of banditry.

In the Monggoljin Banner the strict control of banditry, and the refusal to "turn Chinese" even in the latter years under the Republic, when the Mongols elsewhere in Josoto League were so rapidly being swamped by Chinese, are to be credited largely to the vigor and ability of one man, Bejing by name. (This name, the written form of which is Begejing, is the Mongol pronunciation of "Peking," the Chinese Peiching. In Eastern Mongolia it is not uncommon as a personal name.) "Bejing of the Monggoljin," as he is popularly known, now an old man, organized the Mongols of the region for many years, and saw to it that Chinese bandits did not enter the Mongol-populated regions in the Banner, and also that the Mongol bandits themselves walked gently within the districts patrolled by Mongol self-defense corps.

There is one county town, Fuhsin or Fouhsin, New Abundance, formerly known as Shui Ch'üan-rh, The Springs. It was established in 1903. The county is perhaps most distinguished for having produced T'ang Yü-lin, Governor of Jehol until the Japanese campaign which brought the province under Manchukuo. He was border-bred and a bandit from his youth up, and an early associate of Chang Tso-lin, the Old Marshal of Manchuria. Unlike some of the Old Marshal's other associates, he never showed any talent for civil organization, and remained rapacious to the end.

THE INDEPENDENT LAMA BANNER

Shiretu Khurie Banner

The Mongol name of this Banner means The Table-land Monastery. The Chinese transcription is Hsi-lieh-t'u K'u-lun. This is the place-name, not the religious name; for temples and monasteries have a religious or formal name, but have a place-name by which they are commonly known. *Shire,* written form *sirege,* is "a table"; *shiretu* is an adjectival form. *Khurie* is "an enclosure," and is particularly used of temple enclosures. It is regularly corrupted to *k'u-lun* by the Chinese, as in Ta K'ulun, Great Monastery, for Urga.

There is another Shiretu monastery, north of Kueihua, with a small quasi-autonomous territory of its own, forming an enclave within the Suiyüan Tumet Banner lands. It is commonly known as Shiretu Jo, which also means Table-land Temple, *jo* being the Mongol version of a Tibetan word, rendered *chao* in Chinese. Whether there is any connection between the two Shiretu monasteries, I have not been able to find out; but I suspect that when the present Josoto Tumets migrated from Suiyüan this monastery may have been established as a branch of the Suiyüan foundation. The family which monopolizes the religious succession is of Suiyüan Tumet origin; but on the other hand the succession at the Suiyüan Shiretu Jo is not monopolized by a family. In the *Ta Ch'ing Hui Tien*,[6] in a list of "reincarnations" or Living Buddhas, two Shiretu Khurie Living Buddhas are mentioned, but without anything to indicate either differentiation or relation.

There are a number of "autonomous" monastery-precincts scattered through the Mongol territories that have a peculiar status. The Mongol usage is to regard all monasteries and lama temples as autonomous, in the sense that they are not under secular law; so that even when a Banner, or a sub-division of a Banner, dedicates a part of its territory to a monastery "of its own," that territory is virtually ceded to the religious foundation. Certain religious foundations, however, have possessions which give them something like the magnitude of tribes, exercising the secular functions of tribes in an ecclesiastical form.

Such foundations can often be traced back to the time before the Mongols came under the Manchus. In the fifteenth century a number of different regional and tribal groups among the Mongols were trying to build up dynastic powers in rivalry against each other. In so doing, they developed a method of creating rival Church patronages, in order to fortify secular power with religious authority. When the Manchus became overlords of the Mongols, they put an end to this by working temporal and ecclesiastical

[6] Li Fan Yüan 12, *chüan* 737.

power against each other, in pursuit of their general policy of limiting and preventing Mongol cohesion. They exalted the authority and prestige of Living Buddhas as a counter-balance to the power of ruling princes, and one of their devices for making this effective was to bar the "sons and brothers" of ruling princes from being selected as "reincarnations," in order to prevent the concentration of the two kinds of authority in any one person or family.[7]

It may be said here that there is nothing in the "theory" of "reincarnation" to prevent the close association of religious and temporal power. On the contrary, it is an excellent device for transforming high religious office into dynastic succession. The theory, simply stated, is that a Living Buddha is the reincarnation of a particular sanctity, or manifestation of the divine. When he dies, the sanctity or "virtue" is reincarnated in another person. In other words it is the permanent quality of sanctity, not the human person of the previous saint, that is reincarnated. There is much the same kind of difference, in "higher criticism," between the technical and the popular understanding of the nature of Living Buddhas as there is between the vulgar and the adept interpretation of the function of images of saints, in Christian theory.

Between the earlier Mongol tendency to integrate Church and State and the later Manchu policy of differentiating them, the typical Mongol religious foundation emerged as a kind of pseudo-tribe, with its monks or lamas forming its

[7] *Ta Ch'ing Hui Tien,* Li Fan Yüan 13, *chüan* 738; also *Wei Tsang T'ung Chih, chüan* 5.

255

ecclesiastical corporation, and yet with a kind of tribal aspect because of its territorial possessions and the laymen inhabiting them. The laymen attached to a religious foundation are *shabinar*, "disciples," who are often called "serfs." They are, in reality, *subjects*, taken out of the tribal life and paying taxes (largely in the form of services) and owning allegiance to a monastery, the head of which is the equivalent of their "chief."

In certain cases, notably that of the Shiretu Khurie Banner now under discussion and that of the Chagan Nom-on Khan Banner or Banner of the Khan of the White Law, or White Scripture, in the Kokonor region, the tribal structure was allowed to develop more completely. In both cases what really happened was not that a princely family was allowed to monopolize a religious succession, but that hereditary princely rank was conferred on a religious dignitary.

The succession in Shiretu Khurie Banner has long been established as a regulated form of nepotism. The Living Buddha, having princely rank but being, *ex hypothesi*, a celibate, is allowed to transfer the succession to one of his nephews. The theory is that he "comes to life again" in the person of the nephew; or rather, according to the analysis given above, that the quality of which he is a manifestation is manifested afresh through his successor. This form of succession is mentioned as early as 1729,[8] when it is ordained that a "grandson" (the term is allowable for a grand-nephew) be appointed; with the alternative of ap-

[8] *Ta Ch'ing Hui Tien, loc. cit.*

pointing an "able" man from the monastery's religious establishment.

While the Living Buddha of this monastery has long had the rank of Jasak Lama (written form, *blama*) or Ruling Lama, it is only since the Republic that the territory has been recognized and listed as a fully independent Banner. Under the Manchus, as has been said, it had autonomy within its own boundaries, but in dealing with the central Government was considered subordinate to the East Wing Tumet (Monggoljin) Banner.

The territory forms a northward projection from the Monggoljin Banner, and according to the Japanese maps has an extension of about seventy miles from north to south, with a maximum width of about thirty miles. Although so small, it has been remarkable in recent years for the vigor of its spirit of independence. According to Mongol statements it has a total population, including lamas and laymen, of a little more than 12,000. Although the ruling family is Tumet, and the original tribal "following" was perhaps also Tumet in the beginning, the general population is now drawn from all the surrounding tribes, as is usual in such religious territories.

The Prince Lama long ago set himself against Chinese encroachment, and refused to allow Chinese to settle among the Mongols on any terms whatever. All the Mongols are agricultural, and the standard of literacy is high. The Prince-Lama has sent many boys to China and, it is said, to Japan for higher schooling. Many of the Suruk Mongols, on whose old territory the Banner borders, withdrew into this Banner to escape Chinese pressure. The Banner supports about 500 troops, and in case of necessity the whole adult population "including women" can be called to arms.

There is an old trading town on the edge of the Banner territory, called K'ulik'ou—a name which appears to be compounded from a Chinese corruption of the word *khurie,* with the addition of the word *k'ou,* "mouth" (of a valley). In 1908 this was made a county town, under the name of Suitung, Pacification of the East. According to Mongol information, the local Mongols gave so much obstruction that the county was not able to function, and was therefore moved far to the North, into Naiman Banner. (I have marked both sites of Suitung on the map.) The Shiretu Khurie Banner regularly collected the taxes demanded by the Chinese authorities and forwarded them to the county, but refused to let Chinese tax collectors enter the Banner. The Chinese traders in the little town of K'ulik'ou were permitted to remain, but were not allowed to leave the town unless provided with passes; while Mongols were not allowed to live within the town.

The defiant independence of this small Banner is an example of what the Mongols can accomplish under Mongol leadership. The fact that the leadership in this Banner has been ecclesiastical disproves the popular theory that lamaism *necessarily* precludes Mongol independence and makes education and a vigorous political life impossible. It is obvious that the Lama Church *can* be reinvigorated from within and *can* be coördinated with a healthy tribal organization.

The Banner was visited by Hedley in 1906.[9]

Tanggot Khalkha Banner

This Banner, formerly subordinated for administrative purposes to the East Wing Tumet (Monggoljin) Banner, is popularly known as Tanggot Khalkha (Chinese transliteration, T'ang-ku-t'e K'a-erh-k'a, or Ha-erh-ha) or "Tibetan Khalkha" Banner. The reason for this I have never been able to discover. The Mongols use the term Tanggot (Tangut) for the people who founded the Hsia or Western Hsia dynasty, which ruled from Kokonor across Kansu to the Ninghsia region in the twelfth century, and was destroyed by Chingghis Khan in his last campaigns at the beginning of the thirteenth century. In modern use, the term applies to the part of Tibet adjoining Kokonor.

This tiny territory, of not more than 7 or 8 by 12 or 15 miles, is said to have a population of about 500 people. There are practically no Chinese, as the surrounding districts are all held by Mongols. The "tribe," which has a prince of its own, was founded by immigrants from the Jasakto Khan division of Outer Mongolia, who fled to Inner Mongolia and offered submission to the Manchus in 1662, during the wars between the Northern (Khalkha) and Western (Ölöt) Mongols. They were then attached to

[9] See Bibliography.

the Monggoljin Tumets for administrative purposes, but under the Republic have been recognized and listed as an independent Banner. They form, with the northern part of Monggoljin Banner, the Shiretu Khurie territory, the East Wing or Chokhor Khalkha Banner and the southeastern part of Naiman Banner, a block of unassimilated Mongol territory surrounded by Chinese settlement.

Chapter XIV

THE WESTERN OR JO-ODA LEAGUE DIVI-
SION OF HSINGAN AND THE LOST MONGOL
TERRITORIES ASSOCIATED WITH IT

THE name of Jo-oda or Hundred Willows, commonly written Joo-oda; properly Jagon-oda, is said by Mongols to derive from the name of the place where met the tribal assembly which formed the League. The Chinese transcription is Chao-wu-ta. The League contains eight tribal groups—Aokhan, Naiman, Bairin, Jarod, Aro-Khorchin, Ongniod, Keshikten and Khalkha, divided into thirteen Banners.

It has already been pointed out that in tribal history the Jo-oda Mongols belong rather with those of Jerim League than with those of Josoto. Their territory forms a rough triangle, pointed north, occupying about two-thirds of Jehol province. The Shira Muren or upper Liao flows right across the League from west to east, dividing it roughly in half. The river, for most of its length, has been made the boundary between the part of Jo-oda retained within Hsingan province and the part abandoned, so to speak, to Chinese colonization; at the western end, however, one

of the southern headstreams of the Shira Muren is taken
as the boundary, in order to include the whole of Keshikten Banner within the western division of Hsingan. South
of the river, in the "lost" territories, many Mongols remain;
their status being like that of the Mongols in the "lost"
territories of Jerim League. The "lost" Banners are: two
Ongniod Banners, three Aokhan Banners, and the Naiman
Banner and Khalkha Banner.

The territories north of the river are still strongly Mongol in character. In all of these Banners there is a certain
amount of Chinese settlement, but the Chinese are nowhere really formidable in numbers. They had begun to
gather headway just in the last years of Chinese rule, and
the extension of the railway from T'ungliao to K'ailu
would have greatly increased their economic range. The
uncolonized parts of Jo-oda are generally comparable to
the uncolonized parts of Jerim, except that on the whole
more of the Mongols are nomadic and fewer are farmers.
The territories that have been allotted to Hsingan are: the
Keshikten Banner, two Bairin Banners, Aro-Khorchin Banner and two Jarod Banners.

It will be convenient to list the "lost" Banners first.

THE ONGNIOD TRIBE

The Mongol written form is Ongnigod; the Chinese
transcription is Weng-niu-t'e. The tribe formed a single
Banner until after it went over to the Manchus in 1632.
The original territory of the whole tribe, according to the
Mongol Pastures, extended 300 *li* east and west by 160 *li*

north and south, or about 100 by 53 miles. The tribe had been subject to the Chahars before coming under the Manchus. Although the two Ongniod Banners are designated as West and East, their relative geographical positions are better described as south and north.

Whether there is any connection between the tribe and the thirteenth century Ongut of the Kueihua region, I do not know.

Ongniod West Wing Banner

or Right Wing Banner. This is the junior Banner, having been formed out of the East Wing Banner in 1635. A portion of its territory was detached and allotted to the Imperial Hunting Park. The Banner has been swamped by Chinese, and the Mongols are now in a hopeless minority. The important town of Ch'ihfeng or Red Peak, a translation of the Mongol name Olan Khada, written form Olagan Khada, stands in its territory. It was made a county town as long ago as 1778.

Ongniod East Wing Banner

or Left Wing Banner. It is not so thickly settled by Chinese as the West Wing Banner, because the land is poorer. The county town of Ch'üanning, Completed Peace, was founded in the middle of this Banner in 1932. The original settlement was called Wutanch'eng; this name being perhaps compounded from a Chinese rendering of the Mongol *oda*, "willow," and the Chinese word *ch'eng*, "a walled city." From Wutanch'eng eastward, in the angle between the

Shira Muren and its main southern affluent, the Laoha Ho, there is actually a good deal of open pasture remaining, in which Ongniod, Aohan and Naiman Mongols keep up the nomadic life.

THE AOKHAN TRIBE

This tribe formed a single Banner until after the foundation of the Chinese Republic. It came under the Manchus in 1627. Before this it had been tributary to the Chahars. The original extension of the tribal territory was 160 *li* east and west by 280 *li* north and south, as given in the *Mongol Pastures*. The Mongol name may perhaps be connected either with the word *aoga,* "strength," "might," or with the word *aogan,* "elder," "senior." This is a word which presents no difficulty to the Chinese ear or tongue, and consequently the Chinese are able to give it the accurate rendering of Ao-han.

A Prince of Aokhan was concerned in the land war between Chinese and Mongols in 1891. The Banner was not subdivided until 1913, when it was split into East and West Wings. Still later the East Wing was again divided, to form a South Banner. These divisions, occurring under the Republic, are a good illustration of the modern Chinese policy of combining encroachment with the creation of new princes and the support of the princes as a class.

Aokhan West Wing Banner
or Right Wing Banner. The territory contains no large towns. The population is thin, and the Mongols are said

not to be hopelessly outnumbered. The princes, ever since the rising of 1891, are said to have been feckless; and this is said to be true of all three Aokhan Banners.

Aokhan East Wing Banner

or Left Wing Banner. This Banner might as well be termed North as East. There is a certain amount of open pasture in the north, where it borders with Ongniod East Wing; but the Mongols are poor and it is said that their future is hopeless, though as yet there are no large towns and the Mongols are not badly outnumbered.

Aokhan South Banner

or Front Banner. (The designation "Wing" is not used of "Front" and "Rear" Banners.) Just within the borders of this Banner there stands the county town of Chienp'ing, Founding of Peace, formerly Hsinch'iu, New Embankment. The Chinese are more numerous than in the other two Aokhan Banners.

THE NAIMAN TRIBE

One Banner

This name, like Aokhan, presents no difficulty for the Chinese, who transcribe it straightforwardly as Nai-man. The name, which means "eight" in Mongol, occurs in history, and this Banner, according to tradition, fought against Chingghis in the period when he was uniting the Mongol tribes. The Banner, after being subject to the Chahars, joined the Manchus in 1627 and fought against the Chahars.

The *Mongol Pastures* gives the size of the Banner as 95 by 220 *li,* or about 31 by 73 miles.

Naiman Banner is described by Binsteed in 1913 as being half occupied by Chinese. The villages of Mongols and Chinese are interspersed, but in the southeast there is a fairly large area of practically solid Mongol occupation. Chinese coming in from K'ailu, just over the northern boundary of the Banner, have isolated these Mongols, and the isolation will probably be completed by a railway running up the Shira Muren valley from K'ailu to Dolon Nor, on the edge of Chahar territory.

The region still strongly held by Mongols owes its existence to the energy and capability of one man, who took on himself the unofficial leadership of the tribe when the former and present princes proved incapable. This man, now in his old age, is named Bejing or "Peking," like his counterpart and old ally Bejing, the Monggoljin Tumet who has already been mentioned. Originally a lama, he openly renounced his religion and set himself to rally the Mongols of his Banner. He gathered together as many of them as possible in order to form a community which it would be hard for the Chinese to penetrate and assimilate. The result has been that these Mongols, although encircled by Chinese and leading a settled life, have held stoutly to their Mongol national feeling. They have raised their own self-defense corps and kept their villages reasonably free from banditry. They form, with Shiretu Khurie Banner, the northern part of Monggoljin Tumet Banner, and so forth, an enclave in which the Mongols, in spite of their isolation, have managed quite unofficially to keep out most of the Chinese influence, by virtue simply of their own self-reliance and the emergence of capable leaders.

There are no large towns in the Banner territory.

Khalkha East Wing Banner

or Left Wing Banner. The Chinese rendering of Khalkha is K'a-erh-k'a or Ha-erh-ha. The Banner is popularly known among the Mongols as Chokhor Khalkha or Smallpox Khalkha. I have heard this explained by Mongols as meaning that the people of the Banner are so few that they are scattered over the land "like pock-marks." I suspect, however, that the Banner may have suffered heavily in a smallpox epidemic. Its boundaries as given by the *Mongol Pastures* run 125 by 230 *li,* or about 41 by 76 miles. At present, judging by the Japanese maps, they do not run over more than about 15 by 35 miles. It may be therefore that the tribe did suffer from a severe epidemic, after which part of its territory was given over to Naiman Banner.

The Chokhor Khalkha, like the Tanggot Khalkha, came in as the following of a petty prince from Jasakto Khan Aimak in Outer Mongolia. They migrated in 1664, two years after the Tanggot Khalkha. They are known apparently as Left Wing Banner in order to distinguish them, not from the other Khalkha group in Jehol, but from Khalkha Right Wing Banner, popularly known as Darkhan Beile Banner, in Olanchab League (nominally part of Suiyüan province) which migrated into Inner Mongolia from the Tosiyato Khan Aimak of Outer Mongolia in 1653.

The Banner is described by Binsteed in 1913 as being completely colonized by Chinese; but according to present Mongol accounts the Chinese influence is not dominant, and the Banner belongs with the unassimilated southeastern group already described. Binsteed may possibly have been speaking in terms of the old limits of the Banner.

There are no towns or even large villages in the territory.

The Mongols who have been included in the western division of Hsingan province have now to be described.

THE KESHIKTEN TRIBE

One Banner

The Mongol written form is Gesikten or Gesikteng; the Chinese rendering is K'o-shih-k'o-t'eng. It is referred by the Mongols to the word *gesik*, "grace," and especially "Imperial grace." The Keshikten tribe joined the Manchus in 1635, after the Manchus had defeated the Chahars, who had been their overlords for a while. The original extension of their territory is given in the *Mongol Pastures* as 334 *li* east and west by 357 *li* north and south, or about 111 by 119 miles. A part of it was detached and assigned to the Imperial Hunting Park.

The southern part of the Banner has been heavily penetrated by Chinese, but owing to the strong policy of the prince the Mongols have kept up a good front. They are now mostly concentrated in the north, where they have stoutly opposed any farther advance. In the extreme north they are still nomadic; toward the south they are settled farmers. The Keshikten Mongols are considered by other Mongols to be among the most genuine, uncompromising and at the same time progressive in Jehol. They are certainly, within the limits of a defensive policy, the most powerful in Jo-oda. The county town of Chingp'eng, Lengthwise Shed, was founded in this territory in 1914. Since then, the threat of further colonization has been countered by open defiance, and officials sent up to survey proposed land grants have been thrown out.

The Banner borders both on Silingol League and on the All-Blue Banner of the Chahar Mongols. This probably explains why the whole Banner has been included within the autonomous province, although in the south it has been fairly thickly settled by Chinese. Its position is of strategic importance, and there are obvious advantages in demonstrating a generous policy of Mongol autonomy in Manchukuo to the Mongols of Western Inner Mongolia.

THE BAIRIN TRIBE

The Mongol written form is Bagarin; the Chinese rendering is Pa-lin. The name may be connected with the Mongol word *baga,* "small," or perhaps with the verb *baharamoi,* "to rejoice." The tribe formed one Banner until after it came under the Manchus. After being subject to the Khalkhas of Outer Mongolia the Bairin Mongols were attacked by the Chahars in 1628. They then turned to the Khorchins of Jerim League for support, and followed the Khorchins in offering allegiance to the Manchus. They served in the conquest of China in 1644 and were

organized into two Banners in 1648. The relative position
of the two Banners is south and north rather than west and
east. The original extension of the whole tribal territory
is given in the *Mongol Pastures* as 251 by 233 *li*, or about
83 by 77 miles. In 1913, according to Binsteed, there were
no colonists in the Bairin Banners, but a few settled Mongols were to be found in the south of West Bairin, near
the Shira Muren.

Bairin West Wing Banner

or Right Wing Banner. Popularly known as Great Bairin.
There has not been much colonization, but the county of
Linhsi, West of the Forest, was founded in 1908, and in
the vicinity of the little town there is a certain amount of
Chinese settlement. There is also a Catholic Mission, working among Chinese colonists. "Mongol banditry," caused by
the pressure of colonization on the south, has done much
to hinder the further penetration of the Chinese. It was in
this district that the patriot Babojab was killed.

Bairin East Wing Banner

or Left Wing Banner. Popularly known as Little Bairin.
The Mongols of this Banner are predominantly pastoral.
The county of Lintung, East of the Forest, was founded in
1925, but colonization has been inconsiderable. Lintung is
built near the ruined city called by the Mongols Borokhoto
(written form, Borogo Khoto) or Destroyed City. It was
probably the Northern Capital of the Liao or Khitan dynasty. It is called by local Chinese Ko Su-wen Ch'eng, or

City of Ko Su-wen, after a Chinese hero of the Sung dynasty who fought against the Khitans and is said to have destroyed the city.

THE ARO-KHORCHIN TRIBE

One Banner

The Mongol name means Rear or North Khorchin. The Chinese rendering is A-lu-k'o-erh-ch'in. The territory is reckoned in the *Mongol Pastures* as 130 by 420 *li,* or about 43 by 140 miles. The Banner is known as North Khorchin because it was established at one time on the borders of Barga and Outer Mongolia.[1] An old name for the main body of the Khorchin Mongols, distinguishing them from the then northern group, was Nonni Khorchin. The Aro-Khorchin, after being tributary to the Chahars, went over to the Manchus in 1630. They then formed two Banners, but in 1635 one of the two princes was deposed, by the Manchus, for habitual drunkenness, and the two Banners combined as one.

The Banner is little affected by colonization, or even by agriculture, the majority of the Mongols being pastoral. The county of T'ienshan or Heavenly Mountains was established in the south of the Banner in 1926, and the county town removed to a new site the following year; but the Chinese have not increased in numbers or influence.

[1] See pp. 157-158.

THE MONGOLS OF MANCHURIA

THE JAROD TRIBE

The Mongol name may be connected with the verb *jaromoi,* "to serve," (as troops, for instance). The Chinese rendering is Cha-lu-t'e. The tribe consisted originally of a single Banner. Its territory is given by the *Mongol Pastures* as 125 by 460 *li,* or about 41 by 153 miles. The tribe was at one time subject to the Khalkhas of Outer Mongolia. It then joined the Khorchins, in order to escape conquest by the Chahars, and proceeded to alliance with the Manchus in 1628.

Prior to this, however, the Jarod had formed a series of marriage alliances with the Manchus in 1614, before Manchu alliances with the Mongols had become general. In 1619 they broke away from this alliance and went to the aid of the Ming dynasty of China, fighting against the Manchus. Shortly after this, the expanding power of the Chahars forced them over to the side of the Manchus once more. Their history thus illustrates the kind of tribal warfare preceding Northern Barbarian conquests of China, the nature of which has already been discussed. In 1623 they were defeated by the Manchus and finally in 1650, after the conquest of China, they were organized in their present two Banners.

Jarod West Wing Banner

or Right Wing Banner. The county town of K'ailu, the name of which may mean either Beginnings of Culture or The Opening Up of Barbarian Regions, and which also refers to the syllable *lu* in the Chinese transcription Cha-lu-t'e, was founded in 1908 just within the southern boundary of this Banner. Apart from this district there is little Chinese colonization and not very much Mongol agriculture. The boundary of Hsingan province has been moved north a few miles in order to leave this district to the Chinese. If Chinese rule had continued in Manchuria for a few more years, K'ailu would have been the main passage for colonists moving westward into Jehol.

Jarod East Wing Banner

or Left Wing Banner. The Banner in general is much the same as West Jarod, but there is more Mongol agriculture. A certain number of farming Mongols driven out of the neighboring Darkhan Wang Banner of Jerim League have moved into East Jarod. Binsteed described the Mongols of both Jarod Banners, in 1913, as poor. He says of East Jarod that they lived largely in "yurts"—the Mongol *ger* or felt tent—which had been converted into permanent dwellings; that they had garden agriculture and that the Banner was "thickly colonized" by Chinese. It may be that the Chinese were largely driven out during the risings of the period between 1913 and 1918. The county of Lupei, North of Lu, was founded in 1924 to promote colonization in the northern part of the Banner, but not much progress was made.

This completes the list of the Banners of Jo-oda League.

Chapter XV

MONGOLS BORDERING ON MANCHUKUO

THERE has already been a discussion of the frontier significance of Hsingan province, the autonomous Mongol policy in Manchukuo and the proclamation of a sovereign who could easily be made the focus of a movement to unify all the Mongols. Autonomy for the Mongols in Manchukuo under a "legitimist" Manchu Sovereign is a standing invitation to all the Mongols of Outer and Inner Mongolia to have done with Russia and China alike and revive the old Manchu-Mongol alliance that once dominated China and Central Asia as far as Kashgar—but with "Manchurians" in place of the almost vanished Manchus and with dynamic control in the hands of Japan.

It will be enough here to give a brief list of the Mongols who actually border Manchukuo.

OUTER MONGOLIA

All of Outer Mongolia except the Altai-Kobdo region [1] is occupied by the Khalkhas, who are divided into four

[1] For list of these tribes, see *China Year Book*, edition of 1933 or 1934.

275

aimak. The name Khalkha means "a barrier," and also "the gate of a barrier." It is thus equivalent to the Chinese *kuan,* which appears in Shanhaikuan, the Sea and Mountain Barrier. The name of the town of Kalgan is a corruption of Khalkha, the full Mongol name being Gorban Aimak-on Khalkha, Barrier of the Three Peoples—Mongol, Manchu and Chinese. In the case of the Khalkha tribes, the name is said to indicate that they were the northernmost barrier of the Empire; of the Mongol Empire, that is.

The Khalkhas who border on Hsingan province belong to the twenty-three Banners of Sechin Khan Aimak. The name Tsetsen, appearing on maps, is a corruption of this. The Chinese rendering is Ch'e-ch'en.

The following four Banners are marked on the map:

East Wing Rear Banner, Center-West Banner, and Front Banner, West Wing Rear Banner.

The Mongol written form of this name is Sil-on Gol, or North-slope River, from the name of a river in the eastern part of the League. The Chinese transcription of the name is Hsi-lin-kuo-le. There are five tribes in the League, each having two Banners. The tribes are as follows:

Ujumuchin

Also written Ujumchin. Chinese transcription Wu-chu-mu-ch'in. Some Mongols derive this from the word *ujum,* "grapes." Some refer it to the verb *ujemui,* vernacular *ujine,* "to look," "to see," and explain it as "the watchers." Others derive it from *ujughur*, vernacular *ujur*, "the sharp end," and interpret it as "the outposts."

Hochit

Mongol written form, Hagochit, from a plural form of *hagochin*, "old." Chinese transcription, Hao-ch'i-t'e.

Abaga

This is a Mongol word meaning "uncle." The Chinese rendering is A-pa-ko.

Abahanar

From a plural form of *abaga*, "uncles." The Chinese render it as A-pa-ha-na-erh. Mongols, in common speech, often group the four Banners of these two tribes together as Durben Abaga, the Four Uncles.

Sunid

The Chinese transcription is Su-ni-t'e.

The Banners are distributed as follows, from east to west: East Ujumuchin, West Ujumuchin; East Hochit, West Hochit; East Abahanar; East Abaga; West Abahanar; West Abaga; East Sunid, West Sunid.

The Silingol League is nominally a part of Chahar province, but the Chinese have not been able to master it yet, and instead of there being Chinese officials in its territory, representatives of the Mongols reside at Kalgan to deal with the Chinese authorities. As there is neither Mongol agriculture nor Chinese colonization anywhere in the

League, and as the princes are powerful and at the same time afraid of the revolutionary ideas of Outer Mongolia, the Silingol territory is a stronghold of the old nomadic society and the old tradition. It is therefore a kind of hinge on which turn the politics of Inner Mongolia as a whole. The present autonomy movement in Chinese Inner Mongolia, affecting not only Silingol but the partly colonized League of Olanchab, is plainly an effort to secure guarantees against further colonization from the Chinese, under the more or less covert threat of joining Manchukuo. This, however, is not a constructive move, for if China makes enough concessions, the Mongol princes are likely to play for safety and time. The result in the end would be disastrous, for the princes of Silingol would find that when the next stage of action began, the initiative would have passed completely out of their hands; and with it, to a great extent, the power of initiative of all the Mongols.

THE CHAHAR MONGOLS

The Mongols write this name as Chahar, and the Chinese transcription is Ch'a-ha-erh. The commonest vernacular pronunciation in Mongol is, however, Jakhar, and Mongols derive the name from the word *jakha,* "border," and explain it as meaning Borderers.

The Chahars, after succeeding the Tumets as the chief power in Inner Mongolia, and attempting to form a Mongol Empire on a major scale, were defeated at the beginning of the seventeenth century by an alliance of Eastern Mongols and Manchus. They were then deprived of their hereditary princes and organized, as previously described, on a system combining the Manchu regimental Banner and the Mongol tribal-territorial unit. Each of their Banners is administered by an appointive official.

The following eight Banners form part of Chahar province. They are about 70 per cent colonized by Chinese, the colonization being least in the easternmost Banners: All Blue (containing the important trading town of Dolon Nor, the written form of which is Dologan Nagor, Seven Lakes); Bordered White, All White, Bordered Yellow, and the four Herdsman Banners. A few small groups from Outer Mongolia were also granted holdings in this territory, but they have now been practically wiped out by colonization.

The following four Banners form part of Suiyüan province: All Yellow, All Red, Bordered Red and Bordered Blue. They are heavily colonized by Chinese. A certain number of the Mongols have settled to agriculture.

Less than forty years ago the Chahar Mongols came right down to the Great Wall, about 30 miles north of Kalgan. They have now been driven about 70 miles farther back. Yet weak administration and bad economic handling have so ruined the colonized country that miles of fields taken from the Mongols have been abandoned, while others have been ruined by destruction of the top growth of herbage, allowing the sand to break out. Bandits range over the whole of the colonized belt, and the trade of Kalgan is not so great as it was when the merchants dealt with rich nomad herdsmen instead of economically help-less peasants.

The colonization of the Chahar country was almost en-tirely the result of railway construction, and is a striking illustration of the power of railways to extend the economic reach of Chinese settlement—though not to improve the economic structure of agriculture. The railway, beginning at Peking, reached Kalgan in 1911, Fengchen in 1915, Kuei-hua (Suiyüan) in 1921 and Paot'ou in 1923.

The retreat of the Chahars has largely obliterated the old quasi-tribal distinctions between the different Banners. The breaking down of their social organization has driven many of them, as "masterless men," into the ranks of the bandits. Moreover the remnant of their tribal lands is too small for a sound pastoral economy. Camps are too close together, the country is over-grazed, there is not enough scope of movement between winter and summer ranges, and the effects of drought and cattle plague are greatly enhanced. Even the pastoral Chahars, therefore, cannot be compared with Mongols living under natural Mongol conditions.

Chapter XVI

CHINESE "COUNTIES" (*HSIEN*) FORMED OUT OF MONGOL TERRITORY: RAILWAYS AFFECTING COLONIZATION

THE following list, the figures for which I have extracted from the *Tung-pei Nien-chien* or *Northeastern Year Book*, published at Mukden a few weeks before the Japanese occupation in 1931, will I hope give some idea of the distribution of Chinese colonization areas, their proximity to territories remaining in Mongol occupation, the numerical importance of their population, and their relation to railway expansion. They represent Manchuria at the very end of Chinese control.

The settlements in the north of Barga, along the Amur, hardly affect the Mongol question. They have not been important in displacing old populations with Chinese colonists, and the range of their occupations, including gold-washing and surreptitious trade across the river with Siberia, is not typical of agricultural pioneers.

The Nonni valley regions also are not typical. It should be remembered that the great majority of the people here displaced are not true Mongols—except on the lower

Nonni. Their problems could in fact have been more adequately treated in a study of the old Manchu population in Manchuria, and the tribes related to it; in which case the whole Amur-Sungari-Ussuri basin should be taken into account, instead of the restricted Nonni valley.

In the column of place-names, it will be seen that many places have two names, one of which is in parentheses. In such cases the name which comes first is that which is on the map. The other is either an old Frontier name which has now been displaced, or a new official name which has not yet come into general use.

Many of the names are also followed by two dates. The first of these is the date of the establishment of the county, as a county. A date in parentheses refers to some earlier Chinese official organization. This of course does not preclude the fact that often, long before the first introduction of official control, the place had been reached by Chinese, either as traders or as tenants of the Mongols, in the period when the Mongols themselves were promoting agriculture.

There are two columns for the square-mile area of each county. These figures illustrate the difficulty of dealing with statistics in the present state of weak statistical organization in China. In the first column is given the area as reported by one of the provincial government organs; in the second, the area as reported by the county authorities themselves. The remarkable discrepancy between some of these pairs of figures must often be due to local reorganization, taking land from one county and allotting it to another, which has not been properly checked between county and provincial

officials. For the province of Jehol there are no county figures, and the figures as given by the provincial authorities
are perhaps largely theoretical. The original figures are all
given in square *li,* which I have reduced to square miles
at the rate of nine square *li* to one square mile.

In the column for population I have again given two sets
of figures, one for the town itself and one for the county as
a whole. This will give a general indication of the degree
of urbanization; but it is not an exact indication. In some
rural districts a large part of the farming population lives
in the county town for most of the year, on account of
bandits. In other districts, the method of keeping to a large
number of scattered, fortified, stronghold-villages and
manors is more popular.

The Chinese colonization of Mongol lands appears mis-
leadingly simple when thus reduced to a list of towns and
counties. I advise the reader to consult this list with a ques-
tioning mind, and to be particularly curious about the *rate*
of colonization. What has been previously said about the
period of colonization tolerated by the Mongols, and the
period of rapid railway-promoted colonization, should also
be referred to as a check. In estimating the importance and
the social and economic character of any town in Manchuria, the size of the town will only begin to have full
meaning for the experienced observer when he has compared it with the date of establishment, the distance from
the nearest railway, and the date of that railway.

The dates of construction of the various railways (listing

only railways that affect Mongol regions in Manchuria) are
as follows:

Shanhaikuan-Mukden

This is a section of what used to be the Peip'ing-Liaoning
(Peking-Mukden) line. It does not pass through old Mongol territory, but when first constructed it affected colonization just west of the Willow Palisade. The section from
Shanhaikuan to Mukden is about 175 miles long. It was
completed in 1907 under a British loan agreement.

Chinchou-Peip'iao

This is a branch of the above line. It affects a region of
early Chinese settlement in Tumet West Wing Banner. It
was built largely to exploit the Peip'iao coal mines, but
will now be projected to Jehol City.

Tahushan-T'ungliao

Formerly operated as a branch of the Peking-Mukden
line. It ran first to Changwu and then to T'ungliao, through
traffic being opened in 1927. The distance is 157 miles. It
runs through the old Suruk Mongol lands, Bintu Wang
Banner, across a corner of Bo Wang Banner, and then
through Darkhan Wang Banner. It connects at T'ungliao
with the following line:

Chengchiat'ün (Liaoyüan)-T'ungliao

This line runs entirely through Darkhan Wang Banner,
for 70 miles. It was built under a Sino-Japanese agreement
and completed in 1921, as a branch of the following line:

THE MONGOLS OF MANCHURIA

Ssup'ingkai-Liaoyüan-T'aonan

Built under a Sino-Japanese loan agreement. Completed to Chengchiat'ün (Liaoyüan) in 1918 and to T'aonan in 1923. It runs from the South Manchuria line across a corner of Bo Wang Banner and then through Darkhan Wang and Jasakto Khan Banners, for a distance of 194 miles. It connects with the Chinese Eastern through the following:

T'aonan-Angangch'i

Built by the South Manchuria Railway acting as contractors for the Chinese. It runs through Jasakto Khan, Tusiye Gung, Jalaid and Yeghe Minggan Banners for a distance of 141 miles. Completed in 1926.

T'aoan-Solun

This branches off from the above line at T'aoan, 20 miles from T'aonan. Construction was begun in 1930, but has only been completed for about 40 miles, running all the way through Jasakto Khan Banner.

Chinese Eastern

This railway was begun in 1897 and opened to traffic in 1903. Originally Russian and then under Russo-Chinese management, its status under Manchukuo has yet to be finally determined. The Western Line runs for 339 miles from Manchuli to Harbin, through Barga, the Buteha lands, Yeghe Minggan, Durbet and North Gorlos Banners. Thence it continues by the Eastern Line for 583 miles to

Pogranichnaya (Suifenho), whence it connects with Vladivostok. The Southern Line runs for 149 miles from Harbin to Hsinching (Ch'angch'ün), about half this distance being through South Gorlos Banner. The Chinese Eastern differs from other Manchurian lines in being of the broad Russian gauge.

Tsitsihar-K'oshan

Construction of this line, as a Chinese enterprise without foreign loan, was begun in 1928 and completed almost to K'oshan, about 1931. The length of the main line is about 100 miles, with a branch of about 25 miles running to Hala, on the Nonni. This line and its branch affect all the Daghors on the eastern side of the Nonni. The line is the beginning of a strategic approach to the Amur valley.

South Manchuria

The construction of this line was begun by the Russians in 1896. It was taken over by Japan in 1904 and converted from the Russian gauge to standard gauge in 1907. About 80 miles of this line lie in old Mongol territory, in the Banners of Bo Wang, Darkhan Wang and South Gorlos. As the line passes close to the Willow Palisade, all the territory traversed was colonized before the railway was built; but it stimulated colonization farther to the west.

CHINESE COUNTIES AND COUNTY TOWNS ESTABLISHED IN MONGOL TERRITORY IN MANCHURIA

CHINESE COUNTIES AND COUNTY TOWNS ESTABLISHED IN MONGOL TERRITORY IN MANCHURIA

Name	Date	Square Miles		Population		Remarks
				Town	County	
BARGA REGION						
Manchuli (Lupin)	1914 (1908)	11,274	44,416	....	548	Population figure evidently a mistake; but colonization unimportant. Railway and frontier town only.
Shihwei	1920	11,608	3,583	372	3,542	Colonization unimportant.
Ch'ikan	1922 (1920)	9,752	16,666	218	1,885	Colonization unimportant.
Hailar (Hulun)	1920 (1908)	15,277	8,516	7,975	23,493	Small agricultural community adjoining town. No expanding colonization.
NONNI VALLEY REGION						
Mergen (Nenchiang)	1913 (1908)	16,883	30,266	2,835	14,585	Largely Daghors.
Noho	1913 (1909)	9,939	2,177	31,490	105,777	Formerly East Butcha territory; Daghors now being swamped by Chinese.
Puhsi	1915	13,423	4,482	2,306	23,009	Formerly West Buteha territory; Daghors losing ground.
Kannan	1926	3,793	2,644	1,965	44,096	Largely Daghors.
Chinghsing	1914	2,274	2,160	2,900	34,567	
Tsitsihar (Lungchiang)	1913 (1905)	8,534	3,911	27,000	113,441	Garrison town since 17th cent.
Fuyü	....	529	529	....	20,821	Hsien organization not completed in 1931.
Ian	1923	1,651	1,466	4,051	17,485	
K'oshan	1915	3,224	158	19,852	132,582	
K'otung	1929	1,930	260	....	....	
Tetu	....	2,156	2,156	....	....	Hsien organization not completed in 1931.
Paich'üan	1906	4,388	1,277	4,959	209,842	Hsien organization not completed in 1931.

Mingshui	1923	2,157	301	6,614	104,068	
Ch'ingkang	1904	2,277	733	....	149,109	

JERIM LEAGUE REGION

Solun	1917 (1914)	1,632	1,333	418	1,428	Remains in Hsingan province.
T'ailai	1917 (1913)	3,775	289	17,918	90,708	Jalaid Banner land.
T'aikang	1926	2,627	2,627	....	2,518	Durbet Banner land.
Lintien	1917 (1914)	2,996	239	9,461	67,145	Durbet Banner land.
Anda (Anta)	1913 (1904)	4,128	2,696	11,337	68,123	Durbet Banner land.
Chaotung	1913	3,401	1,731	51,199	199,190	North Gorlos land.
Chaochou	1913 (1906)	5,137	3,555	7,452	251,699	North Gorlos land.
Talai	1913 (1904)	2,739	15,555	15,969	86,062	North Gorlos land.
Ch'ienan	1927	1,150	1,167	3,022	37,975	South Gorlos land.
Nungan	1882	3,079	1,894	21,457	318,190	South Gorlos land.
Tehui	1910	2,366	....	....	376,034	South Gorlos land.
Ch'angling	1907	2,055	1,946	9,794	147,782	South Gorlos land.
Hsinching (Ch'angch'ün)	1913 (1802)	2,566	3,522	94,362	478,539	South Gorlos land. Now capital of Manchukuo.
Huaite	1877	1,451	1,451	20,546	324,297	Darkhan Wang Banner land.
Shuangshan	1929	472	608	4,915	61,863	Darkhan Wang Banner land.
Lishu	1914	1,028	1,028	16,741	385,532	Darkhan Wang Banner land. Actually a very old settled region.
Chengchiat'ün (Liaoyüan)	1913 (1902)	702	412	40,993	112,417	Darkhan Wang Banner land.

JERIM LEAGUE REGION

Name	Date	Square Miles		Population Town	Population County	Remarks
Ch'angt'u	1913 (1866)	1,875	2,266	2,004	418,514	Bo Wang Banner land.
K'angp'ing	1880	2,933	2,255	4,302	158,107	Bo Wang Banner land.
Fak'umen (Fak'uhsien)	1913 (1906)	972	920	9,946	268,129	Extends into Bo Wang Banner. Earliest settlement much older.
Changwu	1902	1,217	1,217	9,293	100,627	Suruk Mongol land.
Tungliao (Payint'ailai)	1921 (1918)	2,444	2,222	41,995	152,943	Darkhan Wang Banner land. May revert to Mongols.
Tanyu	1917 (1912)	1,269	1,114	21,000	50,241	Tosiyato Wang Banner land.
K'ait'ung	1904	1,777	1,322	4,652	60,559	Jasakto Khan Banner land.
Ankuang	1905	1,238	1,162	1,220	76,742	Tusiye Gung Banner land.
Taonan	1913 (1905)	1,822	2,322	41,707	132,939	Jasakto Khan Banner land.
T'aoan	1904	1,050	978	8,458	74,453	Jasakto Khan Banner land.
T'uch'üan	1908	3,771	3,771	3,377	63,383	Tosiyato Wang Banner land.
Chentung (Ch'akannao)	1909 (1908)	2,077	1,333	2,977	39,143	Tusiye Gung Banner land.

JOSOTO AND JO-ODA LEAGUE REGIONS

Name	Date	Square Miles		Population Town	Population County	Remarks
Weich'ang	1914 (1875)	66	....	3,181	110,169	Sq. m. figure evidently a misprint. Imperial Hunting Park land.
P'ingch'üan (Pakou)	1778 (1729)	7,500	....	12,534	252,457	Kharchin West Wing Banner land.
Lingyüan (T'atzukou)	1778 (1738)	7,800	....	8,796	359,296	Kharchin East Wing Banner land.

	Year				
Ch'aoyang (Santsot'a)	1778 (1738)	8,888	23,313	654,199	Tumet West Wing Banner land.
Fuhsin	1903	3,955	2,239	158,731	Tumet East Wing (Monggoljin) land.
Ch'ihfeng	1778	20,000	21,919	165,500	Ongniod West Wing Banner land.
Ch'uanning	1931	....	....	....	Subdivided from Ch'ihfeng *hsien*.
Chingp'eng	1914	4,800	4,268	35,548	Keshikten Banner land. Remains under Hsingan.
Linhsi	1908	1,653	....	34,905	Bairin West Wing Banner land. Remains in Hsingan.
Lintung	1925	....	....	....	Bairin East Wing Banner land. Remains in Hsingan.
T'ienshan	1926	2,222	....	9,200	Aro-Khorchin Banner land. Remains in Hsingan.
K'ailu	1908	....	....	....	Jarod West Wing Banner land.
Suitung	1908	7,666	2,800	185,047	Said to be in Naiman Banner land. Marked twice on map.
Chienp'ing	1903	889	2,100	120,000	Aokhan East Wing Banner land.
Lupei	1924	4,333	793	13,708	Jarod East Wing Banner land. Remains under Hsingan.

Bibliography

(Only sources referred to in the text or notes are here listed)

Reference in Text	Full Reference
Annals and Memoirs of the Court of Peking	*Annals and Memoirs of the Court of Peking,* by E. Backhouse and J. O. P. Bland; London, 1914.
Baddeley	*Russia, Mongolia, China,* by John F. Baddeley; London, 1919.
Binsteed	*The Tribal and Administrative System of Mongolia,* by Lieut. G. C. Binsteed, in *Far Eastern Review;* Shanghai and Manila, July, 1913.
China Year Book	*The China Year Book,* ed. H. G. W. Woodhead; Shanghai, Chicago, London. The material on Mongolia varies in different issues. The more important numbers are: 1914 (Binsteed's material); 1921 (fresh material on Outer Mongolia); 1926 (Constitution of Outer Mongolian Republic); 1933 (re-written by Lattimore); 1934 (added article on Chinese Turkistan, by Lattimore).
Empire in the East	*Empire in the East,* by various hands, ed. Joseph Barnes; New York, 1934.
Foreign Affairs	*The Unknown Frontier of Manchuria,* by Owen Lattimore, in *Foreign Affairs;* New York, Jan., 1933.
Franke	*Beschreibung des Jehol-Gebietes,* by Dr. O. Franke; Leipzig, 1902.
Gazetteer of Kirin	*Chi-lin T'ung-chih,* or *Gazetteer of Kirin;* preface dated 1891.
Giles	*China and the Manchus,* by Herbert A. Giles; Cambridge, 1912.
Gold Tribe	*The Gold Tribe, "Fishskin Tatars" of the Lower Sungari,* by Owen Lattimore; Memoirs of the American Anthropological Association, No. 40; Menasha, 1933.

BIBLIOGRAPHY

Reference in Text	Full Reference

Gughe Sodor — *Yeghe Yuwan Olos-on Mandoksan Turu-in Gughe Sodor,* or The Azure Chronicle of the Rise of the Dynasty of the Great Yüan (Mongol) Nation; printed in Mongol at Peip'ing; no date, about 1929.

Hedley — *Tramps in Dark Mongolia,* by John Hedley; London, 1910.

High Tartary — *High Tartary,* by Owen Lattimore; Boston, 1930.

Howorth — *History of the Mongols,* by Sir H. H. Howorth; London, 1876-88.

Hsingan Monthly — *T'un-k'en Yueh-k'an,* or *Colonization Monthly;* Hsingan Reclamation Project, Vol. I, No. 1 (no date); Mukden & T'aoan, about 1930.

Hsingan Report — *Hsing-an T'un-k'en Ch'ü Ti-i Ch'i Tiao-ch'a Pao-kao,* or *Report on the First Inspection of the Hsingan Colonization District;* Mukden, 1929.

Krijanovsky — *New Political Subdivisions of Outer Mongolia;* note on an article in *Siberian Soviet Encyclopædia* (Novosibirsk, 1932?); by N. N. Krijanovsky; *Geographical Review;* New York, Jan., 1934.

Kuo Tao-fu (Merse) — *Meng-ku Wen-t'i Chiang-yen Lu,* or *Discussion of the Mongol Question,* by Kuo Tao-fu (the Chinese name of Merse, a Hailar Daghor); Mukden, 1929.
Modern Mongolia; translated from the Chinese journal, *Progress;* by Kuo Tao-fu, in *Pacific Affairs;* Honolulu, Aug., 1930.

Lindgren — *Northwestern Manchuria and the Reindeer Tungus,* by E. J. Lindgren, in *Geographical Journal;* London, July, 1930.

Manchuria, Cradle of Conflict — *Manchuria, Cradle of Conflict,* by Owen Lattimore; New York, 1932.

Manchuria in History — *Manchuria in History,* by Li Chi, in *The Chinese Social and Political Science Review;* Peiping, July, 1932.

Marco Polo — *The Book of Ser Marco Polo,* by Sir Henry Yule; 3rd ed., revised by Henri Cordier; (reprinted) London, 1921.

Merse — *See* Kuo Tao-fu.

294

BIBLIOGRAPHY

Reference in Text	*Full Reference*
Mimeograph MS.	*Ch'üan Meng Meng Ch'i Yen-ko Chih*, or *Note on the Derivation of the Leagues and Banners of All the Mongols*, by P'ao Wei-han (the Chinese name of Sangbo, a Kharchin Mongol); Peiping, misdated 1910, actually written about 1930.
Mongol Pastures	*Meng-ku Yu-mu Chi*, or *Records of the Mongol Pastures;* preface dated 1859.
Mongol Ten-day Journal	*Monggol-on Arban Edur-un Daromal*, or *Meng-ku Hsün-k'an*, or *Mongol Ten-Day Journal;* Nanking, 10 Oct. 1931. (In Mongol and Chinese.)
Northeastern Year Book	*Tung-pei Nien-chien*, or *Northeastern Year Book;* Mukden, 1931.
North Manchuria	*North Manchuria and the Chinese Eastern Railway*, by various hands; Harbin, 1924.
Open Court	*Chinese Turkistan*, by Owen Lattimore, in *The Open Court;* Chicago, March, 1933.
Pelliot	*Chrétiens d'Asie centrale et d'extrême-orient*, by Paul Pelliot, in *T'oung Pao*, XV; Leiden, 1914.
Shirokogoroff	*Social Organisation of the Northern Tungus*, by S. M. Shirokogoroff; Shanghai, 1929.
Sokolsky	*The Tinder Box of Asia*, by George E. Sokolsky; New York, 1932.
Ta Ch'ing Hui Tien	*Ta Ch'ing Hui Tien*, or *Institutes of the Ta Ch'ing (Manchu) Dynasty;* edition of 1818.
Table of Mongol Leagues and Banners	*Monggol Chigolgan Hosigot-on Helhiye Holboga-in Iletkhil*, or *Meng-ku Meng Ch'i Hsi-t'ung Piao*, or *Summary Table of the Mongol Leagues and Banners;* Nanking, 1930. (In Mongol and Chinese.)
Tung Hua Lu	*Tung Hua Lu*, or *Annals of Eastern China;* Peking (reprint edition), 1887.
Turanians and Pan-Turanianism	*A Manual on the Turanians and Pan-Turanianism;* London, no date, about 1919. (Anonymous—a compilation.)
Unofficial Record of Heilung-chiang	*Hei-lung Chiang Wai Chi*, or *Unofficial Record of Heilungchiang;* printed about 1894, written about 1810.

BIBLIOGRAPHY

Reference in Text	*Full Reference*
Unofficial Record of Kirin	*Chi-lin Wai Chi*, or *Unofficial Record of Kirin;* 1895.
Wei Tsang T'ung-chih	*Wei Tsang T'ung-chih*, or *Gazetteer of Central Tibet*, 1896.

Mongol words have been compared with Kowalewski's *Mongol-Russian-French Dictionary* (Peiping photostat edition of 1932, of the Kazan edition of 1844); but I have used a simple transcription. I have also used the *Mongol-Chinese Dictionary* recently published in Peiping (no date).

Manchu words have been checked with the glossary of von der Gabelentz: *Sse-schu, Schu-king, Schi-king in Mandschuischer Uebersetzung*, etc.; Leipzig, 1864. Here also I have used a simple transcription.

Chinese words and characters have been compared with the *Chinese-English Dictionary* of Giles; London and Shanghai, 2nd ed., 1912.

Index

Abaga, 277
Abahanar, 277
Absorption, 112
Ach'eng, 199
Agriculture, 22, 43, 63-5, 69, 71-2,
    74, 78-9, 85, 89, 93-4, 98,
    104-5, 107, 113, 198, 203,
    244, 249, 257, 271, 273, 277
Agricultural Colonies, 84
    Communities, 112, 197-8, 215-6,
        222-3, 238
    Development, 195
    Economy, 87, 93, 218, 238
    Mongols, 116, 195, 217, 222
    Villages, 196
Aigun, 172, 178, 180-2, 188
    Banners, 180
Aimak, 145, 153
Alakshan, 26, 102
Alashan, 26
Albasin, 157
Altai, 74, 246
Altan Khan, 48, 59, 249
Amorsana, 160, 190
Amur, 49, 84, 156, 172, 177, 281,
    286
Ancient Frontier, 45
Anda, 48, 196, 249, 288
Ankuang, 218
*Annals and Memoirs of the Court
    of Peking,* 231, 293
Anta, 288
Antagonism, 86

Aokhan, 240, 261, 264
    Banner, 262, 265
    East Wing Banner, 265
    South Banner, 265
Argun, 51, 169
    River, 156
Aristocracy, 82
Aro-Khorchin, 261, 271
    Banner, 262
Ascendency, 113
Ashihho, 199
Asia, Central, 59, 75, 275
Assimilated, 87
Astrakhan, 25
Australia, 22
Autonomy, 117, 119, 125, 129
    Movement, 30

Babojab, 124, 223-4, 252, 270
Baddeley, 48, 58, 157, 177, 185,
    193
Baikal, 161
Bairin, 234, 261
    East Wing Banner, 270
    Tribe, 269
    West Wing Banner, 270
Balance, 75
Bandit Leader, 206
Banditry, 115, 131, 224, 229, 252
Bandits, 118, 223, 252, 279-80
Bands, Chinese, 108
Banner, 146, 152
Bao T'ungl'ing, 206

INDEX

INDEX

China (Cont.)
  and Mongolia, 16
  Policy of, 99
China Year Book, 61, 145, 251, 275, 293
Chinchou, 251
  -Peip'iao Railway, 284
Chinese, 39, 54, 61, 63, 65-6, 74, 81-2, 94, 101
  Agriculture, 82
  and Barbarians, 94, 100
  Banks, 108
  Bannermen, 59, 67, 181
  Becoming, 82
  Colonization, 84, 87, 93, 105, 117, 119, 143, 194, 204, 207, 210, 213-4, 218, 261, 273, 277, 281, 283
  Colonists, 281
  Eastern Railway, 99, 117, 119, 143, 158, 173, 196-7, 214, 285-6
  Emperor, 48
  History, 55, 93
  Immigrants, 85, 87, 94
  Immigration, 19, 80, 83, 90, 93
  Mongols, 81
  Pale, 48, 58-9, 67-8, 70, 72, 80, 85, 204, 207, 234, 239
  Peasant, 93
  Policy, 99
  Republic, 18, 100, 111-2, 264
  Revolution, 106, 116, 119, 123
  Settlement, 260, 262
  Slaves, 181
  Trader, 92
  Turned, 247
  "Turning," 95, 226
  Turkestan, 25, 74-5, 101, 130, 135, 137, 145, 149, 160, 191, 227, 231
  Volunteers, 224

Chingan, 212
Chingghis, 43, 45, 56, 60, 149, 196, 265
  Bogda, 140
  Khan, 143, 183, 193, 245, 259
  Wall, 158, 169
Ch'inghai, 102, 237
Chinghsing, 287
Ch'ingkang, 288
Chingp'en, 269, 290
Chintan Society, 115
Chipchin Banners, 162
Chipchins, 159, 179
Chokkor Khalkha Banner, 260, 267
Ch'uanning, 263, 290
Ch'ung Te, 245
Cities, 63
City Building, 64
  Manchu, 66
Civilization, 63, 69-72
Civil War, 106
Clan, 175, 187
Climatic Change, 54
Coal, 251
Colonist, Chinese, 92-3, 178
Colonists, Non-Frontier, 181
  Refugee, 22, 112-3, 189, 251
Colonization, 63, 72-3, 78-9, 83, 86, 90, 97-9, 100, 103, 106, 108, 110, 113-4, 129, 130, 196-8, 202-4, 207, 211-2, 223, 230, 239-41, 261, 268-71, 273, 277, 279-81
  Chinese, 22, 102, 114, 207
  Within China, 73
Communism, 17
Communist Faction, 129
Conquest, 54, 56, 75, 269, 272
Continental Power, 123
Counter-Revolution, 32
Court, The Open, 237

299

INDEX

INDEX

301

INDEX

302

INDEX

INDEX

304

INDEX

Mongol (Cont.)
  Kuomintang, 129
  Land, 109
  Landlord, 80
  Lands, 116
  Land Tenure, 76
  Language, 247-8
  Mongol Pastures, 48, 195, 197,
    201-4, 208, 216, 226, 231,
    244, 250, 262, 264, 266, 268,
    270-2, 295
  Mongol Policy, 21, 31, 139
  Population, 40, 45, 215, 218, 227
  Princes, 203
  Processes, 176
  Question, 40-1, 103, 281
  Rebellion, 114
  Rebellions, 116, 131
  Revolutionaries, 125
  Rising, 20
  Surut, 116
  Mongol Ten-Day Journal, 166, 295
  Mongol Territory, 41, 97, 99, 126,
    243
  "Turning," 231
  Unification, 55
  Unity, 123
Mongolia, 24, 57, 107, 123, 136,
    139, 286
  Chinese Inner, 30
  Eastern, 223, 252
  Eastern Inner, 123-4
  Inner, 16, 18, 25-6, 40, 50, 94,
    101, 106, 112, 114, 119-20,
    122, 127-8, 138, 278
  Kuomingtang, 129-30
  Manchurian, 26
  Outer, 16-8, 24, 32, 34, 42, 47,
    57, 61, 74, 89, 114, 119-20,
    122, 125, 127-8, 136, 141, 152,
    155, 214, 218, 243, 267-8,
    271-2, 275, 278-9

Mongolia (Cont.)
  Surut, 284
  Western, 130, 160
  Western Inner, 218, 269
Monggoljin, 222-3
  Banners, 250-2, 257, 266
  Tumets, 166, 260
Mongols, 19, 24, 29-30, 38, 43,
    45, 47, 51-2, 55, 57, 60-1, 65,
    70, 72-3, 75, 78-9, 85, 94,
    101, 107-9, 111, 113-4, 137,
    139, 173, 214, 245-6
  Agricultural, 116, 195, 217, 222
  Barga, 119, 124, 131, 133, 153
  Chahar, 20, 26, 102, 207, 234,
    239, 245, 269, 278-80
  Chinese, 81
  Code, 60
  Eastern, 16, 57-60, 124-5, 278
  Gorlos, 196
  in Manchuria, 109
  Inner, 41
  Jo-oda, 261
  Kharchin, 121, 232, 237, 239
  Khorchin, 226, 232
  Manchurian, 124, 138
  Nomadic, 262
  Northern, 73
  of Jehol, 236
  of Jerim, 193
  of Manchuria, 38, 42, 60, 75,
    89, 108, 117, 119, 138, 176
  Olot, 259
  Sibe or Sibege, 225
  Suruk, 221-4, 257
  Western, 73-5, 145, 190, 259
  Young, 111, 128, 130, 224
Monasteries, 254
Mortgage, 81-3
Mortgaged, 79
Mortgaging, 80

INDEX

306

INDEX

Pastoral, 63, 270
  Communities, 215
  Economy, 87, 93-4, 138, 210, 280
  Mongols, 90, 92
Pastures, 264
Pauchan Lama, 122
P'ayint'ailai, 208
Payint'ala, 208
Peasant, 91-3
Peip'iao, 251, 284
Peip'ias, 244
Peiping, 130
Peking, 38, 48, 57, 129, 147, 280
  Manchus, 70-1, 97, 148
  Meridian, 123
Peking-Mukden Railway, 99, 100, 116, 284
Peking-Suiyüan Railway, 20
Pelliot, 240, 295
Periods, 66
Petuna, 199, 227
Philosopher's Stone Society, 115
P'ingch'uan, 247
Pogranichnaya, 286
Policy of China, 97
Population, 222, 234, 257, 265, 281, 283
Powers of Western World, 135
Prester John, 249
Pressure, Western, 39, 99
Primogeniture, 111
Prince, 76-8, 83, 111, 146, 166, 168
Princely, 76
Princes, 20, 27, 33, 68, 70, 78, 87, 102-3, 105, 110-1, 115-6, 122, 127, 129, 139, 141, 150, 200, 264, 279
Prince's Land Deeds, 104, 116, 151, 279

Princes of Inner Mongolia, 18
  Outer Mongolia, 18
  Silingal, 278
Princes, Sealless, 150, 207, 225
Principality, 77
Private Ownership, 82, 104
Privileged Class, 83, 86, 89
  Position, 94
  Propaganda, 247
Progress, 132
Provincial Officials, 112
Provisional Government of Manchuria, 97
Puhsi, 287
P'u Yi, 28, 123, 140

Railway Expansion, 101, 109, 281
  Exploitation, 143
  Politics, 37
  Promoted colonization, 283
Railways, 19, 99, 100, 106, 143, 172, 202, 213, 240, 266, 279, 283
Rebellion, 110, 128, 131, 224
Rebellions, 124
Reclamation Army, 214
Refugee Buriat Banners, 163
  Buriats, 165
Regional Autonomy, 27
  Balance, 75
  Feeling, 66
  Group, 69
Regionalism, 39, 103
Regional power, 68
Reincarnation, 255
Reincarnations, 255
Reindeer, 164-5, 184
  Buriat, 25
  Culture, 189
  Economy, 43
  Nomads, 189
  Tungus, 169

INDEX

INDEX

INDEX

INDEX